Lions of the Dan

LIONS of the DAN

THE UNTOLD STORY OF ARMISTEAD'S BRIGADE

J. K. BRANDAU

NEW YORK

LONDON • NASHVILLE • MELBOURNE • VANCOUVER

Lions of the Dan

The Untold Story of Armistead's Brigade

Published in New York, New York, by Morgan James Publishing. Morgan James is a trademark of Morgan James, LLC. www.MorganJamesPublishing.com

ISBN 9781642793086 paperback
ISBN 9781642793093 eBook
Library of Congress Control Number: 2018912153

Cover Design by:
Megan Dillon
megan@creativeninjadesigns.com

Interior Design by:
Chris Treccani
www.3dogcreative.net

Effie Adwood Hamlett, a granddaughter of James Lafayette Oakes, was born June 11, 1901, in Elba, now Gretna, Pittsylvania County, Virginia.

She primed tobacco in hot sun with eleven siblings as their family had done for generations.

She loved her Lord and her family and fretted over all "the meanness" in the world.

Effie once declared, "Oh. Our family didn't come from no place. We'uz just plain ol' Americans."

This book is dedicated to Effie and all others who regard themselves simply as Americans.

For man also knoweth not his time: as the fishes that are taken in an evil net, and as the birds that are caught in the snare; so are the sons of men snared in an evil time, when it falleth suddenly upon them.

—Ecclesiastes 9:12 KJV

The years 1861–1865 in the Un-United States of America was such a time.

CONTENTS

ACKNOWLEDGMENTS

Here a little, there a little, bits and pieces comprise the whole.

Ernest Norman Oakes Sr., Marie Oakes Murphy, Edith Oakes Chapman, Jane Oakes and Virginia Doss Oakes provided essential information on the Oakes family.

Anna M. Craik, Carl L. Sell Jr., Robert E. L. Krick of the Richmond National Battlefield Park, and John Heiser of Gettysburg National Military Park supplied remarkable letters.

C. Edmonds Allen shared Edmonds family insights.

Kent Masterson Brown showed the author Gettysburg as he had never seen it before.

The helpful staffs of the American Civil War Museum, the Library of Virginia, the Mercer Museum, the National Park Service, the Virginia Military Institute Archives, and the Virginia Museum of History and Culture aided research.

The Pittsylvania Historical Society, the Williamsburg Civil War Roundtable, and the Gettysburg Civil War Institute educated and inspired.

David Hancock and his staff at Morgan James Publishing recognized the importance of this work. Lori Paximadis expertly edited the manuscript.

The author's wife, Sharon, provided loving support throughout the process.

All had essential roles in bringing this story to print.

For the many surprising discoveries, experiences and friends made along the way, thanks be to God!

INTRODUCTION

Each of the original thirteen American colonies had unique beginnings. Whether for profit, religious refuge, or debtor exile, all were products of the same English kingdom. Theirs was a rigid, classed society, a brutal system of authority and subjection. Cruel bondages and impressments were commonplace.

Distinct cultural alignments North and South began at the end of the English Civil War as Virginia planters earnestly embraced African slave labor. Its perfidious legalization traces directly to Virginia's royal governor Sir William Berkeley. If not his brainchild, Berkeley, at least, ranked chief enabler.

Slavery benefited both regions economically, first through triangular trade, later through expansion of the cotton industry. The long-term consequence was a nation divided against itself: agriculture versus industry, racial slavery versus immigrant labor, aristocrats versus commoners, state sovereignty versus federal authority. All resulted in two incompatible societies battling in Congress.

Abraham Lincoln repeated Christ's warning that a house divided cannot stand.[1] States disadvantaged by lopsided representation considered disunion. Communities armed themselves against specters of servile insurrections and interregional interferences. The election of 1860 energized fracture. States in the Deep South quit the Union. The chief executive exercised his last remaining option to quash rebellion: force of arms. The situation exploded into all-out war.

Each side claimed divine sanction. The conflict grew into a monster with a life of its own. Those who lived by the sword suffered the ordeals required to wield it. They died by the sword and its attending plagues.

Delusions, war, famine, and pestilence—the Four Horsemen of the Apocalypse—rode rampage in the Un-United States from 1861 to 1865, "trampling out the vintage where the grapes of wrath are stored." Over 150 years later the world still stops to stare at this first modern, total war.

Midway into the conflict on July 3, 1863, at Gettysburg, Armistead's brigade charged over the stone wall atop Cemetery Ridge. Popular history notes the point of their repulse as the high-water mark of the Confederacy. Artists' renderings portray Brigadier General Lewis A. Armistead as an icon of Southern heroism with hat raised high on his sword leading his men at the climax of Pickett's Charge.

In most Civil War chronicles, Armistead's brigade appears for that one moment and then vanishes away. Although Armistead perished at Gettysburg, his brigade continued intact and fought until Appomattox. The unit was unique in composition and leadership. Some of them endured the full four years of that brutal war.

All five regiments of Armistead's brigade were Virginia regiments. Forty-five of fifty companies haled from Southside Virginia, a region more geographically proper to North Carolina than the Old Dominion. A full quarter of Armistead's men came from Pittsylvania County, the largest county in Virginia. One Pittsylvania unit, the Chatham Greys, fought from Big Bethel to Appomattox.

Logic dictates that a concise record of Armistead's brigade center on the officers and men of the 38th Virginia Volunteer Infantry, the Pittsylvania Regiment. Human interest directs attention to Company B, the Pittsylvania Vindicators from Callands Post Office and four brothers Oakes, their cousins, friends, and neighbors from that tobacco farming community.

The officers of the 38th Virginia were aristocratic, slave-owning, planter stock. At first muster, all but one of its field officers were direct descendants of the native chieftain Powhatan through his daughter Pocahontas. The exception was its colonel, a direct descendant of Robert "King" Carter.

In contrast, the majority of its rank and file were poor, common, non-slave-holding tobacco farmers. Until Fort Sumter, they were pro-Union. The combination makes the 38th Virginia Infantry and their families an extraordinary microcosm of antebellum Virginia.

After the war, survivors returned home to scratch livings from poor soil as they had done before called to fight. Except for one article by their last colonel and one transcribed speech by a captain, none wrote postwar accounts. If others shared experiences, they did so privately with comrades or around their firesides. Family and community identified them with Armistead's brigade of Pickett's Charge. That seemed legacy enough for them.

Their charge at Gettysburg was only one of many battles and exploits. Postwar glorifications of Armistead and Pickett at Gettysburg eclipsed their men and their overall record. Their amazing story now rises above the overlaid lost cause myths.

The wartime record of the 38th Virginia survives disjointedly as rosters, reports, letters, incidental mentions, and one diary. Firsthand accounts diminished as attrition culled the unit's few chroniclers. The rank and file were marginally literate. No doubt, many letters scribbled or dictated in the field perished over time. Extant letters survived generations of farmhouse storage. Some found their ways into archives. Some remain in private hands.

This history owes much to Colonel George K. Griggs, who kept a diary that covers his four years with the regiment.[2] G. Howard Gregory's book provided additional bones upon which to flesh out this story.[3] Much information surfaced in recently published works. Nothing less than divine appointments provided access to other resources. Thanks be to God, the Revealer of Mysteries!

This work evolved from the casual interest in an ancestor forty-plus years ago. Its research amounted to a second career, which included a seven-year sidetrack writing about the Hall murder case.[4]

For verity, the author personally surveyed every battlefield and traveled every route taken by the 38th Virginia. He draws upon two score years as a scientist and researcher, a score as a primitive camper, and a decade of Civil War reenacting starting in 1986 under the tutelage of noted Civil War historian the late Brian Pohanka. The advent of the internet revolutionized information access. Dr. Peter Carmichael's personal invitation to the Gettysburg Civil War Institute afforded unique opportunities to rub elbows with the finest scholars in the field. Many of their works are referenced herein.

The forty-year parade of bits and pieces that form this record suggests there are more facts to rally. No doubt more treasures remain undiscovered in attics and archives. Every troop movement has its stragglers. Regrettably, the now-or-never decisions of life order this work forward without them.

Follow the 38th Virginia Infantry, the Pittsylvania Regiment, its gallant leaders, eager volunteers, dutiful citizens, and reluctant conscripts on every march, every camp, and every fight from beginning to end. Share their sufferings and heartbreaks in triumph and defeat. To know these men and their situations is to glimpse Armistead's brigade, Pickett's division, and Confederate Virginia as they were.

CHAPTER ONE

Southside Virginia: An Antebellum Primer

Highborn adventurers seeking wealth established the first permanent English settlement at Jamestown in 1607. Early Virginia colonists suffered grievous hardships, losses, and imminent failure. Salvation through John Rolfe's tobacco is legendary. Rolfe married Pocahontas, daughter of Chief Powhatan. Their stories are essential Virginia history.[5]

Tobacco, an eighteen-month crop, required prodigious labor. Planters first employed indentured servants. From 1618 onward, the colony filled demand through its headright system. Many were commoners lured by empty promises. Most were desperate lowborn, debtors, petty thieves, or street urchins, the off scourings of English society.[6]

The first Africans arrived in 1619. An English ship had taken these prize from a Portuguese vessel and exchanged twenty for provisions at Old Point Comfort. Since English law prohibited holding Christians in permanent bondage, this entitled evangelized Africans to indentured status.[7] Therefore, the first Africans may have entered the colony as indentures.

Captured Turks, African Muslims, and others classed heathen entered the colony as non-statutory, permanent slaves.[8] Some obtained indentured status upon conversion to Christianity. Generally, the colony favored indentured labor, for permanent bondage, purchased at premium, was less profitable due to the colony's high mortality rate.[9]

Technically, indenture contracts expired, while permanent bondage did not. In practice, treatment proved the same either way. By 1620, the sale of contracts between planters had already reduced indentures to chattel.[10]

The odds of indentures surviving servitude to realize freedom dues were slim. Those who survived hardening in Virginia and subsequent toils often had terms extended by courts through a master's fabricated complaint.[11] Some fled to take their chances in the wild.[12] A minority fulfilled their servitude to work allotted parcels alone or in partnership with other freedmen. These, in turn, acquired indentures and expanded their tobacco holdings.

In 1624, King James revoked private charter and made Virginia a royal colony. It was the first colony in what was to become the British Empire. The king died the next year, and son Charles inherited the throne. The Stuart kings, though Protestant, resisted Protestant reforms and alienated Puritan subjects. Many sought refuge in Virginia.

By 1640, a considerable Puritan population established themselves in the colony, particularly south of the James River. Virginia (and the entire South) may have developed differently and in parallel with New England had it not been for Sir William Berkeley (pronounced Barclay).

Sir William was a courtier, playwright, and favorite of King Charles I. Puritan reforms enacted by Parliament stopped Berkeley's income, thus arose an intense, personal contempt for that sect. Berkeley finagled royal appointment as governor of Virginia and proprietor of North Carolina. He arrived in Jamestown in 1642 just as civil war erupted between the king and Parliament. Local outbreak of the Third Anglo-Powhatan War in 1644 eclipsed the bloody struggle at home. Berkeley successfully defended the colony and restored peace. By that time, Parliamentary forces controlled England.

Sir William remained fiercely loyal to the king and maintained control of the colony after the Regicide in 1649. In the name of the crown, as well as personal vendetta, Berkeley persecuted Virginia's Puritans. This drove many to Maryland. At the same time, many Royalists, casually referred to as Cavaliers, left England for refuge in Virginia.

In 1651, Parliament dispatched three warships to demand Berkeley's surrender. Only then did Sir William relinquish control to Virginia's Puritan faction and peacefully withdrew to his plantation, Green Spring.

Virginia colonists continued to prosper under Puritan governors Richard Bennett, Edward Digges, and Samuel Mathews.[13] In 1653, Oliver Cromwell became Lord Protector of England, Ireland, and Scotland. Berkeley bided his time until Cromwell died in 1658. Sir William then wrestled control from the frail Governor Mathews. When Mathews died in January 1660, Berkeley resumed governorship. Later that year, England restored the throne. King Charles II recognized Berkeley's loyalty and declared Virginia a dominion: thus, its epithet, Old Dominion.

Sir William's plantation exile provided him opportunity to experiment with alternate cash crops. Despite possibilities, nothing challenged tobacco's profitability.

To the chagrin of common colonists, Sir William confiscated public lands for distribution as proprietorships and grants to Royalist chums and noble spawn. English tradition willed titles, lands, wealth, and virtually everything to eldest sons while siblings received token inheritances, if anything at all. Virginia offered Cavalier offspring disinherited by birth order unique opportunities for wealth.

By 1660, servant longevity had increased sufficiently to make permanent slavery competitive with indentured labor. Berkeley, his political cronies, and Royalist transplants provided themselves means to work their holdings most cost effectively by formally legalizing permanent slavery in 1661. Additional laws governing hereditary slavery and racial slavery followed. Provisions for Christian conversion affecting slave status vanished. African slavery in Virginia mirrored the classic Roman pattern rather than biblical guidelines.[14]

At this same time, King Charles II formed the Royal African Company to monopolize the colony's African slave trade. The king then assured demand by cutting off the supply of indentures.[15]

The most notable beneficiary of Berkeley's new, evolving social order was Robert "King" Carter, born in 1663. Carter would die in 1732 the richest man in the colony, leaving over three hundred thousand acres in lands, many plantations, a thousand slaves, a fortune in liquid currency, and a Cavalier dynasty. Intermarriages of his and other wealthy Royalist planter clans, like the Randolphs, were the unofficial, untitled, but nevertheless very real aristocratic class celebrated as the First Families of Virginia (FFV).

Berkeley rigorously enforced tenants of the Church of England and persecuted dissenters. In 1672, George Fox visited the Puritans of Nansemond County. Virtually all became Quakers. Berkeley stepped up harassments with ruinous fines, confiscations of property, and expulsions from the colony. Persecution drove nonconformists west into the frontiers of Southside Virginia and North Carolina.

Berkeley's dominion ignored, slighted, and oppressed all but the wealthy planter class. Rebellion erupted in 1676 led by Nathaniel Bacon, Berkeley's nephew by marriage. The roughly 50:50 Anglo:African racial composition of rebelling freemen reflected the relative color blindness of contemporary commoners.[16] Berkeley fled to the Eastern Shore. Bacon and his rebels burned Jamestown.

Soon thereafter, Bacon succumbed to disease, and the revolt collapsed. Berkeley returned and summarily hanged conspirators. The number and personages executed appalled Charles II, who recalled his superannuated representative to England to give account. Sir William returned to London but died before having audience with the king.

Berkeley governed Virginia for twenty-seven years, the longest and most influential tenure of any Virginia governor. He is best noted for having established Virginia's bicameral legislature. However, it was also Sir William who purged the colony of its Puritan element, fostered Virginia's Cavalier class, and codified permanent, hereditary racial slavery.

Puritan versus Cavalier mindsets had polarized England into bloody civil war.[17] The respective American derivatives North and South would eventually do the same.

* * *

The First Families of Virginia were the wealth and power in the Commonwealth. They populated leadership and learning. FFV gentry were stewards of Virginia culture and history. FFVs mothered Founding Fathers and presidents.

Proud FFV progeny perpetuated time-honored delusions of a fanciful Cavalier past referred to simply as Old Virginia. One wrote, "What is certain is, that life in Virginia, at the time, was an ideal life, simple wholesome and happy."[18] In reality, few, if any, lived such a life. What is certain is that only an FFV possessed such potential.

Virginia's yeomanry (descendants of commoners, indentures, Puritans, dissenters, Scotch-Irish, Germans, etc.) embraced Cavalier legacy by default, if at all. For them, life was brutal, all-consuming at best. For them, precious little memory conveyed beyond a generation.

By 1860, the average Virginian looked back as far as the Revolutionary War. It was as if the Declaration of Independence marked the beginning of time. The colonization of Jamestown was ancient lore. The epithet *Old Dominion* was well known but its origin vague. Fables about Captain John Smith and Pocahontas, Bible stories, and oral traditions from the Revolution constituted most pedestrian history.

In effect, "old times there" were forgotten!

* * *

Virginians in the Albemarle Basin were particularly forgetful of old times. Southside Virginia is geographically more North Carolina than Virginia. By 1860, few gave thought to why ancestors settled in such isolation. It was home.

Blue Ridge mountain rivulets form the headwaters of the Dan River. The lazy stream crosses the Virginia–North Carolina border six times before joining the Roanoke River, which then crosses the border again to eventually empty into the Albemarle Sound. The collective watershed geographically isolated Southside Virginia from the colony's Chesapeake Bay economy. The region therefore became refuge for Quakers (converted Puritans), Baptists, Methodists, dissenters in general, runaways, and outcasts of every description fleeing effective reach of the English crown and Anglican authorities.

In 1714, Governor Alexander Spotswood built Fort Christanna in Virginia's Southside near present day Lawrenceville to establish regular trade with Indians. Spotswood encouraged settlement in the region by Scotch-Irish and Pennsylvania Dutch as buffer between native tribes and proper English civilization. The formation of Brunswick County followed in 1720. Its boundary then stretched to the Blue Ridge Mountains.

Serious English settlement of the area began after the official survey of the Virginia–North Carolina border by William Byrd II in 1728. Population growth required subsequent divisions into additional counties: Lunenburg in 1746, Halifax in 1752, and Pittsylvania in 1767.

Pittsylvania County, the largest county in Virginia, was named in honor of English prime minister William Pitt, First Earl of Chatham. The popular Pitt had recently secured repeal of the much-hated Stamp Act. The new county seat assumed the name Chatham.

Two score years prior, Byrd described what became Pittsylvania County as a veritable "Garden of Eden." Settlers discovered the truth was that the climate, soil, and topography was good for growing the tobacco weed and little else.[19]

Regional geography stunted growth, for the law required all tobacco to be inspected before sale. The sole cash crop of the colony required expensive, torturous transport overland to a government inspection site with Chesapeake Bay access: Lynchburg, Petersburg, or Norfolk. The situation discouraged establishment of towns in Southside Virginia.

Consequently, subsistence farmers on this frontier depended heavily on necessities from either nearby plantations or from a unique system of Scottish stores.[20] Scottish financiers backed warehouses in Richmond and Norfolk. These supplied their trading posts throughout Virginia's Southside, which, in turn, served as middlemen for tobacco exchange. The proprietor of the Scottish store in Chatham was Scotsman Samuel Callands. Independence from Great Britain made Callands an independent store owner.

When Patrick Henry County split off from Pittsylvania in 1777, the county seat moved to the more central village of Competition. By 1788, Callands's store occupied the original brick courthouse/gaol vacated by county government. Callands's store and post office thrived as center for local community. By 1852, the original Chatham, the first county seat, had become known simply as Callands.[21] Locals then referred to Competition, the new county seat, as Chatham.[22]

* * *

In 1793, the General Assembly established a tobacco inspection warehouse on the Dan River at Wynne's Falls, the site of a ford and trading post. That same year, upon approval of formal town layout, the legislature changed its name to Danville. Work also began that year on the Dismal Swamp Canal to connect the Albemarle Sound to Hampton Roads. Eight years later, the new waterway opened river trade throughout Southside Virginia. Another event in 1793, no less important to the area, was the birth of Benjamin William Sheridan Cabell.

B. W. S. Cabell was born of FFV stock at Repton on the James River. Cabell studied law at Hampden-Sydney. In 1811, he moved briefly to Kentucky with his father but returned to Virginia with his aunt Elizabeth. At the outbreak of the War of 1812, Benjamin Cabell secured a commission as ensign in the 3rd Regiment Virginia Militia. He eventually served on the staffs of generals Joel Leftwich and John Pegram. After the war, Cabell ascended to colonelcy in the Virginia Militia. He married Sallie Epps Doswell in 1816.[23] The couple moved to Danville, a mere fledgling town.

The Cabells lived in a modest abode at the foot of Main Street.[24] Pocahontas Rebecca Cabell, the first of ten children, was born there June 29, 1819. Her name reflected Cabell's direct descent from John Rolfe and Pocahontas.

Colonel Cabell was energetic and visionary. In 1820, he and another Mason established the Roman Eagle Lodge. The first meeting inducted other Danville principals, including Dr. George Craighead and James Lanier. The brotherhood consolidated town leadership. Soon thereafter, Benjamin Cabell named his first son John Roy after friend John B. Roy, the first Worshipful Master of the lodge and head of local tobacco trade.[25]

Cabell's leadership and clout promoted development of the Dan River. Cabell was responsible for the first mill race,[26] bateaux navigation to Danville by 1825, construction of the boat basin,[27] the stone canal around the falls, and the first cotton mill in 1828.[28] When Danville's first newspaper went defunct, Cabell cofounded and edited its successful successor.[29]

Cabell's second daughter, Virginia, was followed by son Powhatan Bolling, which name again emphasized noble colonial lineage.

William Lewis Cabell was born New Year's Day 1827. Cabell named this son after his gristmill partner and future uncle by marriage.[30]

Cabell acquired land suitable for a plantation overlooking the Dan River on the north bank opposite Danville. There he built Bridgewater.[31]

Following a stillbirth came son Algernon Sydney named for that distinguished Puritan.[32] Next son George Craighead was named after another friend, the prominent town doctor. The last three Cabell children were Sarah Epps, Joseph Robert, and Benjamin Edward.

Colonel Cabell served multiple terms as delegate in the Virginia General Assembly (1823–1827 and 1829–1830).

* * *

The Great Eclipse crossed the South in 1831.[33] In Southampton County, an evangelized slave named Nat Turner embraced it as a sign from above. His deadly slave insurrection rocked Southside Virginia. Shockwaves jolted every slave state. Reactionaries in Virginia pushed to abolish slavery.[34] Not only did their legislative efforts fail, but the Virginia General Assembly passed counter-legislation that banned manumission and made abolitionist activity a felony.[35] Abolitionist groups tolerated until then fled north. Paranoia spread. Legislatures throughout the South passed ever increasingly stricter laws restricting slave assembly, worship, transit, and education with severe penalties and ruthless enforcements. Southern racial slavery reached its ultimate, most repressive, and cruelest form. The perfidiously twisted biblical justifications for the South's "peculiar institution" defied Scriptural contexts. Christian denominations split North and South.

* * *

Danville approached five hundred inhabitants. It was the only recognizable town in all Southside Virginia.[36] Legislation authorized election of a town council. This first body included familiar names Colonel Benjamin Cabell, Dr. George Craighead, and James Lanier, Danville's first mayor. Cabell also served in the Virginia State Senate (1830–1833).

Despite his holdings in the Roanoke Navigation Company, Cabell began advocating railroad construction in 1835. Twelve years later, the Richmond & Danville Railroad received charter.

Cabell was appointed major general of the Virginia Militia in 1843. In 1850, he served as a pallbearer for John C. Calhoun's Richmond procession. In 1856, Cabell officiated alongside Mayor William T. Sutherlin to welcome the first train into Danville. That same year, the nation elected his cousin John Cabell Breckinridge vice president of the United States.[37]

Benjamin William Sheridan Cabell, Major General of Virginia Militia, cornerstone of Danville, and father of six Confederate officers. (Courtesy Albert and Shirley Small Special Collections Library, University of Virginia)

Mid-nineteenth-century Virginia offered limited opportunities to wealthy planter offspring. For those not positioned to inherit land, career options were generally doctor, lawyer, engineer, or military officer.[38] General Cabell set a pattern of excellence emulated by his sons, who chose from best opportunities.

John graduated from Virginia Military Institute (VMI), attended the University of Virginia, and interned with Dr. Craighead to become a local physician. Powhatan attended the University of Virginia; studied medicine in Philadelphia, London, and Paris; and became a physician. The general secured an appointment for William to the United States Military Academy.[39] Algernon married into a respected Arkansas family and became a planter. George graduated from the University of Virginia, practiced law in Danville, became the local Commonwealth's attorney in 1858, and served as newspaper editor.

Had Danville not already been so named, the town might well have been dubbed Cabellville.

* * *

In the South cotton was king. Nevertheless, bright leaf tobacco ruled Pittsylvania County. In 1840, the county ranked number one in the state for tobacco production.[40] The entire tobacco chewing world preferred plugs and twists from the area. The nicotine weed made the Dan River watershed one of the few areas in Virginia with a growing slave population. Pittsylvania County ranked third largest in the state.

Only 5 percent of Virginia's white population owned slaves. Scarcely half that number owned more than four. Most slave labor resided on large plantations owned by less than 1 percent of the white population, virtually all of whom belonged to FFVs.[41]

Of Pittsylvania County's thirty-two thousand residents, 45 percent were slaves. The county was home to the Hairston family, which likely possessed the largest slave holdings in the South.[42] Pocahontas Cabell married into that family.[43]

Southern patricians viewed themselves as highborn descendants of Cavaliers and Norman conquerors.[44] Male FFV progeny considered themselves aristocrats, Christian gentlemen, custodians of civilized society, and paternal stewards of inferiors, both white and colored.

Southerners viewed Northerners as Saxon mongrels interbred with other European substrata and driven by a Puritan contentiousness. They considered Northerners self-righteous, greedy, and meddlesome. Historically, Northern speculation and unsecured bank notes caused the Panic of 1819. Crippling tariffs devised by the North upon the South enriched the former at expense of the latter. Biased taxation incited the Nullification Crisis of 1832, which had nearly resulted in disunion and civil war.

Northern banks precipitated the Panic of 1837, which poisoned Danville's economy. Tobacco factories shut down. The local economy gradually recovered over the next twenty years only to be slammed again by the Panic of 1857. As elsewhere in the South, Northern financial manipulations, exploitive tariffs, and abolition pressures fueled resentments at all levels of free Virginia society.

Money was power everywhere. Regional investments varied. In the South, powerful bloodlines ruled and slaves accounted for the bulk of their wealth. Abolition threatened their affluence and class. In this, Northern abolitionists appeared the greatest of hypocrites.

In 1641, Massachusetts became the first colony to legalize slavery, fully twenty years before Virginia. Although the North gradually abandoned slavery, it did so as Northern industry transitioned to a more profitable wage enslavement of immigrants, including women and children. Brutal hours, poor working conditions, and starvation wages yielded all the benefits of bond slavery with none of the responsibilities and costs of owning labor.

Once chattel bondage withered in the North, it paved the way for political crusades against Southern slavery.[45] All the while, Northern states shamelessly exploited free labor and Southern markets, and enforced racial exclusion laws![46]

Southerners perceived the North as a foreign power that threatened their socioeconomic stability. Aristocrats feared destruction of their wealth and class. Commoners feared social uncertainties and competition with freedmen. Both classes resented Northern interferences. These resentments grew and festered for over four score years.

Secession issues were as old as the United States Constitution. The original colonies coveted their identities. State sovereignties made the United States an optional cooperative.[47] Western Pennsylvanians threatened secession in the Whiskey Rebellion. New Englanders considered secession when politically disadvantaged by the Virginia Dynasty during the War of 1812.[48] Since the 1830s, cotton states threatened secession as an expedient to preserve slavery.

Secessionist firebrand Virginia governor Henry Wise observed, "Wherever black slavery exists there is found at least equity among the white population."[49] Such proslavery sentiment was Cavalier speak for class immobility of both whites and blacks. Slavery elevated common whites above their society's lowest labor class. At the same time, some slaves looked down on poor whites.[50] As one slave noted, "Poor whites was just like stray goats."[51] The majority of Southern whites were poor.

Everyone in Cavalier society knew their place. The nail sticking up got beat down. For generations, tobacco and cotton lords fought to preserve their wealth and class. Wealthy planters blocked every initiative for emancipation and drove compromise after compromise in Congress, forestalling the inevitable day of reckoning.

The incalculable cruelties and moral depravities intrinsic to the South's "peculiar institution" were norms on plantations and screened from public view.[52] The emphasis wealthy planters placed on Northern tyrannies kept public attentions off the far greater tyrannies in the stratified society in which common Southerners lived.

Pittsylvanians considered themselves Virginians, Southerners, and Americans, in that order. Common white Pittsylvanians lived simple, agrarian lives. They were poor, non-slave-holding tobacco farmers, descendants of colonial dissidents, outcasts, and non-English immigrants. Some owned their single-family subsistence farms. Others were tenants. Families, friends, and neighbors lived mutually dependent lives in a narrowly defined world of court days, market days, and Sunday meetings. Subsistence farming afforded no time for high-minded notions. Any political mindset simply mirrored that of their ruling class.

Pittsylvanians lived sheltered existences as subjects of a Cavalier realm. They were like lions in the wild: free within a range, content to be left alone, and posing no threat to anyone unless provoked, wounded, or driven to bay.

* * *

In 1859, three years after its completion, the Richmond & Danville Railroad boasted nineteen locomotives. Six pulled passenger cars. Thirteen pulled freight. Engine no. 10, named the *Pittsylvania*, logged 14,003 miles in a year hauling tobacco and goods. That September its boiler burst. The explosion destroyed the engine and killed its engineer.[53] No one grasped the foreboding analogy as social, economic, and political pressures surged within its namesake.

The very next month, John Brown's raid on Harpers Ferry stoked fears of servile revolt throughout the South. Virginians rallied to defend their communities. Pittsylvania militias like the Chatham Greys, Spring Garden Blues, and Turkey Cock Grays exchanged peacetime fraternity for serious military musters. Volunteers flooded the ranks of the Danville Blues.[54] Overflow formed a second company the Danville Grays.

General Benjamin Cabell and Danville's mayor William T. Sutherlin recognized these prides of lions lacked qualified leadership. Sutherlin, a wealthy tobacco industrialist, was born and raised in Pittsylvania County and educated at the Danville Male Academy.[55] Sutherlin, under Cabell's advisement, acquired his alma mater to establish a military school and hired two military instructors. One was young Edward Edmonds.[56]

Edward Claxton Edmonds was born January 21, 1835 in Paris, Virginia. Ned was one of four sons of Dr. John R. Edmonds and his wife Helen, née Carter, direct descendant of Robert "King" Carter. Edmonds grew up a near neighbor to General Walker Keith Armistead's family. This kindled his keen military interest as a boy.

Ned graduated from VMI, class of 1858. After graduation, he married Margaret Tutwiler.[57] Edmonds taught mathematics at the Staunton Male Academy until accepting the new headmaster position. Edmonds, his pregnant wife, and three servants (one male, two female) moved to Danville.

On New Year's Day 1860, pro-Unionist John Letcher succeeded secessionist Henry Wise as governor of Virginia. Weeks later young Edward Edmonds turned twenty-five as headmaster of the newly opened Danville Military Academy.

The school was an imposing, three-story brick structure at the north end of town. It stood between the Grove Street Cemetery and W. T. Sutherlin's new mansion.[58] Open country for training lay just beyond. General Cabell's nineteen-year-old son, Joseph Robert, was among the first enrolled. Youngest son Benjamin Edward was a year shy of eighteen, the minimum admission age.[59]

The cadets grew proficient. Edmonds and his cadre provided drill expertise at local militia musters.[60]

On May 6, Edmonds's wife gave birth to daughter Molly. Dr. Robert E. Withers attended delivery.[61] Withers was also senior officer in Danville's militia.

* * *

The 1860 presidential campaign peaked tensions. The Democratic Party split into three factions fielding separate candidates. Ballots reflected local sentiments. Pittsylvania's slave-holding class voted for Vice President John Cabell Breckinridge, the Southern Democratic Party candidate. Cabell kinship, no doubt, bolstered county support.

Common folk favored the Constitutional Party candidate. Thus, John Bell carried Pittsylvania County by wide margin and won Virginia. Stephen Douglas received a few nods.

Not one soul in Pittsylvania County voted for Abraham Lincoln.

Lincoln won the presidency with 59 percent of the electoral votes but only 40 percent of the popular vote. The Northern tyranny that Southerners feared had placed a pro-abolition Republican in the White House. Virginia remained pro-Union, but the election pushed the cotton states into revolt. South Carolina seceded in December.

Virginia's governor John Letcher upheld the right of secession but steadfastly asserted benefits of union. Despite the weight of pro-Union sentiments in the Commonwealth, Tidewater radicals in the Virginia General Assembly called for a secession convention.

In early January 1861, Southern sympathies and economic interests prompted New York City to consider secession to form an independent city-state.[62] Within days, Mississippi, Florida, and Alabama left the Union. Georgia and Louisiana seceded before the end of that month.

Pittsylvania County elected pro-Union delegates William T. Sutherlin and William M. Tredway. The Virginia Secession Convention convened at the capitol in February, two days after Texas left the Union.

By mid-March Lincoln's inaugural address whittled away pro-Union support. Lincoln expressed tolerance for slavery but emphasized federal authority over the seceded states.

On April 4, Virginia's convention entertained a motion for secession. Those in favor of Union soundly defeated the measure by a two to one vote. Yet, in the unstable climate, no one moved to adjourn.

On Saturday, April 13, news reached Richmond that South Carolina had fired on Fort Sumter. Excited citizens filled the streets. Bands assembled and played "Dixie." Crowds waved the Confederate Stars and Bars. Some appropriated a cannon from the Tredegar Iron Works and fired salutes.

At the governor's mansion, shouts for Letcher moved the executive to address the crowd.[63] Letcher promised actions faithful to Virginia but reminded everyone that Virginia was still in the Union. Boos and hisses erupted. Letcher gracefully stepped back inside.

The crowd repaired to the portico of the capitol to hear fiery secessionist leaders. Demonstrations continued throughout the day. Richmond remained in turmoil Sunday. After worship services, itching ears crowded Capitol Square again for more speeches. Radical secessionists met in hotels to discuss strategies. Pro-Unionists rethought positions.

The attack on Fort Sumter left President Lincoln one, and only one, option to preserve the Union. On Monday, April 15, Lincoln called for seventy-five thousand volunteers to quell the rebellion. He set Virginia's quota at three regiments. Decades of state sovereignty issues climaxed. Governor Letcher refused to provide the men. He also banned federal troop transit through Virginia to subjugate seceded states.

The reaction should not have surprised Lincoln. Twenty-seven years earlier, President Andrew Jackson met similar resistance from then Virginia governor John Floyd regarding like contingency against secessionists in South Carolina.[64]

Until the call for troops, the benefits of Union had always carried greater weight. Cooperation threatened Southern honor. Cavalier culture coveted honor above all else. Indeed, Virginia gentlemen still settled personal affronts with duels. All believed the seceded states had properly exercised their rights. In effect, Lincoln had declared war on his own people. Emotions exploded.

The Secession Convention met in secret next day. Lincoln's demands silenced pro-Unionists. Pittsylvania County Delegate William T. Sutherlin declared, "I have a Union constituency which elected me by a majority of one thousand, and I believe now that there are not ten Union men in that county to-day."[65] Elsewhere in the city, the Spontaneous People's Convention opened to bring added pressure on the official body.

Zealots rushed atop the capitol, pulled down the US flag, and ran up Confederate colors. After dark, Governor Letcher ordered the Stars and Bars replaced with a Virginia state flag.[66] The response marked the limit of the governor's control over the situation.

On April 17, the convention in secret session passed the Ordinance of Secession. The news spread like wild fire. Richmond burst into jubilation. Local militias marched. Bands struck up "Dixie" and "La Marseillaise." Bright, new Confederate banners waved in crowds abandoned to the moment.

Former governor Henry Wise, ardent secessionist, usurped Letcher's authority and ordered the Virginia militia to seize the Gosport Navy Yard in Portsmouth and the federal arsenal at Harpers Ferry. The militia obeyed without question and set the tasks in motion.

Official repeal of Virginia's ratification of the Constitution of the United States required approval by public referendum scheduled for May 23. Blind exuberance misdirected attentions and trampled all notions of an independent, self-determined, national Virginia. The state was ripe for picking.

Alexander Stephens, vice president of the Confederate States of America arrived to encourage alliance with the Confederacy. Stephens proposed the Confederate capital be moved from Montgomery, Alabama, to Richmond. This was despite the fact that until North Carolina, Tennessee, and Kentucky seceded, Virginia was an island surrounded by Union states.[67]

The convention embraced the idea.

On April 24, John Tyler, former president of the United States, signed the treaty admitting Virginia to the Confederate States. In anticipation, President Jefferson Davis had already ordered troops to Richmond. The 1st South Carolina Regiment arrived that evening to cheering onlookers. The convention ratified the treaty next day, a month prior to the secession referendum.[68]

Passions trampled due process.

The Commonwealth of Virginia had joined the Confederacy.

CHAPTER TWO

The Second American Revolution

The telegraph in Danville clickety-ticked that Virginia had seceded. The excitement fell short of that euphoria in Richmond. Nevertheless, word spread rapidly throughout Pittsylvania County that a second American Revolution had begun.

The Danville Military Academy closed. Its cadets departed to join hometown militias. Locals joined the Danville units. Star pupil Joseph R. Cabell enlisted as a private in the Danville Blues.[69] Elder brother George C. Cabell was already its captain.

The two Danville companies mustered as one battalion under the command of Dr. Robert E. Withers. Danville Military Academy's principal Edward C. Edmonds was adjutant.[70]

On April 23, the battalion boarded the train to Richmond. Withers left his wife and eight-hour-old unnamed daughter. The mother would call her Virginia Secessia.

Ten hours later, the men detrained at the Richmond & Danville Railroad depot in the new Confederate capital. They marched three miles to the camp of instruction at the Hermitage Fair Grounds. Due to insufficient tents, the unit billeted in the fairground stables. The next day, the battalion marched back to the customs house across the street from the capitol where the state accepted the unit into service.[71] The battalion returned to camp and trained under VMI cadets.

The battalion acquired other companies to become the 18th Virginia Volunteer Infantry Regiment. Dr. Withers was its colonel. Henry A. Carrington replaced Edmonds as second in command. George Cabell became major. Governor Letcher sent Edmonds back to Pittsylvania County with full colonelcy to organize another regiment. The Cabell family figured prominently.

Dr. John Cabell, eldest son of General Benjamin Cabell, agreed to raise a company. At Edmonds's request, Colonel Withers released Major Cabell's brother, former cadet Pvt. Joseph Cabell for captaincy in another new company. One speculates that had Dr. Powhatan Bolling Cabell not succumbed to a Comanche arrow wound eighteen months prior, there may have been a third Cabell organizing a company.[72] Yet, Cabell involvements did not end there.

Henry A. Carrington, who replaced Edmonds when the Danville Battalion merged into the 18th Virginia, was first cousin to Chatham attorney Isaac H. Carrington. Their mothers were daughters of the late William H. Cabell, former governor and chief justice of the Virginia Supreme Court. Governor Letcher commissioned recent widower Isaac Carrington major to assist Edmonds. The major then arranged for lateral transfer of his youngest brother 1st Lt. Edgar Carrington from a Charlotte County cavalry troop.

Carrington's law partner and cousin James Whittle hosted brother Powhatan Bolling Whittle, who had recently resigned his commission in the Georgia militia. The governor commissioned Powhatan Whittle lieutenant colonel of Edmonds's new regiment.

The new organization afforded these leaders unique opportunities to enter state service as field-grade officers. In contrast, local physician and friend Dr. Rawley Martin, a first lieutenant in the prewar Chatham Greys, retained junior officer rank when the state ordered his company to Richmond.

Powhatan Bolling Whittle was born and raised at Millbank in Mecklenburg County.[73] He was a direct descendant of Powhatan (through Pocahontas) and colonial figure Colonel Robert Bolling, as were also the Cabells and the Carringtons. Whittle graduated from the University of Virginia in 1850. He practiced law with his brother Lewis in Valdosta, Georgia. When that state seceded, Whittle was a lieutenant in the Jackson Artillery. He transferred to the Macon Volunteers headed to Virginia. Upon arrival, he resigned and offered himself in defense of his native state. Standing six feet, six inches tall, Powhatan Whittle presented an imposing figure.

On May 20, Powhatan wrote his brother Lewis: "We are succeeding rather slowly. The men of this region do not seem to enlist as readily as persons in the South."[74] Enlistments increased after ratification of secession May 23.

Governor Letcher allotted Edmonds two Pittsylvania companies already in state service: the Kentuck Grays, organized the previous year, and the Cascade Rifles, activated April 24.[75]

John Taylor Averett, former headmaster of nearby Ringgold Military Academy and trustee of Danville's Union Female College, was a second lieutenant in the Kentuck Grays. Edmonds promoted Averett to captain as regimental quartermaster.[76] The colonel filled the regimental commissary captaincy with eldest brother William Bell Edmonds. The regiment took shape as five new Pittsylvania companies prepared to join the two already in Richmond.

* * *

Dr. John Cabell practiced medicine at Callands, the original county seat. The well-respected physician solicited enlistments throughout the neighborhood.

The Oakes were typical of Pittsylvania families on small tobacco farms. As was common in the South, James Washington Oakes and his wife, Evaline, née Oakes, were married first cousins. Their multigenerational, non-slave-holding family raised tobacco, lived in a small log house, cooked on open hearth, and drew water from a spring at the bottom of a steep gulley.[77] Although devout Christians, their family had long since forgotten their Puritan roots in a century of scratching livings from red clay. Four of their ten children were males of military age. Charles and James were married. Thomas was recently widowed and a single parent. His mother and sisters cared for his son. Brother John was unmarried. Tom and John still lived on and worked their parents' farm.

Secession, militia activations, and threat of invasion signaled excitement, adventure, and escape from farm drudgeries as much as any patriotic calling. When Dr. Cabell visited their farm, Tom and John Oakes eagerly volunteered. Friends and neighbors did likewise. Three Fuller brothers and five Adkins brothers promised to go. Commitments were for one year. Few expected to be away that long.

On Thursday May 23, the men of Callands assembled at the old county clerk's office for the formal vote on secession. Dr. John Cabell formally enlisted recruits into his company, which he named the Pittsylvania Vindicators. Most enlistees had no idea what a vindicator was, but it sounded powerful and manly.

Women feverishly sewed uniforms and haversacks for their new soldiers. Less than two weeks later, sixty farm boys stood before the old clerk's office. They mustered into two ranks clad in gray roundabouts trimmed in infantry blue and brass buttons.[78] Matching gray kepis completed their outfits. They lacked arms and accoutrements. The undisciplined group more closely resembled schoolboys on a lark than a martial force.

Local dignitaries praised their crusaders. A pastor invoked blessings on them and their yet-to-be-issued arms. Captain Cabell mounted his steed. The newly elected officers herded the farm boys into a column of fours. Upon command, the company stepped off and guided onto the road to cheers, blown kisses, and waves farewell from families, sweethearts, and friends. The boys in gray doffed caps, returned waves, and shouted goodbyes. A baggage wagon followed as did also the officers' body servants.

The young men relished the novelty. Few imagined it could be years before they might see home again…if ever.

The company tramped the Franklin Turnpike twenty-one miles to Danville. Those encountered along the way offered refreshments and cheer. They arrived tired and footsore, and spent the night in the hotel.[79] Few had ever stayed in one before. The next morning, the company boarded railcars for Richmond. For most, it was their first train ride.

The iron horse pulled the clacking conveyance through the countryside at a thrilling twenty-five miles per hour. Wood and water stops were the only delays in the ten-hour ride. Those able to read announced passing stations: Ringold, Barksdale, News Ferry, South Boston, Clover, Mossingford, Keysville, Meherrin, Jennings Ordinary, Jetersville, Amelia, Coal Fields (now Midlothian), and Powhite. At Manchester the train crossed the trestle spanning the James River and pulled into the Richmond depot.

The Pittsylvania Vindicators detrained and marched through the city to the Hermitage Fair Grounds, renamed Camp Lee.[80] There they officially entered state service June 4. Three other Pittsylvania companies, the Cascade Rifles, the Kentuck Grays, and the Laurel Grove Riflemen had already arrived. More were expected. Captain George King Griggs of the Cascade Rifles had received temporary charge of the Pittsylvania Battalion. Griggs had attended VMI two years before marrying into the county. Griggs began drilling the men on June 5.[81]

The sun regulated life back home. Only affluent families owned clocks and timepieces. Drums ordered life in camp. From first call to tattoo, the army rose, ate, worked, and slept to signals from musicians. Chores were as much a part of soldiering as with farming. Wood and water needed fetching as at home. Camp discipline stressed additional care of personal toilet, uniform, and gear. It was the first time most ever had to cook anything.

There was much to learn about military courtesy, forming ranks, marching by squad, company, battalion, the manual of arms, and nine-step loading sequence. Muskets were novelties, hardly appreciated as lethal weapons. The Pittsylvanians drilled five hours a day. One hour was before breakfast. Doctors sent Stephen Holland home due to a prior medical condition that limited his drill.

Military rules and regulations restricted the farm boys to camp. Passes allowed visits to the city. New soldiers strutted among the adoring public. Richmonders received them everywhere as heroes. Some, like Pittsylvania Vindicator John Hutson, posed in uniform for a photograph to send home.[82]

Anyone caught outside camp without a pass ended up in the guardhouse. The men gladly surrendered personal freedoms for a season to ensure liberty in the future.

There was food aplenty, but there was no cornbread nor fried chicken. Some grew homesick, but the new recruits adjusted.[83]

VMI cadet William Bond Prichard drilled the Pittsylvania Vindicators. The affable third-year cadet from Petersburg earned their respect.[84]

Officers had to equip themselves. Captain Griggs bought a Navy pistol for $65.[85] The rank and file spoiling for the fight outfitted themselves with supplemental arms, mostly Bowie knives. Rare few had money for a pistol. Some had brought old kill pistols from their farms.

The city offered endless activities for curious, immature farm boys away from home for the first time: some wholesome; some not so much. Those bent on proving manhood were particularly susceptible to vices common to soldiers: cursing, drinking, gambling, and whoring. Language in camp became especially vexing to those determined to maintain Christian conduct.

There was preaching in camp every night. Most paid little attention.[86] Impetuous youth focused rather on terrestrial glories.

News of victory reached camp late June 10. Union forces from Fort Monroe had attacked the Confederate position on the York-Hampton Highway at Big Bethel Church. Southern troops led by Colonel John Bankhead Magruder had soundly routed a superior Yankee force. With the news came nagging fears that the war might end before they got their chance to fight.

The Whitmell Guards arrived in camp June 11. By then, the Secession Guards also drilled. Each company grew as recruiters at home enlisted more volunteers.

Sundry Union scouts and marauders captured near Manassas Junction trickled into the city's makeshift jails.[87] Developments renewed excitement and anticipation of adventure.

On June 13, the Chatham Greys entered the opposite end of the city. Those lions of the Dan escorted their Yankees captured at Big Bethel. They paraded them through streets lined with gawkers. The Pittsylvanians delivered their prisoners to the customs house. The public gathered to view the curiosities. Newspapers reported a few of the prisoners were Virginians. Some felt the "traitors" should be hanged.[88] Nothing came of that. The Pittsylvanians in Camp Lee envied their Chatham neighbors. It whetted appetites for similar glory.

On June 14, Colonel Edmonds officially took command of his six companies from Pittsylvania County; a seventh was due any day. The Pittsylvania Regiment entered state service officially as the 38th Virginia Volunteer Infantry Regiment.

Edward Claxton Edmonds, Colonel, 38th Virginia Infantry. (Courtesy C. Edmonds Allen)

The Pittsylvania Regiment was the picture of stratified Southern society. Its field officers were high-bred Cavalier stock, accompanied by body servants. Class and nepotism determined command appointments. Hence sprang dissatisfactions among certain officers over Griggs's command until Edmonds's arrival.[89]

The rank and file were as common as the dirt they farmed. Soldiering bestowed a unique respectability they had never known. For the first time in their lives, they were part of something bigger than themselves.

As the regiment consolidated, the Pittsylvania Vindicators from Callands became Company B. Most assumed company alignment in alphabetical order. They were mistaken. The infantry manual defied common logic. Facing the regiment, Company A was on the far left, Company B on the far right, and Company C, the color company, was left center. Standard company order was A F D I C H E K G B. The first five companies constituted one battalion; the second five another. In marching column, Company A was always first, Company B always last.

The Cabell Guards arrived June 21.[90] Joseph Cabell had initially named his company the Lincoln Tormentors, but members insisted their title honor his family.[91] The point was moot. In the regiment, they were simply Company E.

Strong winds blew through camp that night. Dust and dirt covered everything. Soldiers noted this in letters home as a significant event.[92] Once accustomed to service, such weather rarely rated mention.

On June 22, Powhatan Whittle wrote from camp acknowledging arrival of his new saddle, delivered by two of his brother's slaves. Whittle still sought a mount. He would go into town that evening and examine a horse his brother recommended. Powhatan, like other officers, had to buy his uniforms out of pocket. He asked for a loan until the state paid him. Whittle said he had not felt well for days due to the heat. Carrington was well. He, too, had not yet purchased a horse.[93]

Training and drilling proceeded. Days turned into weeks as routine replaced novelty. Homesickness spread. On June 28, a heavy rain gave welcomed diversion to some who pulled off their clothes and ran around in it "like so many ducks."[94]

On June 29, the 38th Virginia Infantry fell in as a full regiment for the first time. Two companies from Mecklenburg County, Whittle's home county, and one from Halifax County completed ten companies.

Colonel Edmonds inspected the men. The colonel radiated command presence. Lean and fit, one might not class Edmonds as short per se. However, paired with the six-foot-six Lt. Colonel Whittle, the contrast was sufficient for his men to call Edmonds their "little colonel."

All members of the Pittsylvania Regiment hailed from Southside Virginia. Though mere whelps, they were lions of the Dan.

* * *

Federal threats mounted along the Potomac River. General Jackson defended Winchester with four brigades, roughly 18,000 men on paper. Measles, mumps, and other diseases common to military camps drastically reduced effective strength. Control of the region was tenuous.

On July 1, the 38th Virginia Infantry completed its training. The state transferred the regiment to Confederate service. They were officially soldiers of the South.[95]

Skirmishing erupted at Falling Waters on July 2. General Joseph E. Johnston pleaded with President Davis for reinforcements. That took time. Regiments trickled into the field as they exited camps of instruction.

The Fourth of July was unlike any previous Independence Day. The men of the 38th Virginia were in Richmond, the capital of Virginia and a new nation. They were part of a second Revolution. They believed it a rebirth of liberty as profound as the first. They were ready and eager to fight for Southern independence.

By July 5, the Pittsylvania Regiment prepared to move. Army life thrilled the young soldiers. Thus far, the work was easier than farming. There was always plenty to eat: rice, onions, cucumbers, biscuits, peas, beef, and salt pork.[96] Real adventure seemed assured.

Drill instructor William Prichard sought field service. Captain John Cabell recognized the VMI cadet as fit executive for the company from Callands. On July 7, Prichard became first lieutenant in Company B.

Rumors intensified of deployment to Winchester. 1st Lt. Edgar Carrington completed his transfer from cavalry and arrived in camp. Colonel Edmonds posted the major's brother as executive officer in Company H, the last open position appropriate to his rank. His company commander Captain Joseph Terry, a blustery, middle-aged lawyer from Chalk Level, resented the major's young brother.

On July 9, the 38th Virginia received orders to join General Jackson's Army of the Shenandoah. Colonel Edmonds's reaction can only be imagined. He and his fellow VMI alumni studied under Thomas J. Jackson. They remembered him as that gangly, eccentric professor some called "Tom Fool."[97]

The regiment formed as lively as crickets and marched to the Richmond, Fredericksburg & Potomac Railroad (RF&P) platform at the edge of camp.[98] Soldiers crammed into the stifling hot railcars. Sweat soaked their uniforms. The seventy-eight men of Company B boarded last.

The camp's band played trackside. The whistle blew. Couplings banged. Cars lurched. Steam gushed. Wheels rolled forward. The bell clanged. Wood smoke and sparks belched from the stack. The band struck up "Dixie." Song and cheers burst forth from the tobacco farmers as the train chugged away.

Everyone missed the cosmic ironies. Many lions of the Dan were descended from seed purged from the Virginia colony. Now the fruit of those loins fought for Old Virginia. The Pittsylvania Regiment was not from a land of cotton. And old times? Theirs had been forgotten!

CHAPTER THREE

Elusive Glory

Rushing air cooled sweat soaked men. Relief was brief. At Hanover Junction (now Doswell), a baggage car derailed while switching to the Virginia Central Railroad. After a two-hour delay in stifling heat, the train chugged to Gordonsville where it switched to the Orange & Alexandria Railroad for Manassas Junction. The train switched again to the Manassas Gap Railroad for Strasburg.

The men detrained late that night in a downpour. Colonel Edmonds halted the regiment in a field and bivouacked. Wet men slept fitfully. They rose early July 11. Uniforms dried as they marched the macadamized Valley Turnpike eighteen miles to Winchester. Their wet blankets and gear felt heavier by the mile. The men were not used to exertion. Captain Griggs noted, "A good many gave out on the march from Strasburg."[99]

Breathtaking Shenandoah panoramas competed with heart-wrenching scenes of refugees fleeing south. Federal threats had forced civilian evacuations and abandonment of homes. The new soldiers grew anxious to repay those responsible.

The 38th Virginia reached the outskirts of Winchester by three p.m. The regiment camped at Stephenson's farm. On paper, the 38th Virginia joined the 4th Brigade under General Edmund Kirby Smith.[100] However, the rest of the brigade was away countering Union movements.

The Winchester area was beautiful. The regiment camped beside a stream. There was abundant food and plenty of fresh "limestone water." There was, however, no shelter. An officer in the 38th Virginia wrote, "A great many of our soldiers have been lying on the ground here without tents and nothing but their blankets." Fortunately, the weather cooperated. The men were "just beginning to experience the realities of soldier life."[101]

Tents arrived and gave legitimacy to camp. Rigorous chores, inspections, and drills heightened order and readiness. The rank and file received little outside news. Delayed expectations bred impatience and carelessness. On July 13, one soldier accidentally discharged his sidearm in camp, killing another.[102] Colonel Edmonds immediately banned pistols among privates.[103] No one objected. It was enough work to maintain one's musket properly.

After three days in camp with little excitement, one wrote that soldiers dismissed the likelihood of a fight.[104] Troops continued to arrive from Richmond. The 10th Alabama camped nearby.

On July 15, the 38th Virginia struck tents and took positions about a mile north of Winchester. They remained in line of battle in an open field throughout the night. The men stood fast the next day pelted by a heavy rain with nothing but blankets for shelter. After two days in position, the area fouled for lack of sanitation. The regiment returned to camp on July 17. Tents remained in wagons, but at least they cooked rations, slept beside fires, and used sinks.

The 8th Alabama, 9th Alabama, 11th Alabama, and the 19th Mississippi arrived. These newest regiments had also been rushed to the front. They joined Kirby Smith's command until a fifth brigade could be formalized.

Late next day, the 38th Virginia received orders to move again. They left camp at five p.m. The entire brigade marched. Colonel Edmonds halted the regiment after two miles because of road congestion. Edmonds announced the brigade was ordered to Manassas Junction, then threatened by attack. Their march in the direction of Washington resumed with an exuberance that made good time over the hilly roads and across streams. The regiment halted about midnight. They marched again before daybreak.

The men forded the knee-deep Shenandoah River and spent most of the day ascending the grade to Ashby Gap (1,100 feet). They crossed the mountain at sunset and passed through Paris, Edmonds's hometown, at twilight. The colonel stopped briefly to pay respects to his uncle Lewis Edmonds and family at Belle Grove.[105] Ned had stayed there often as a boy.

His footsore men continued down the valley toward Piedmont Depot (now Delaplane). They halted that evening in a miles-long queue of regiments awaiting transport. They were hungry from their two-day, twenty-five-mile march. Colonel

Edmonds provided a cow courtesy of Uncle Lewis and ordered it killed and distributed. The men devoured it in less than an hour.[106]

Night passed. No train arrived. The column sat idle.

The first delivery of an army to a battlefield by train made history, but it was anything but efficient. The Manassas Gap Railroad was poorly maintained. Its locomotives and tracks were incapable of moving loaded cars at speeds over five miles per hour. Troop transport began on July 19 when Jackson's brigade rode from Piedmont Depot to Manassas Junction. Next, the train transported Bartow's Georgia brigade. Exhausted engineers, who had worked over twenty-four hours, quit and went home. Authorities scrambled to find substitutes. This they did. Also, a second train joined the operation.

Bernard Bee's brigade boarded and chugged away. The next load conveyed the 1st Maryland, 3rd Tennessee and 10th Virginia of Kirby Smith's brigade. This left behind the 13th Virginia and 38th Virginia next in queue. Behind them were the remaining five regiments attached to Smith.

The operation was slower than command anticipated. The thirty-mile Manassas run required six hours. Empty trains returned faster, but engines still required wood and water stops. Rail travel was quicker than marching, unless one waited days for a train.

At one halt, members of the 10th Virginia jumped off to pick blackberries and dawdled back aboard. Impending battle, stifling heat, hunger, thirst, derailments, and other delays stoked tensions. By evening July 20, stresses peaked such that upon a minor collision, the army summarily executed the engineers as saboteurs.[107] Staff scrambled to find replacements.

Early July 21, the 13th Virginia boarded and departed. These endured a miserable ride in crowded, hot freight and cattle cars. Several derailments added delays. As they neared Manassas Junction, gunfire scared the train's crew. The frightened engineers stopped their engine and ran for their lives fearing the same fate as the "saboteurs." The 13th Virginia completed the trip on foot and deployed to guard a ford.

General Kirby Smith and his 1st Maryland, 3rd Tennessee, and 10th Virginia reached the battlefield in time to reinforce the Confederate left at a crucial moment. Smith was wounded. Colonel Arnold Elzey took command. While these fought hard throughout the hot afternoon, the 38th Virginia sat stranded waiting for the next train.

At Piedmont Depot, Chaplain Cosby in the 38th Virginia held Sunday service. Word spread from the telegraph office that the battle raged. Men grew restless. Time palled. No trains returned. Anxieties and frustrations mounted. Finally, the telegraph clickety-ticked the news. Victory! The Yankees had been routed! All cheered the success of Southern arms.

* * *

Three thousand troops had missed the battle waiting for trains.[108] The would-be heroes received the triumph with mixed emotions. They had missed the big fight. Perhaps they had altogether missed the war and their chance for glory.

Trains arrived before daybreak July 22. Officers roused their men and crowded them onto railcars. Jubilation masked ambivalence having been denied a role in the action. The Pittsylvania Regiment detrained at Manassas Junction in high spirits and marched to a reserve position. They hoped to march on Washington.

The regiment halted on Henry House Hill. One corporal counted 150 dead Yankees lying where they fell.[109] Although Colonel Edmonds and his regiment missed the battle, his family had not. Virtually the entire battlefield was ancestral land.

In the near distance, the Carter mansion, coincidentally named Pittsylvania, overlooked Bull Run. It was the home of Colonel Edmonds's maternal grandparents. Shot and shell had scarred his mother's birthplace. Troops had trashed fences, trampled crops, scattered livestock, and frightened servants away. Dead soldiers littered the fields. Wounded and dying filled the house and outbuildings.[110]

Edmonds and his men stood before the ruins of the Henry house, where vicious fighting had trapped ailing widow Judith Carter Henry in her home. Artillery had smashed the house to splinters and killed the old woman. She was Edmonds's aunt Judith! His mother's eldest sister!

Confederates had made their final stand on the high ground between the Henry house and the Robinson farm. The owner James Robinson was a free mulatto, son of a white Carter and black servant. Robinson was Edmonds's kin.[111] Though common in the South, such relationships were seldom advertised.

Beyond the violent death of Aunt Judith, other ironies surely struck Edmonds. The victory there promised to forever link his new nation's struggle with his family seat. Also, that old, "Tom Fool" instructor from VMI had reportedly saved the day. He would soon to be known to all as "Stonewall" Jackson.

Despite hopes of an attack on Washington, no such orders came. Instead, the 38th Virginia received orders to march in the opposite direction.

A summer storm erupted. The 38th Virginia marched eight miles soaked by a cloud burst. They bivouacked in woods on Broad Run next to the Orange & Alexandria Railroad near Bristoe Station. Officers sent a detail back to Winchester for baggage. The men lived under tree canopies, crude brush arbors, and lean-tos until their wagons brought tents and tools for a proper camp. "Camp Edmonds" was near Brentsville, the Prince William County seat. Its only attraction was its tavern.

In addition to camp duties, details from the 38th Virginia guarded about two hundred wounded prisoners nearby. The glory the Pittsylvania volunteers craved eluded them. Indeed, history scarcely notes the 38th Virginia in that first Manassas campaign. They remained the only untried regiment in the 4th Brigade. Not a single man in the 38th Virginia had yet fired a shot.

Many assumed the war won. The general feeling was that the stellar victory at Manassas (Bull Run) assured recognition from England and France. That would force peace.[112] Even farm boys knew that meant the end of the war and lost opportunities for excitement, adventure, affirmation, and glory. Most young 1861 volunteers had joined for those reasons.

Thomas Jefferson Hines, Private, Company D, 38th Virginia Infantry. (Courtesy Library of Virginia)

Older privates like Tom Hines, Company D, 38th Virginia were pragmatic. The literate, thirty-five-year-old husband, father, farmer, and nominal slave owner had enlisted to defend his property rights. Peace suited him. Hines ended his next letter, "…far from home but in hopes not for long."[113]

* * *

The men's constitutions had not yet attained those of seasoned campaigners. Two weeks of marching and bivouacs in wet clothes took its toll in sick men. Company B, 38th Virginia lost a man to pneumonia on July 25. Ironically, his given name was Doctor Adkins.

On July 29, a soldier in the 38th Virginia reported plenty of food and blankets.[114] However, even after arrival of proper shelter and formal establishment of Camp Edmonds, many suffered colds or worse.

Colonel Cadmus Wilcox of the 9th Alabama assumed command of the provisional 5th Brigade, consisting of four Alabama regiments and one from Mississippi.[115] The new brigade also added the 38th Virginia. In effect, this culled the untried Pittsylvanians from the bloodied veterans of the 4th Brigade.

The Pittsylvania volunteers were a thousand among tens of thousands dispersed along Broad Run from Manassas to Thoroughfare Gap. Men often relieved themselves when and where convenient. Camp runoff contaminated water supplies with the inevitable result that men sickened by the thousands and died by the hundreds with typhoid fever.

Until then, losses had been incidental. Now pestilence took an alarming toll. Company B was uniquely blessed that their captain was a physician. Nevertheless, Company B suffered typical losses. Chesley Jackson and John Thompson died August 9, followed by William Grant the next day. Messmates cared for Cpl. John Hutson as he lay in his tent with typhoid. This was common care throughout the Army of the Potomac.

Green Adkins sponged Hutson to lower his fever. The sick twenty-year-old weakened and could not eat. Hutson took hold of Adkins's hand and told him he was happy, at peace with God, and felt like going to heaven.[116] Despite encouragements from friends, Hutson failed to rally and died three days later.

Captain John Cabell wrote the dead youth's father. Hutson "had endeared himself to each and every member of the company by his manly course and gentlemanly bearing…He was a soldier in every sense of the word, one who never flinched from duty."[117]

John Henry Hutson, Corporal, Company B, 38th Virginia Infantry. (Courtesy Cynthia Kay Hall)

Joe Hutcherson died a week later. Captain Cabell wrote another letter, then another, and another.

Lack of clothing in the 38th Virginia exacerbated the situation as uniforms wore out. In Company E, Captain Joseph Cabell wrote W. T. Sutherlin, appointed quartermaster for Danville, that his men were "nearly naked."[118] Cabell also took sick. His adjutant Lt. George H. Sutherlin wrote his elder brother W. T., "Our regiment is now suffering more from sickness than it has at any time since we have been out. We [the regiment] have over 300 cases typhoid fever so our Surgeon says."[119] George also contracted typhoid. The surgeon transferred him to a Richmond hospital. Sutherlin struggled two months. He rallied and then died.[120]

The regiment served picket duty with greatly reduced numbers. Death from disease thinned its ranks before the Pittsylvanians ever fired their first volley. In Company B, Moses Walker and Alex Mahan died in early September. The deaths only hint at the higher numbers of incapacitated. Most of the Pittsylvania Regiment were sick that month at one time or another. Many received furloughs home for recovery.

On September 22, the 38th Virginia relocated near Centerville. Company B left brothers Tom and John Oakes and others sick in camp on Broad Run. Company E marched away with forty-five, the largest number of actives. Most other companies fielded half that number.[121]

The weather cooled. Soldiers wrote home for warm caps and clothes. Having distanced themselves from the tavern at Brentsville, Tom Hines, enterprising, middle-aged private in Company D, 38th Virginia, added an additional request that his family box up "11 gallons of whiskey."[122]

Cleaner water reduced typhoid, but then, lice-infested soldiers contracted typhus. The summer-like first week of October aggravated infestation. This infection claimed six lives in the regiment.[123] On October 6, Edmonds ordered all unnecessary baggage back to the old camp. Personal trunks had to go. The order did not sit well with the older company commanders, who disagreed with the young colonel on a number of points.

A tropical storm brushed the region on October 7 and 8. Heavy rain and wind made camp life miserable. Yet, a different storm brewed as contentions over the colonel's most recent orders came to a head. Edmonds threatened to resign. Captain Joseph M. Terry, Company H, the blustery lawyer nearly twice Edmond's age, hoped he would.

Terry assembled the company commanders in Captain John S. Wood's tent to consider actions if Edmonds refused to resign. None dared express opinion openly. The meeting ended without resolution.

On October 9, Captains Terry and John Cabell preferred charges. Court-martial proceedings opened October 11 with Major Carrington as provost; Captain Townes as chair; Captain Griggs as secretary; and Lieutenant Prichard as judge advocate.

Many feared desertions in the ranks if Colonel Edmonds resigned or was reduced in rank. The court-martial concluded on October 14 with the matter dropped.[124]

In Colonel Edmonds's absence, Captain Terry reduced 1st Lt. Edgar Carrington to 2nd Lt. This was retribution, no doubt, for refusal to side with Terry in his cabal against Edmonds.

* * *

Colonel Edmonds took leave during the controversy. On October 13, the Edmonds family held a memorial service at Upperville Methodist Church for their beloved Judith Henry, slain at Manassas.[125] Also in attendance were their neighbors Francis "Frank" Stanly Armistead and his elder brother Lewis Addison Armistead.[126]

The brothers had resigned commissions in the U.S. Army to serve their native Virginia. Both had arrived in Richmond mid-September from separate posts in the West. Both were commissioned majors in the Confederate Army. Lewis had just received promotion to full colonel in command of the newly formed 57th Virginia Volunteer Infantry Regiment, comprised largely of Pittsylvanians and other Piedmonters like those under Edmonds.

Ned Edmonds and Frank Armistead were the same age and friends growing up.[127] Lewis was eighteen years older and already enrolled in West Point when the boys were born. Ned remembered Lewis as Brevet Major when last home in 1852 to settle matters when the Armistead estate burned. Lewis returned to the West to fight Indians.

Association with the Armistead family had kindled Edmonds's military interests. General Walker Keith Armistead's experiences in the Battle of Fallen Timbers, the War of 1812, the Seminole War, as well as Lewis's exploits in Mexico, fired imagination. The general died in 1845 second in rank to General Zachary Taylor.

Upon reaching sixteen, the late general's record secured Frank's appointment to West Point. Ned enrolled in VMI three years later following his father's suicide. Edmonds's education prepared him to head the Danville Military Academy.[128]

The memorial service for Judith Henry coincided with the Armistead brothers being home on furlough to bury their mother.[129] It was yet another sad event in a long line of tragedies for Lewis Armistead. He had lost two wives and two children while on posts serving in the U.S. Army.

There was no time to linger with family and friends. Edmonds hurried back to camp.

The war would soon reunite Ned Edmonds and Lewis Armistead.

* * *

Members of the 38th Virginia fired their first shots at the enemy when Federals drove in their picket line on October 16. The regiment braced themselves for an attack that never came. The following day, Wilcox's brigade became official.[130] The 38th Virginia was part of that brigade in Gustavus W. Smith's division camped on Cub Run near the Fairfax-Loudoun County line. The weather turned cold. The men had only ragged summer clothing.

On October 30, the Pittsylvania Regiment marched to Centerville for an assembly with other Virginia units. Governor Letcher presented each a state flag. The new blue banner bore the Virginia state seal and its motto, *Sic Semper Tyrannis*. The General Assembly had approved the device on April 30. No official state flag existed prior to secession. The prototype first appeared thirty years earlier at the head of troops putting down the Nat Turner Rebellion. All considered it a fit banner for their crusade. Virtue stood armed with spear and sword at the ready with her foot planted on a tyrant, like they imagined Old Abe.

On November 1, a week after first frost, the quartermaster in the 38th Virginia issued great coats. That same day, doctors discharged Booker Adkins, Company B for chronic rheumatism, the most common, noninfectious malady. The remaining Adkins brothers and cousins received their warm coats with the rest of the company.

In advance of Confederate elections, congressional candidate John Goode of Bedford County spoke to the men. All were ordered to attend. The weather warmed that evening ahead of a rain squall. Wind blew. Tents toppled. Perhaps it was a politician-induced slumber, but some did not realize their shelter blown off until awakened by drenching rain.

Colonel Edmonds's wife and her sister visited the muddy camp briefly on November 4. Traveling to and from lodging with relatives accounted for most of their day.

November 6 was Election Day. Everyone cast a ballot for president, vice president, and congressman. It was mere formality. There was only one candidate per office. The following day, Captain Griggs of Company K, a devout Baptist, paid $2.50 from his own pocket for five pints of medicinal whiskey for the sake of his many ill men.[131]

Despite hardships, esprit de corps was sufficiently high in the 38th Virginia that Major Carrington wrote a friend on November 15, "If there is one thing utterly impossible, it is this army can be whipt by any force the Yankees can bring against us."[132]

* * *

The national flags of the Union and Confederacy were scarcely distinguishable when limp. A single flag's identity had decided victory at a crucial moment at Manassas. Generals Johnston and Beauregard determined the Southern cause should never again be jeopardized by the confusion. Johnston requested states provide flags for their troops. Virginia and North Carolina had complied. Meanwhile, Beauregard ordered a distinctive battle flag designed.

The chosen shape was square rather than rectangular. Twelve stars, one for each Confederate state, showed bright on the arms of a dark blue Saint Andrew's cross outlined in white on a blood red field edged with gold fringe.[133] The flag intentionally incorporated Christian symbolism in the manner of the British Union Jack.

Upon approval of three silk prototypes, procurement fell to Brigadier General William L. Cabell, quartermaster for the Army of the Potomac, brother of Captains John and Joseph Cabell in the 38th Virginia.

General Cabell's Richmond agent purchased all available silk dress fabric. Scarlet silk was in especially short supply being inappropriate for ladies' dresses of the era. Consequently, most flags sported rose or pink fields. Yellow borders replaced gold fringe. As many as four hundred Richmond women worked feverishly to deliver 120 copies.[134]

Snow fell November 24. The next day, General G. W. Smith assembled his division in the wintry landscape at Centerville for review and presentation of new battle flags by Generals Johnston and Beauregard.

Bright sun in clear blue sky reflected off pure white snow. Dazzling light intensified colors. The colonels reported front and center before the general staff and received their bright yellow-trimmed, white-starred, blue-crossed, pink silk devices.[135] The colonels conveyed the new battle flags to their color guards.

The battle flag of the 38th Virginia flared brightly beside their recently acquired state flag. The flower of Virginian womanhood had sewn it for them. All cheered the new standard.

The Pittsylvania Regiment related to their new flag in a special way. Its source was a Pittsylvania Cabell.

The Army of the Potomac officially adopted its colors on November 28. General Beauregard ordered the following read to all troops:

> A new banner is entrusted to-day, as a battle-flag, to the safe keeping of the Army of the Potomac. Soldiers: Your mothers, your wives, and your sisters have made it. Consecrated by their hands, it must lead you to substantial victory, and the complete triumph of our cause. It can never be surrendered, save to your unspeakable dishonor, and with its consequences fraught with immeasurable evil. Under its untarnished folds beat back the invader, and find nationality, everlasting immunity from an atrocious despotism, and honor and renown for yourselves—or death.[136]

In the 38th Virginia, Color Sergeant John Bohanon received promotion to ensign with overall responsibility for the new battle flag and its color guard.

There was no mistaking the new pink and blue device on any battlefield. Personal impressions were never recorded.[137] The distinct pattern was to become the most revered symbol of their cause.

* * *

The rest of the month was routine drill and picket duty. Camp life grew spartan as November ended with orders to ship all baggage to Manassas Junction. Arms, tents, and cook gear comprised group essentials. Individuals retained one uniform, one change of underwear, and two blankets.

Generals Johnston and Beauregard reviewed the troops again on December 3, again in the snow, but colder. December was again characterized by camp chores and picket duties. Many were sick. The continual threat of an unseen enemy, boring routines, cold weather, short days, and long nights tried spirits.

On December 13, Captain Terry, Company H, 38th Virginia resigned. The fifty-one-year-old company commander, a virtual relic in the field, had had his fill of the army and submission to a colonel half his age. The country lawyer returned to his home and law practice at Chalk Level. The popular, young 2nd Lt. Edgar Carrington, recently demoted by Terry, replaced his nemesis as company commander upon immediate election to captain.

The brigade assembled to witness a double execution. Two men from an Alabama regiment had plotted to kill their colonel. Each condemned gave a Roman Catholic priest twenty-five dollars in hopes of saving their souls.[138] The sad affair broke camp monotony and fueled discussions around campfires. The rank and file of the 38th Virginia, mostly Baptists, had never seen an execution before, nor had they ever seen a Catholic.[139]

On December 20, the 38th Virginia formed in response to enemy activity, but no action developed. The men celebrated Christmas. Some scrounged fixings for eggnog. The next day the regiment broke camp and marched to the Manassas battlefield. They halted in a pine thicket at Ball's Ford on Bull Run and began building log cabins for the winter. Details retrieved baggage from the rail depot.

Colonel Edmonds and staff billeted up the hill at the Lewis mansion Portici. The home belonged to Edmonds's kin.[140]

The soldiers crowded primitive cabins. Clothing was adequate. Food was basic and plentiful. Living conditions were not too unlike those in which some had been raised. Once situated, Colonel Edmonds issued furloughs to married men.[141]

Those wintering on the banks of Bull Run faced the routine camp and picket tediums that had so characterized their soldiering to date. There was ample time to reflect.

Eighteen sixty-one had been the year of the volunteer. Adventurous Pittsylvanians answered Virginia's call to arms with enthusiastic hopes of glory. They had drilled, marched, labored, and sacrificed as much as anyone in the army. They had not been bloodied in battle, yet their casualties were many.

Losses in Company B were typical for the regiment. In their six-month deployment, illness and disease claimed one quarter. Fully 10 percent died, and 15 percent were hospitalized or permanently discharged. Many were kin. All were friends.

The simple tobacco farmers reaped no glory envisioned at enlistment, only hardships and bereavements. Personal honor, love of family, community bonds, and faith in God sustained each. They had proven themselves soldiers of Virginia, but these lions of the Dan had not yet roared.

CHAPTER FOUR

Advance to the Rear

Enthusiastic Benjamin Edward Cabell joined his brothers in the war. The youth enlisted in the 38th Virginia the moment he turned eighteen that December. On New Year's Day 1862, the inexperienced lad became second lieutenant in Company E. This was no surprise. His brother Captain Joseph Cabell was company commander. They were FFV stock, brothers of a brigadier general, and sons of a major general in a society where class and nepotism reigned. Winter quarters gave the fledgling officer time to learn his duties.

Communities collected goods for their men in the field. Relatives and trusted servants drove wagons long distances in fickle weather over the bad roads. Visitors often stayed in or near camp to assist as needed. Many abided until the army resumed movement.

An occasional wagon from Callands reached Company B with communal supplies as well as crates and trunks for individuals. Soldiers welcomed comforts from home: sweaters, socks, underwear, blankets, and various edibles. Owners crammed boxes into close quarters to serve double duty as tables and seats. Preserved and baked goods that survived transit supplemented plentiful rations. Candlesticks and lanterns brightened cabins. Sundries from wives, mothers, sisters, and sweethearts boosted morale.

Married officers rotated home on furlough. The rank and file had no such relief. Reduced unit strength and enemy proximity demanded their presence. Drills, inspections, and picket duty summarized a healthy soldier's life. Few stayed healthy. A mumps outbreak added to camp woes.

Cold, wet weather characterized January and February.[142] The 38th Virginia in their canvas-roofed shanties lived in luxury compared to Stonewall Jackson's men suffering bitter cold on their Romney expedition.

Rumors of foreign recognition and end of the war persisted. Notions of peace bred complacency. Inactivity in drab winter surroundings intensified boredoms and home sickness. Illness, disease, and deaths fed discouragements.

The Pittsylvanians reckoned four more months until their one-year enlistments expired. Anticipation lifted spirits, but four months seemed an eternity away.

Drinking, cussing, gambling, and other army vices grew rampant. Southern morality degenerated in camps to such degree that clergy predicted divine retribution on the battlefield.[143] The prophesied defeats came soon and many. Bad news began in February with reports that forts Henry and Donelson had surrendered in the West.[144]

* * *

March brought more daylight and modest relief in the weather.

Lt. Benjamin Cabell had barely served two months when he contracted typhoid. Surgeons transferred him to Richmond, where he died. The death of young Cabell proved double sorrow for his brothers, for the news was too much for their father. Major General Benjamin W. S. Cabell sickened with grief over his namesake and died within a month.[145]

Union threats along the Centerville line and potential landings in Tidewater strained Virginia's defenses. Without consulting President Davis, General Johnston abandoned his Centerville line to move nearer Richmond.

The 38th Virginia received orders to march. Soldiers loaded military gear onto wagons. Individuals held on to what personal effects they dared carry and sent the rest to the rail depot.

On March 8, they torched their cabins and tramped five miles to Gainesville. Men shed superfluous possessions along the way. At Gainesville, they burned stockpiled commissary stores, over a thousand barrels of flour and much bacon.[146] Other troops torched the Manassas Junction Depot. The Pittsylvanians lost their best winter clothing sent there.[147]

Fire consumed anything useful to the enemy. From Thoroughfare Gap to Centerville, mills, meat packing plants, warehouses, and camps constructed for the

Centerville line blazed. Pillars of dark smoke rose throughout the region, savory smoke, the burnt sacrifice of untold tons of rations.

The next morning Colonel Withers, 18th Virginia, took charge of the rearguard composed of one battalion of his regiment (with companies from Danville and Spring Garden) and a second battalion from the 38th Virginia under Lt. Colonel Whittle.[148] The other battalions of the 38th Virginia and 18th Virginia, under Colonel Edmonds and Lt. Colonel Henry A. Carrington, retired with the wagons.

On March 12, the rearguard halted two miles east of Warrenton and formed a line of battle. Their position was especially vulnerable being separated from the main army. When no enemy pursued, officers exercised their men in skirmish drill.

Whittle's battalion entered Warrenton on March 15. The soldiers quartered in the Warren-Green Hotel and the Fauquier County Courthouse. The first contingent of the 38th Virginia had already passed through. Colonel Edmonds had checked in briefly at Edmonium, his paternal ancestral home.[149] His relatives had evacuated leaving only servant caretakers.

For twelve days Whittle's men enjoyed the town's hospitality. Officers intervened to destroy much liquor.[150]

The battalion marched at sunset March 27 to Fauquier White Sulphur Springs on the banks of the Rappahannock River.[151] Weather turned fickle. The next morning, they shook off a frost, crossed over, and burned the bridge behind them. They rose the following day to spring-like temperatures and marched midmorning through Jeffersonton to Rixeville. On the morrow, the men trod the last hilly leg to Culpeper in snow, sleet, and rain. The battalion halted at noon for the day.

Whittle's battalion left Culpeper next day and followed the Orange & Alexandria Railroad. They rejoined Edmonds with the main army camped one mile before Orange Court House. Their brigade (Wilcox's) had been sent to North Carolina.[152] The move left the fragmented 38th Virginia behind, temporarily assigned to the brigade of J. R. Jones.

The arrival of new men bolstered strength. Back on March 10, Governor Letcher fully activated the Virginia militia in response to Johnston's abrupt evacuation of the Centerville line. All former members of the militia who had not reenlisted after secession were drafted back into service. These reported immediately with any serviceable firearm they possessed or could borrow.[153] They were mostly married men with families, a breed apart from 1861 volunteers. The 38th Virginia received twenty-five new men from Callands. Many were brothers and cousins. Company B added an additional Adkins, three Fullers and an Oakes.[154]

The reinforced 38th Virginia lived five to a tent. Camp routines resumed with water and wood details, drills, inspections, and picket duties. Another outbreak of measles reduced unit strength.

Afternoon temperatures in the sixties hinted at spring. Nights remained cold. On April 6, the army acted on reports of enemy activity at Fredericksburg. The 38th Virginia fell in at nine p.m. and marched that direction six hours in the dark. The weather changed dramatically: "…snow, rain and sleet falling the whole while in rapid alternations, and presenting a painful exhibition of the fierce, relentless anger of the savage, ill-tempered and intractable elements."[155] The men bivouacked in a thick wood and miserable conditions. They encountered no enemy and marched back to camp in rain and sleet. The next day it snowed.

News spread of a fight at Norfolk between iron ships.[156] The enemy had taken New Bern, North Carolina. Also, there had been a big battle in Tennessee with staggering losses.[157] General Albert Sydney Johnston was killed. Moreover, a Union army under Major General George B. McClellan had landed at Fort Monroe and threatened Richmond from the lower Peninsula. The Yorktown defense line currently held McClellan in check.

The 38th Virginia broke camp on April 10 and marched to the rail depot at Orange Court House. At midnight, they boarded a train "about a mile long."[158] The men knew not their destination. In view of their retreat and troubling rumors from the West, talk spread within the ranks about the army falling back to Danville.[159]

By dawn, the engine had chugged eight miles to Gordonsville. The train sat idle much of the day before clickety-clacking the remaining sixty miles to Richmond. The men received no food since breaking camp.

On April 12, the first anniversary of Fort Sumter, the regiment detrained at Camp Lee and marched to Camp Winder.[160] The unit ate and rested until late next day.

The regiment marched four miles to Rockett's Landing. A Peninsula destination was apparent. They arrived dockside at dusk and boarded seven river boats. One was the steamer *West Point.*

The James River was tawny and swollen from recent rains. Once loaded, whistles blew, bells rang, and the ships paddled downstream with the current. This was a first boat ride for most. Crowded conditions forced many to stand. Those on deck had fair weather and a full moon. Wheels churned the dark water white and sparks spewed from funnels.

The novel, nighttime cruise down the serpentine course swept around Turkey Island and passed some of the most noted plantations of Old Virginia. They cruised by the dark outline of Fort Pocahontas on Jamestown Island. Three miles beyond, the boats delivered the men onto the wharf at Kings Mill about midnight.[161]

The 38th Virginia marched six miles down the Great Warwick-Hampton Highway to Lebanon Church and bivouacked in a pine forest.[162] This placed them in reserve two miles behind the main defense line.

Major General John Bankhead Magruder, tasked with defending the Peninsula, had engineered a series of dams. These skillfully exploited the Warwick River and feeder creeks to flood expanses in front of earthworks. The fortifications extended from Yorktown to the James River.[163]

The 38th Virginia joined Robert Toombs's Georgia brigade.[164] The next day, the morning of April 15, cannon fire interrupted breakfast. Colonel Edmonds mounted his horse and formed the regiment. He then marched them to close support of defenses. They stood in line of battle anxious for their first fight. Their pink silk battle flag flapped in the breeze. They remained at arms throughout the day and all night. Officers forbade alcohol.[165] There was no relief from the chill, nor from frustration.

Gunfire ceased early April 16. The men suspected something was up. At nine o'clock, Union field artillery opened in earnest as McClellan tested the defenses at Dam No. 1.[166] Confederate batteries replied in kind.

Shells exploded around the 38th Virginia. One observed Colonel Edmonds "seemed as cool as a May breeze." Edmonds rode up and down the ranks calming and encouraging the men. One observed, "A finer little man never rode at the head of a regiment."[167] The 38th Virginia was ready for action.

The pyrotechnic exchange, exciting at first, dragged on for six unnerving hours. At a quarter to three, sounds of musketry joined that of artillery. The 3rd Vermont regiment waded across the waist-deep water "boiling with bullets" to take the nearest trench. Georgia and Louisiana troops counterattacked and retook the position. The Vermonters lost 83 killed, wounded, or captured out of 192.[168] Many wounded drowned where they fell.[169]

Casualties streamed past the 38th Virginia to the field hospital at Endview. Gunfire became intermittent. The Pittsylvanians remained at the ready.

That night, the 38th Virginia filed into "the ditch" to relieve exhausted Georgians and clear the dead. Fortifications of light earth betrayed men silhouetted by moonlight. Day dawned on the 38th Virginia crouched in frontline trenches, deep in mud churned by activity. Earthworks of bright, yellow-buff subsoil glared in the sun.

Behind them on the gentle slope were twin earthen forts with cannon. Before them was the sluggish Warwick River with Dam No. 1 to their left. Dead Yankees littered the open stretch about one hundred yards to the water. The waist-deep river extended another one hundred yards to the opposite bank. The distant shore was clear inland for one hundred yards, except for the standing chimneys of a burned farmhouse.[170] The enemy filled the woods beyond.

Exposure above the embankment attracted fire. The newcomers to "the ditch" tempted fate. Pittsylvanians raised their heads like so many groundhogs for a peek at the enemy. No one resisted. "Balls [flew] thick as hail," reported one private in the 38th Virginia.[171] A bullet struck Joel Tucker of Company F in the chin. The ugly wound was mortal.[172] Most considered it Tucker's bad luck and continued the practice.

Shots rang out throughout the day. Each discharge prompted response. Bullets whizzed like bees. Attentions focused forward on immediate dangers. No one in the 38th Virginia noticed the Confederate hot air balloon rise high in the sky behind them.[173] Cannons belched shot and shell from four o'clock that afternoon until midnight, then silence.

Colonel Edmonds advised his men to "look for a trick." At one o'clock in the morning, the moon came up. A shot rang out. The whole line opened fire and poured rounds into the enemy's position until ordered to cease fire. About five o'clock infantry appeared about four hundred yards away. The whole line opened fire again. Union artillery returned fire. The men loosed "ten thousand balls in among them." That quieted them down.

"Well done my brave boys!" Edmonds praised.[174]

Refreshed Georgians relieved the 38th Virginia. It had been a rough day under punishing fire. Captain Griggs wrote, "The Yankees shot all day. Nearly all broke down from want of sleep. Very cold."[175]

As the 38th Virginia departed, the enemy resumed fire. The Georgians fired back. Union artillery fired high. Iron balls and chards clipped limbs and branches which fell around the retiring 38th Virginia. Elements of Company C broke and ran. Edmonds rebuked the men. It was bad behavior, especially for the color company.

Regiments alternated days between the frontline and camp. The twenty-four-hour reprieve, which included transit to and from camp, hardly prepared a man for the next twenty-four hours in the trenches. The 38th Virginia still had no tents.

The 38th Virginia returned to the frontline April 19. Dead Yankees submerged for days in the river rose to the surface. The Union sent a flag of truce to retrieve their dead. General Toombs inspected the position with Colonel Edmonds. Toombs complimented the men. The Yankees returned to the woods, and the war resumed.

Night time was time to dig. There was much to repair and improve. The men fully grasped General Magruder's epithet, King of Spades.

Soldiers fired at any indiscrete noise or light. Shots directed at sounds rarely hit their marks. A rifle crack followed by a squall signaled a hit. By this measure, most reckoned sharpshooters killed three to five men a day.

Generally, in the daytime, when one fired, the whole line erupted. In time, bullets alone felled trees six to eight inches thick in targeted areas.[176] One hoped the bullets pruned the enemy as well.

Heavy rains began on April 20. The tentless 38th Virginia hunkered down in their pine woods under blankets, oilcloths, and crude lean-tos. They filed back into the trenches next day. The three-foot-wide, two-foot-deep ditch was full of water. One crouched in cold water and mire all day and shoveled mud all night. One either "slaved like a Negro or brined like a ham." Either way, the soldiers were always cold, wet, mud caked, and miserable.[177]

Both Colonel Edmonds and Major Carrington took sick. Edmonds's absence was a blow. One member of the 38th Virginia wrote that day, "We love our colonel dearly."[178]

On April 23, more heavy rain fell. Magruder's chief of artillery Colonel Henry C. Cabell appeared at Dam No. 1. He repositioned the enfilading thirty-two pounders and placed a rifled gun in a new embrasure.[179] He was both near kin to the Cabells in the 38th Virginia and Major Carrington's uncle.[180]

Artillerymen slept beside their guns without benefit of fire throughout the siege. As miserable as this was, it was preferable to the infantry's lot.

Food was less than expected. Men received the "plainest and roughest" rations to date: dry corn in the shuck, pickled pork, flour, and half rations of black-eyed peas. There was no coffee, just brackish water to drink.[181] One described the bacon issued as "yellow as a pumpkin and rank as a mink! I don't think a dog would eat it."[182]

Cooks prepared group mess in the rear areas and then brought it forward. Skimpy portions left many feeling slighted. Siege conditions often prevented delivery. The result was then one meal every other day.

Few in the 38th Virginia had donned a clean shirt since Orange Court House. One scarcely had a "coot or cartridge box" off since arrival on the Peninsula.[183] Moreover, there was no visual discernment of fabric. Wool, linen, cotton, all appeared the same when caked with the yellow-buff trench mud.

On April 25, word arrived that their baggage was detained in Richmond until their fight was decided.[184] This meant no tents and no change of clothes for the foreseeable future. It rained two more days. Finally, the week-long rain ended.

Camp life was miserable, but it was nothing compared to the trenches. Soldiering was anything but the glorious lark first imagined. Most reckoned that if their grandfathers endured similar hardships for independence, they could too. Besides, the end of their one-year enlistments approached.

Crushing news then arrived that Congress had passed the Conscription Act.[185] The law subjected able-bodied men between ages eighteen and thirty-five to military service. Furthermore, it extended all current one-year enlistments to three years.

Discontent festered. The term "volunteer infantry" vanished from vocabularies. Soldiers viewed conscription as an affront to the freedoms for which they fought. This was especially true to those who had faithfully served their year and forced to stay.

One South Carolina officer made known his belief that the law was unconstitutional. Dangerous murmurings spread throughout his regiment and beyond. The commander of the 1st Kentucky pulled his men off the frontline to "reorganize." An address by General Magruder to Kershaw's brigade calmed unrest and persuaded those men to re-enlist. It was mere formality but personal recommitments nevertheless.

Service had become servitude. The men hated the war. They hated the Southern Confederacy.[186] Rich men had picked a fight that poor men fought. Nevertheless, they loved liberty and their homes and needed to fight honorably in their defense.

On April 29, the 38th Virginia held elections in a cold drizzle, for the forced re-enlistment also occasioned the reelection of officers.[187] Nearly a year in the field had given men a clearer perspective on leadership. Company B voted out both its platoon leaders and sent them packing. They elected sergeants Whitmell Adkins and James Warren as second lieutenants.

Alternate days on the frontline and constant exposure continued to take its toll. Sick roll of the 38th Virginia added Captain John Cabell, Company B, himself a physician. The hospital at Endview bustled with activity as if preparing to evacuate. Rumors spread as wagon loads of supplies departed. Everything hinted withdrawal.

On May 1, headquarters transferred the 38th Virginia to Early's brigade comprising the 24th Virginia, the 5th North Carolina and 23rd North Carolina regiments. Jubal A. Early, a native of Franklin County, was educated in Danville and Lynchburg, and graduated from West Point. The army officer turned lawyer had argued against disunion up until secession; thus, his background commended him to the Pittsylvanians.

Like the Pittsylvanians, many men in the 24th Virginia and 5th North Carolina also came from the Albemarle Basin. Early's brigade was one of two in Daniel Harvey Hill's division.

That same day, General Johnston ordered the troops to burn all personal gear except a change of clothing.[188] The 38th Virginia had nothing to burn. They had only what they had worn for over a month. A pullback was imminent. Joe Johnston was retreating again. This was the army commander's second major withdrawal in as many months.

Dark clouds with steady rain rolled in on May 3. At nightfall, Confederate siege guns opened a general barrage. Heavy shells fell all along the Union line and drove the enemy to cover. One Union surgeon called it a "magnificent pyrotechnic display."[189] The bombardment masked retreat.

General James Longstreet coordinated withdrawal along the two main roads. Hill's division supported the bombardment while other infantry and field artillery withdrew. At two a.m. the big guns fell silent. Southerners abandoned their heavy artillery. Gun crews fled at last lanyard pull and hurriedly splashed their way beyond the cavalry screen. Few spiked their guns.

Union listening posts heard only rain. Eerie stillness stoked curiosity. At daybreak May 4, observers ascended in the gas balloon *Intrepid*.[190] Rain and low clouds restricted visibility to only the nearest fortifications and camps. Even so, it was obvious the Rebels were gone. The siege of Yorktown was over.[191]

* * *

Lt. Colonel Powhatan Whittle commanded the 38th Virginia in Colonel Edmonds's absence. The regiment was among the last to quit the line. They passed through the rearguard cavalry posted along the Warwick-Hampton Highway from Magruder's vacated headquarters at Lee Hall to Endview and Lebanon Church.[192] The 38th Virginia joined Early's column and retraced their route of two weeks prior toward Williamsburg.

Rain fell relentlessly. The mire churned by Longstreet's columns impeded Hill's division. Early's brigade marched last with the 38th Virginia and 24th Virginia regiments at the end. These encountered the worst conditions as they slogged the congested quagmire throughout the night. In places men sank knee-deep in water and mud. The thixotropic clay mush sucked off shoes. Exhausted men fell asleep at any halt. At sunrise, the trailing units were scarcely halfway to Williamsburg. One advantage, if there was such a thing, was that each step left the road in even worse condition for pursuers.

Cold rain continued. Guns thundered behind them as J. E. B. Stuart's horse artillery delayed Stoneman's cavalry at the crossing over Skiff's Creek at Blow's Mill. The bridge there was too wet to fire and no time to cut it down. After Stuart's troopers retired, the main Union column crossed and advanced up the Warwick-Hampton Highway. A lesser force moved up the Yorktown Road.

Johnston had no desire to confront McClellan at Williamsburg, only delay pursuit. He ordered Longstreet's division into fortifications prepared by Magruder as a tertiary line of defense. These consisted of fourteen redoubts and redans exploiting key terrain features across the Peninsula at the narrow, four-mile-wide bottleneck between College Creek and Cub Creek. The centerpiece was Fort Magruder, an earthen fort located midway in the line about a mile from town. This guarded the convergence of the two main arteries from the south.

Longstreet was unfamiliar with the layout and left the northernmost positions unoccupied. He had insufficient numbers to man them anyway.

By noon, Early's brigade had slogged the nine miles to Fort Magruder. Shortly after they passed, Union gunboats thundered on the James River. Yankee units began arriving to probe the defenses.

Hill's division moved past Williamsburg. Early's brigade bivouacked two miles beyond the town. All were cold, wet, and hungry. Rations were short. The men ate only what remained in their haversacks. Few had anything. As night fell, the rain slowed and became intermittent. The men slept. All anticipated resuming retreat next day.

On May 5, Hill's division was up again an hour before dawn to renew their trek to Richmond, but plans changed. Longstreet needed help to hold McClellan and summoned Hill's division.

Magruder and his men held his namesake fort. Longstreet's division manned flanking earthworks but lacked sufficient troops to fully cover his line. Redoubts 9 through 14 sat vacant.

Hill's men countermarched to Williamsburg. They halted at the College of William & Mary and stacked arms on the green. Cannons thundered and musketry rattled south of town. Longstreet called for reinforcements on his right. Hill sent Rodes's brigade. Early's brigade waited and listened to the fight.

About three p.m. cannon fire opened east of town. Longstreet ordered Hill to send Early to cover the left flank of Fort Magruder and reinforce the frontline as needed.

Officers ordered men to shed nonessential gear. Companies threw knapsacks, blankets, and cook gear into piles. Early's brigade splashed forward toward the sound of the guns. Each regiment with pink silk colors flying moved in column four abreast at the double quick down the oyster shell paved Main Street (now Duke of Gloucester Street). The town appeared deserted. The few citizens who had not evacuated hid themselves.

Excitement grew in the 38th Virginia as they rushed forward. The Pittsylvania Regiment headed into action!

Major General D. H. Hill and the other mounted officers led the trotting column past the female academy (then a hospital) and out of town onto the main, muddy, rutted road.[193] The 5th North Carolina led the way followed by the 23rd North Carolina, 38th Virginia, and 24th Virginia. The opposing flow of wounded and escorted prisoners stepped aside to make way. Men in ranks focused on keeping up with their units.

The mile-long run in heavy, rain-soaked woolens disheveled ranks. Guns thundered and shells exploded ahead of them at Fort Magruder. Before reaching the fort, D. H. Hill directed the 5th North Carolina left across a muddy, freshly plowed field. The other regiments followed. Another quarter mile put them in a green, knee-high field of wheat. The regiments trampled the crop as lines of battle formed facing the woods. Enemy artillery boomed somewhere beyond the trees.

From his left to right, Early deployed the 24th Virginia, 38th Virginia, 23rd North Carolina, and 5th North Carolina, two untried regiments sandwiched between veteran units. Cannons boomed ahead of them. Shells burst at Fort Magruder to their right rear.

Hill and Early made quick reconnaissance around the right of the woods while the men, "breathless, hot and heavy of foot," recovered from their run.[194] The generals observed Union guns supported by infantry. Hill proposed an attack on the enemy's right rear and galloped to the fort to secure Longstreet's permission. He arrived amid exploding shells.

Hill's visit coincided with General Joseph Johnston's brief presence. Johnston planned only to delay the Federals long enough to ensure safety of his retreating wagon trains and questioned the proposed attack. Longstreet consented under condition that Hill only deal with the nuisance and not delay their withdrawal with a prolonged fight.

Hill rejoined Early and completed preparations. Johnston left for Richmond.

Rather than take the standard position behind his brigade, Early posted himself in front of his old regiment. He ordered his brigade to load and fix bayonets. Steel rattled in flurried motion. Excited men pulled tompions, handled cartridges, drew ramrods, rammed home bullets, capped cones, and fixed bayonets. Muskets came to shoulder arms. The line bristled like a porcupine.

Events moved rapidly, so rapidly that Early did not advance skirmishers. He pointed to the trees and declared the enemy "over there!" He assured the men that once under fire, the safest place would be at the very guns themselves.[195]

Hill, stationed on the far right of the 5th North Carolina, ordered the advance. The signal did not reach Early. He and the 24th Virginia moved forward after seeing the 5th North Carolina in motion. Similarly, the 38th Virginia was last to step off and hurried to keep up across the wheat field.

In the misty haze before them, dense woods in full green leaf concealed a nightmare for maneuver. Forested gullies branched into steep ravines that ran perpendicular to the line of march. As the brigade advanced toward the gunfire, the regiments pushed into the woods and immediately lost alignment and communications in devilish terrain. Field officers dismounted and struggled to manage both troops and mounts.

The 38th Virginia moved down a wet slope thick with slippery leaves, wet underbrush, and fallen timber. Next, they struggled uphill against the same conditions. Beyond the crest, they crossed a farm lane. They again pushed into tangled forest. Soldiers moved tree to tree, down and up another steep, slippery ravine.

Long arms, cumbersome in thickets, were more so with fixed bayonets. Accoutrements snagged. Ranks broke for natural obstructions and struggled to re-form. Inevitably whole companies disintegrated, lost contact, and became disoriented. The 23rd North Carolina faced similar trials but halted frequently to maintain control. The 38th Virginia stumbled forward. Beyond their left, Early with the 24th Virginia attempted to flank the guns.

Earlier in the day, forces under Union general Winfield Scott Hancock, preceded by cavalry under 2nd Lt. George Armstrong Custer, crossed the dam at Saunders Pond. They then occupied the high ground at vacant Redoubt 11. Hancock placed his ten guns immediately west of the redoubt supported by three infantry regiments and two in reserve. Once in battery, the cannon kept up a steady barrage on Fort Magruder and its works.

About five p.m., just as victory seemed assured, Hancock received orders to withdraw. He hesitated and seriously considered disobeying the directive. Nevertheless, Hancock complied. He ordered his guns and infantry to the rear. They moved just as Early's men cleared the woods.

A double surprise greeted Early as he and the 24th Virginia emerged at the edge of a wheat field. First, rather than fall on the enemy's rear, the terrain had skewed their march and exposed their flank before the enemy. Second, the Union was withdrawing.

Early mistook this as retreat and dared not wait for the rest of his brigade. He seized opportunity. The 24th Virginia wheeled left and charged. Exuberant Virginians shouted, "Bull Run!"[196] and "Ball's Bluff!"

Early's men slowed to climb a rail fence. Hancock's men rose from behind the cover of the hill's crest and loosed a murderous volley. Early's horse went down. The general rose and continued to lead on foot. The 24th Virginia pressed forward across the open field of knee-high wheat to the dubious cover of a picket fence. Many went down. Bullets hit Early twice. One pierced his shoulder.

Minutes earlier, three hundred yards to the south, the 5th North Carolina emerged from their end of the woods and prepared to charge the redoubt directly in front of them. This was Redoubt 10, recently manned by the 6th South Carolina. Hancock's gunfire redirected attentions to the real enemy in the distance. The 5th North Carolina wheeled left and charged at the same time as Early. The 5th North Carolina had farther to go and crossed nearly a mile of open field in good order. They took heavy casualties along the way, including three color bearers. Ten minutes into the fight, the 5th North Carolina reached the fence alongside the 24th Virginia, which was by then under command of its major.[197] Cheers broke forth! Opposing lines of muskets roared!

Concurrently, the 38th Virginia emerged from the woods with Lt. Colonel Powhatan Whittle at the forefront encouraging his men into line. Whittle inspired awe. As fearless as his chieftain ancestor, the six-foot-six soldier exhibited a Washington-like presence. For the moment, Whittle seemed as bulletproof as the great Washington. Three balls passed through his coat without injury to his person.[198]

Whittle steadied his line while waiting for his missing companies. The three leftmost companies (B, G, and K) still struggled through the woods. Companies at the far left of the regiment caught the brunt of overshot rounds from the fight before them. Lewis Delaney, Company E took a bullet in a foot and limped to the rear.

One by one the missing companies exited the woods and extended the left of the 38th Virginia. Overshot rounds hit two more men in Company E and one each in Companies I and K. As Company B emerged from the woods and took their place in line, William Lewis received the dubious distinction of being the first combat bloodied soldier from Callands. He too went to the rear.

Report reached Hill that Early was down. Hill abandoned the disjointed attack and ordered withdrawal. The 24th Virginia and 5th North Carolina regiments disengaged just as the 38th Virginia prepared to move forward. Lt. Colonel Whittle herded the 38th Virginia back into the woods. A bullet tore into his right thigh. Whittle retained command.

The 24th Virginia reentered the trees. This left the 5th North Carolina unsupported in the open. The Tar Heels retired obliquely across the open field alone amid a storm of musketry and canister. The slaughter was horrific.[199]

Hancock charged. The Union line advanced down the slope with fixed bayonets. Units stopped occasionally to fire. Overtaken Carolinians surrendered or died.[200]

The fierce attack lasted twenty-three minutes, in which time the 5th North Carolina Infantry suffered a devastating 70 percent casualties. They left behind nearly all their wounded along with their dead and their regiment's colors.[201]

D. H. Hill regrouped the brigade. He found the 23rd North Carolina, the least drilled of the units, halted in the woods, idle, and befuddled. His impression of the 38th Virginia was little better and described them as "huddled up and in considerable confusion." Hill told Whittle to hold fast then galloped off to check on the rest of the brigade. The wounded Whittle relinquished command to Major Carrington who re-formed the regiment.

For reasons unknown, Carrington moved the regiment to the edge of the woods near Redoubt 10.[202] The 6th South Carolina exited that work and made ready to charge. The 38th Virginia prepared to support. Hill discovered the development in time to halt the folly.

The 38th Virginia backtracked to its initial position in the wheat field with the rest of the brigade. Walking wounded staggered from the trees. The re-formed brigade exhibited disconcertingly fewer men and one less battle flag. The two veteran regiments had been mauled. The 24th Virginia had suffered 189 casualties. The 5th North Carolina lost 290 of their 410 men. They resembled a stray company.

Darkness approached, the temperature dropped, and rain continued. The brigade remained in line of battle well into the night.

The Union held the field and weighed their options. Mud bogged down supplies and reinforcements. McClellan chose to consolidate before pressing forward. The battle for Williamsburg was over.

* * *

The 38th Virginia saw little action that day. Lt. Colonel Whittle was its only officer injured. Seven enlisted men were wounded.[203]

With the end of the fighting, the men of Company B shared frustration, disappointment, and embarrassment. Brave men on both sides clashed while they stumbled and slipped in ravines. They had once again missed a fight.

As it happened, approximately 1,200 Confederates with much wet ammunition and no artillery support had blundered into 3,400 Union with artillery. The attack was doomed from the start.

The Confederates slipped away after midnight. Hill's division served as rearguard. Overcast sky and no moon meant blackest night. Guided by an occasional lantern or torch, the column stumbled back through Williamsburg and along the muddy Richmond Stage Road (U.S. Rt. 60). Many struggled to keep up.

The men of the 38th Virginia had only what they carried into the fight. Their knapsacks, blankets, cook gear, and other encumbrances shed before the action still lay in piles on the college green.

Six miles beyond town the 38th Virginia forded waist-deep swamp. Three miles farther on, they halted at Burnt Ordinary (now Toano).

On May 7, they resumed their retreat with no food and "hungry as wolves."[204] Enemy cavalry harvested stragglers, two from the 38th Virginia. General D. H. Hill observed many of his troops were chilled to the bone, hungry, and exhausted. Many had become "indifferent to capture, even death."[205]

Their retreat had only begun.

All wounded in the 38th Virginia marched. Lewis Delaney had the only injury to a lower extremity. He refused to be left for capture and kept up with the regiment despite his foot wound.[206]

The rain stopped. Mud persisted. When Hill's division reached Barhamsville, General G. W. Smith's division took over as rearguard. The bulk of Johnston's army continued up the Richmond Stage Road through New Kent Court House. Hill's division, covering the flank, followed Longstreet's division up Roper's Church Road to the Forge Road (U.S. Rt. 60).[207]

Late that afternoon, Hill's division received orders to countermarch in support of the rearguard at Barhamsville. The 38th Virginia stood at arms for a day. Distant gunfire erupted.[208] The 38th Virginia held fast. Gunfire ceased. The retreat resumed.

Food was scarce. The men subsisted on one ear of corn per man per day. It was dry corn, animal fodder scavenged from corn cribs. Stomachs cramped. Oh, how they longed for that bounty torched on their retreat from the Centerville line!

Hill's division reached the north bank of the Chickahominy at Long Bridge on May 10 and deployed to defend the crossing. The men received a break from marching and their first real provisions since abandoning Yorktown. They had walked for "eight days without anything but parched corn and that very coarse."[209] Ambulances carried sick and wounded into Richmond. Among those from the 38th Virginia were Delaney, with his festering foot wound, and Ensign John Bohanon, taken ill.

Colonel Edmonds and Lt. Colonel Whittle rejoined the regiment that day. Major Carrington resigned. Carrington had served as acting colonel since Williamsburg. Recent ordeals persuaded the thirty-five-year-old attorney to seek a less physically demanding position in Richmond with Inspector General Winder. Carrington, a native of that city and grandson of the late Governor Cabell, became provost marshal for the City of Richmond.[210] By popular vote, twenty-one-year-old Captain Joseph Cabell became the new major.[211]

Captain Edgar Carrington, Company H had transferred from the cavalry to the 38th Virginia at his brother's request. Now that his brother resigned, Captain Carrington respectfully applied for transfer back to cavalry.

Daily drills accompanied constant expectations of attack. Yet another Yankee victory magnified the seriousness of the hour as news circulated that New Orleans had fallen.

On May 15, the 38th Virginia marched four miles in the rain and crossed the Chickahominy. Confederates burned Bottom's Bridge and the rail crossing upstream. Heavy artillery thundered in the distance as Union gunboats on the James River attacked Drewry's Bluff.

The march continued next day in hard rain. On May 17, the regiment had fair weather on muddy roads and halted midday in anticipation of attack. Nothing happened. The next day, they marched to an unprepared site one mile from Rockett's Landing.[212] They had made it to Richmond.

Many arrived "broken down" and "half-starved to death." A considerable number claimed "special furlough pretending to be sick."[213]

Sgt. Henry Talley, Company I said he was nearly worn out marching and was "black as a hog." He hoped to get into town to buy new clothes, but he lost his "pocketbook and all money" at Williamsburg, left in his knapsack on the college green.[214]

On May 20, McClellan's army crossed the Chickahominy. The enemy was at the very gates of Richmond and reinforced daily. Thus far that year, the Confederacy had experienced one setback after another.

The 38th Virginia had known only retreat, hunger, and exposure. They improved their camp site and earnestly embraced drills and picket duty. Bad news continued. Delaney died of gangrene.[215] Rumors spread afresh through Pittsylvania ranks about the army falling back to Danville.[216]

On May 24, Samuel Garland Jr. received promotion to brigadier general and replaced the wounded Jubal Early. Captain Griggs of Company K noted this was "to the pleasure of all."[217] Garland bonded quickly with the 38th Virginia's staff. He was a fellow Piedmonter, a native of Lynchburg, a graduate of both VMI and the University of Virginia, and an established lawyer.

As the defense of Richmond evolved, Hill's division grew to five brigades. Hill reviewed Garland's men. Color Sgt. Peter McDowell trooped the colors for the 38th Virginia in Ensign Bohanon's absence.

On May 30, the 38th Virginia moved to an advanced position, as if staged for attack. Other than an occasional shell, the line was quiet. There seemed little purpose to the incidental fireworks. Rumor spread that this meant the Yankees were pulling back.[218]

They soon learned otherwise.

CHAPTER FIVE

Seven Pines: Day One

McClellan's forces south of the Chickahominy were especially vulnerable with their backs to the river, swollen by recent rains. General Joseph Johnston scheduled attack on the Union position at Seven Pines for dawn May 31. The dark, moonless night before brought an hours-long thunderstorm that was unlike anything in memory.[219] Wind leveled tents. Rain fell in torrents. Heaven's artillery unleashed a spectacular barrage. Lightning killed and wounded men on both sides.

Those staged for attack endured the storm fully exposed. Few slept. At three thirty a.m. musicians sounded assembly. Rekindled watch fires and torches glowed in dense fog and silhouetted rain-soaked soldiers in battle dress. After forming ranks, quartermasters distributed dry ammunition. Each man received a strip of white cloth. General Hill ordered it worn on hats as a battle badge.[220] Mounted officers consolidated regiments.

In the dim dawn, Colonel Edmonds surveyed his wet men from horseback. He led the 38th Virginia to their position in the brigade. The silent column marched in fog onto the Williamsburg Stage Road. Individuals related only to immediate ranks and files. Hooves and boots splashed water and mud. Accoutrements rattled. Two miles beyond the outer defenses the column turned left along the east bank of a small stream. There the regiments formed lines of battle.[221]

The fog lifted to reveal Garland's brigade stretching from the Williamsburg Road north along an ephemeral stream swollen from the storm.[222] Featherston's brigade (G. B. Anderson) stood on Garland's left. Battle flags hung limp on staffs under gray sky. Men breakfasted on soggy rations from their haversacks, for some, their last meal.

Garland's brigade faced east overlooking a field of scrub. The tree line beyond screened them from enemy view. The 2nd Mississippi Battalion advanced 150 yards and deployed as skirmishers. The battered 5th North Carolina anchored Garland's left, followed by the 38th Virginia, 23rd North Carolina, 24th Virginia, and 2nd Florida with its right on the Williamsburg Road.

The men of the 38th Virginia realized themselves in the main battle line. The Pittsylvania Regiment stood at the forefront of an army assembled to save Richmond and, perhaps, deliver the final blow of the war. Tensions mounted.

Dawn grew hours old. Eight o'clock passed without signal. Everyone realized something askew. Other brigades were not yet in position. Officers allowed men to rest in place. Some knelt or sat in mud. Time crawled. Nine o'clock passed. Some dozed. Some prayed. More hours passed. Shortly after noon, Colonel Edmonds ordered the 38th Virginia to their feet. Tensions revived. Next, came orders to load.

1st Lt. Prichard commanded Company B in Captain Cabell's absence. Prichard relayed the command. Ramrods clattered lively in and out of barrels. Each rifle at shoulder arms signaled loaded and ready. The regiment dressed on its colors. Then came more waiting.

Captain Edgar Carrington in Company H mused about his return to cavalry. He longed to get back in the saddle ever since his brother the major left the regiment. He now had his approved transfer in his pocket. Only this day's obligation to the regiment remained.

Finally, at one o'clock, three cannons signaled attack. Even so, Rodes's and Rains's brigades south of Williamsburg Road still struggled through swamp to get into position.

Bugles sounded. Mounted officers waved their swords forward. Garland's brigade of gray and butternut soldiers advanced behind their pink and blue silk banners.[223] Blood red cotton bunting distinguished the new battle flag of the 5th North Carolina. Featherston's brigade (G. B. Anderson) stepped off and overlapped Garland's rear. Tall grass and brush concealed the flood in the field, knee-deep in places. Shoes sloshed full of water. Horses struggled.

Their enemy had been alerted hours before. Nevertheless, the Union units were green volunteers. Opening guns still caught frontline camps eating midday meals.[224]

Federal pickets in the tree line opened fire. Confederate skirmishers fired back. Gun smoke lingered in the humid air. Regiments stopped occasionally to dress ranks disarrayed by the slog through the boggy field. The main body caught up with the skirmish line. Bullets zipped about them and kicked up water in the flooded grass. A few men fell. Unlucky wounded splashed facedown and drowned.

Colonels directed volleys into the woods. The Union picket line broke. Regiments reloaded and sloshed onward encouraged by success.

Battle lines reached the woods. Organization and communication disintegrated as men pushed four hundred yards through brush and briars thick beneath the trees. No infantry opposed them. Shot and shell crashed and exploded in the woods. Sulfurous smoke reduced visibility further. Confusion plagued three regiments. The colonel of the 5th North Carolina collapsed from illness. The 23rd North Carolina halted through a misunderstanding. The commander of the 24th Virginia fell wounded. General Garland rallied each of the units and moved them forward.

The 2nd Florida emerged from the trees first to face a formidable abatis, forty yards deep. Enemy battle lines blazed away at them from two hundred yards away. The 38th Virginia exited the woods next, far to the left of the Floridians.

Enemy volleys pelted the gray-brown troops. Bullets slammed home. *Thud! Crack! Ping!* Projectiles ricocheted off metal, splintered wood, ripped flesh, and smashed bone. Gasps! Cries!

More troops exited the tree line. Officers shouted orders to re-form. They dressed ranks and returned volleys. The standup fight at the abatis shattered all preconceived notions of pitched battle.

In Company B, 38th Virginia, Bart Adkins was hit. A ball shattered Jimmy Hall's right arm. George Lynch took a bullet in his right foot. Each casualty was a friend or kinsman. Many broke ranks to care for wounded comrades. File closers prodded them back into line.

Focus on tasks muted terrors; however, impending summons to God invaded minds. Hundreds on both sides struck bargains with the Almighty. They would serve Him forever hence, if He let them survive the day.

The rest of Garland's brigade joined the fray. Volleys by company crashed from ranks, but the rattle of independent fire dominated. Smoke grew thick in the humid air. Both sides fired blindly or shot relative to last sightings through the smoke clouded abatis. Union howitzers lobbed shells into their midst.

Clammy hands handled cartridges already affected by damp leather. Effectiveness diminished with each round as more and more barrels fouled. Men swabbed bores and picked vents to restore rifles to service. Some wrestled to worm stuck balls. Inevitably, some men double or triple loaded atop unnoticed misfires rendering weapons useless. Thus disarmed, those soldiers either gleaned a serviceable weapon from the fallen or file closers pulled them out of line to tend wounded.[225]

Colonel Edmonds coaxed his line forward. His horse fell shot. Edmonds continued to lead on foot. *Boom!* He dropped, stunned by a spent shell fragment.

Lt. Colonel Whittle took command. His horse, already shot twice, was barely manageable. Whittle's Washington-like figure encouraged the men. Upon a third hit, Whittle's horse dropped dead. Whittle rose and led on foot with a pronounced limp from his still tender wound received at Williamsburg. Major Cabell's horse collapsed dead beneath him.

In Company B, a bullet grazed Sgt. Josiah Fuller. Dan Fuller and Leo Grubbs fell.

Colonel Edmonds shook off his painful contusion. The little colonel resumed command and "led in most handsome manner."[226]

Featherston's brigade (G. B. Anderson) exited the woods and commingled with Garland's brigade. Regaining control, Anderson obliqued his command to the left then wheeled right to press the enemy's flank. Defense of the abatis crumbled. Garland's brigade filtered through the entanglements aided by paths cut by the enemy's own artillery fire. They re-formed their battle line and resumed attack.

Just as victory seemed assured, the 100th New York, the 104th Pennsylvania, and three companies of the 11th Maine fixed bayonets and charged the Confederate left. Their attack supported by artillery checked the Rebels' advance.

The blue line of the 104th Pennsylvania climbed over a split rail fence and halted. Their companies fired into the gray line. Both sides held their ground. Casualties mounted. One of the two color bearers in the 104th Pennsylvania planted the national colors upright as he crumpled to the ground shot. To the left of the 104th Pennsylvania, two-thirds of the officers and one-half of the battalion of the 11th Maine were killed or wounded. Bullets pierced the Maine regiment's colors eleven times before splintering the staff.[227]

The perforated colors of the 38th Virginia dropped when a bullet killed Color Sergeant Peter McDowell. Color Corporal Luke Tarpley raised them and carried on.

Southern infantry fixed bayonets and countercharged. Companies B, G, and K of the 38th Virginia engaged hand to hand the leftmost companies of the 104th Pennsylvania. In Company B, 38th Virginia, John Stokes and Dick Gregory went down. A clubbed musket broke Bill Hall's left arm. The guide with the 104th Pennsylvania's flank marker turned to escape. A rifle butt struck him in the back of the neck and knocked him down.[228] Captain Griggs, Company K, seized the flag.[229]

The enemy withdrew firing. A bullet pierced Griggs's coat. Another grazed his scalp. Griggs led his men onward.

Color Sergeant Hiram Purcell of the 104th Pennsylvania retired with his colors as his men in blue scrambled back over the rail fence. However, the national flag of the 104th Pennsylvania remained upright in the ground ripe for capture.

Purcell, his major, and others dashed back through a hail of bullets. The major fell dead. Purcell, already a flag in one hand, snatched up the abandoned colors with this free hand and rushed back. A bullet struck him down as he crossed the fence, but he had rescued the colors. Purcell would survive to receive the Congressional Medal of Honor for his deed that day.[230]

The 104th Pennsylvania lost all its officers. Their entire battered brigade quit the field in disorder. Their sacrifice bought time for the rest of their division to fall back into their earthworks.

Working sketch for "Rescue of the Colors" by William Trego; action portrays Sgt. Hiram Purcell rescuing the colors of the 104th Pennsylvania. Not depicted in the moment, the 38th Virginia clashes hand-to-hand capturing the 104th's left flank marker flag. (From the Collection of the Mercer Museum Library of the Bucks County Historical Society)

After two hours of hard fighting, Garland's and Anderson's men reorganized. Files closed and command structure realigned. They resumed attack and charged the enemy's earthworks.

In Company B, 38th Virginia, Reub Hankins and Tom Bradner took hits. Lt. Prichard received a flesh wound. Every soldier's mouth was black from tearing cartridges. A bullet grazed John Oakes's lower lip. Black smudge permanently tattooed Oakes's wound.[231]

Resistance collapsed and Garland's men charged over the muddy red clay works to find only dead and wounded enemy. The rest had skedaddled. Major Cabell claimed an artillery piece. The fight for the entrenchments proved less difficult than that for the abatis, largely due to the delayed but timely support from Rodes's and Rains's brigades on their right.

Garland's brigade advanced through the enemy's deserted tent city. Many broke ranks to grab items on their way through. Breaches of discipline impeded progress and required reassembly beyond the camp. The brigade then moved forward to a second, larger abatis. There was no challenge this time. Files worked their way through the obstructions and re-formed. Featherston's brigade (G. B. Anderson) did the same and posted to Garland's left.

The fighting had raged three full hours. Incredibly, General Joseph Johnston was unaware that Hill had attacked until then. Due to the strange phenomenon called acoustic shadow, Johnston failed to hear the gunfire though only two miles away.

By four thirty p.m. Garland's and Anderson's men were exhausted and their ammunition spent. They held fast for three more hours while Rodes's brigade pressed the fight in the distant right front. Jenkins's brigade from Longstreet's division arrived and engaged the enemy beyond their left front. The fighting ceased after dark. Relief from Huger's division arrived. Hill ordered Garland's men to the rear.

To the soldiers' disappointment, they passed the enemy's camp they had won at great cost. Now their relief occupied it. The 9th Virginia and 14th Virginia of Armistead's brigade enjoyed the spoils of Garland's fight and picked through the abandoned goods and equipment with gusto. Garland's men marched back to their initial position tired, powder blackened, and hungry, and slept on wet ground.

The 38th Virginia had performed gallantly in their first real battle. Their pink silk flag bore battle honors stitched in bullet holes, shrapnel tears, and abatis snags. They had routed the enemy and captured his camp. Trophies included an enemy's flank marker and a howitzer.

Captains Griggs and Jennings were wounded. Captain Carrington was dead—killed with his approved transfer to cavalry in his pocket.[232]

The cost in blood was high. Company B reported Lt. Prichard and thirteen men wounded, about 20 percent. The wing company had fared better than those centermost. The regiment lost 42 percent killed, wounded, and missing. That same figure applied to the whole brigade.

* * *

News circulated that General Johnston had been wounded and replaced by General G. W. Smith. Fighting resumed next day. Garland's brigade again moved forward beyond the Union earthworks taken the previous day. They halted just past the landmark double houses and stood at arms. Fallen brothers, cousins, and friends made the conflict more personal than ever.[233] The Pittsylvanians preferred to fight and end the war rather than sit idle in the mud, but sit in mud they did. They saw no fighting on the second day but waited expectantly as gunfire erupted in the woods nearby.

Confederate blunders that morning ended the battle. Jefferson Davis removed G. W. Smith from command and gave the army to General Robert E. Lee.

Lee ordered everyone back into their original works. The Union reoccupied theirs. Both armies resumed the same positions as before the costly, bloody, hard-fought battle.

The move made Seven Pines a hollow victory. Many wondered about Lee's thinking. Moreover, they questioned Jefferson Davis's thinking. Both army and citizenry knew Lee as that same "Granny Lee" who had failed to hold western Virginia. Now "Old Granny" oversaw the entire defense of Richmond.

Lee directed energies in improving fortifications and establishing a new outer defense line. This earned him the mantle King of Spades throughout the South. Apprehensions grew. Newspapers expressed concerns over waging war with pick and shovel. Everyone knew a purely defensive strategy meant certain defeat.

However, Lee knew stronger positions enabled defense by fewer forces and thus freed men for maneuver.

The defenders labored with vigilance while the Union Army improved and expanded their works on both sides of the Chickahominy. The threat to Richmond increased daily. Soldiers of the Pittsylvania Regiment spent the next three weeks alternating days between picket duties and digging. There seemed no end to the backbreaking toil with picks and shovels.

Local slave owners had already benefited from the work. Much of the existing defenses had been dug by slave labor rented to the government at $30 per month per slave. The larger numbers of private soldiers rallying to the defense of the capital was the better bargain at $11 per month per man to both dig and be shot at. It was another example of a rich man's war and a poor man's fight but not one apparent to the rank and file.

The Battle of Seven Pines had turned all of Richmond into a hospital. Sick and wounded filled most available space in the already overcrowded capital. Tobacco warehouses became hospitals, as did private residences. The wounded, dead, and dying overwhelmed the system. Newspapers published casualty lists. Families searched everywhere for wounded loved ones.[234]

In the less hectic weeks prior to the flood of casualties, it was not unusual for doctors to assume comatose patients dead. Newspapers recorded several revivals en route to burial. Knockings inside coffins alerted undertakers to a live corpse.[235] Statistically, some must have been buried alive. This was horror as ghastly as any from the pages of Poe.

On June 3, mud miseries returned with week-long rain. Major General D. H. Hill and Brigadier General Garland reviewed the brigade amid showers on June 5.[236] Both generals delivered speeches. General Garland announced appointment of Rev. John Poulton as chaplain for the 38th Virginia. The assignment provided personal ministry within the regiment.

General Hill presented a new battle flag to the 38th Virginia. Color Corporal Luke Tarpley accepted the new colors in Ensign Bohanon's absence and promised to carry them until death.[237] With that Tarpley received promotion to Color Sergeant.[238] Blood red cotton bunting replaced pink silk. Cochineal red! The color of courage!

* * *

June 8 was the first Sunday since the big fight. Richmond faced imminent capture. Besiegers outnumbered defenders three to one. Indeed, God's deliverance was everyone's prayer.

Virginians reserved Sundays for rest and worship. Since its founding, Virginia codified Sabbath observance.[239] Military officers traditionally restricted labors on the Lord's day.

Commanders recognized the spiritual well-being of men was important to morale. Colporteurs distributed religious tracts to soldiers eager for reading material. Guest chaplains held Sunday services in camps. Sermons and tracts addressed camp vices. Smoking, drinking, cursing, gambling, and whoring topped the list.

Strategically, clean living transcended benefits to individuals. Leaders believed a God-fearing army courted favor from above. Religious interests spread throughout the army. The war blended religion and politics into a toxic emulsion.

Ordained ministers were the most learned and respected members in nineteenth-century communities. These intellects were as prone as any to contemporary infatuations with *Ivanhoe* and "Horatius at the Bridge."[240] Cavalier notions of chivalry and honor fused with beliefs in divine sanction for the war. Clergy preached a Gospel tailored to the moment. Listening ears had been raised on the ubiquitous, extra-biblical notion of Heaven as ethereal extension of present society—Southern society. The message preached was that defending the South was the Lord's work. Holy! Just! Good!

Few had reason to doubt men of God who presented their revolution as a crusade. However, the greater love hath no man than to lay down his life was not the same love Jesus preached. It was Southern honor in disguise.

During the war, many would accept Christ as personal Savior. Hardships and sufferings would spawn genuine conversions on a scale that produced great Christian revivals in both armies. However, in the early days of the war, Southern-bred fishers of men tossed their nets on the wrong side of the boat.

Culture that twisted Holy Scripture to justify brutal, Roman-styled slavery easily cast the Prince of Peace in a Mars-like roll.[241] Yea, verily. Men convinced of sacred duty will do anything.

* * *

On June 14, a skilled hand with brush and black paint applied battle honors to the Pittsylvania Regiment's new battle flag. "Williamsburg" and "Seven Pines" attested to "good conduct and bravery at those places."[242] The same brush applied the unit designation "38th Va" in stylized, black letters.

Lt. Prichard, Sgt. Fuller, and other wounded returned to Company B. Bill Hall and his brother Jimmy both received discharges. Bill had a badly broken left humerus. Jimmy lost his right arm. Both went home heroes.

On June 17, headquarters reassigned the 38th Virginia to Huger's division. By the end of the day, Colonel Edmonds learned his regiment was in Armistead's brigade under the command of his neighbor the recently promoted Brigadier General Lewis Addison Armistead.

The 38th Virginia now camped with other Southside Virginia regiments. The 53rd Virginia and 57th Virginia both contained Pittsylvania companies. Men in the 57th Virginia had brothers, cousins, and neighbors in the 38th Virginia.

Until his promotion April 1, Lewis Armistead was colonel of the 57th Virginia.[243]

CHAPTER SIX

The 57th Virginia, Armistead, and His Brigade

When Virginia seceded, the state consolidated existing militia companies into battalions and regiments. The Danville Blues, Danville Grays, and Spring Garden Blues became respectively Companies A, B, and I of the 18th Virginia Infantry. The Chalk Level Grays and Turkey Cock Grays became Companies H and I of the 21st Virginia Infantry. The Chatham Greys became Company B of Montague's Battalion (later Company I, 53rd Virginia Infantry).

By June 1861, two other existing and five new Pittsylvania County companies became the core of the 38th Virginia Infantry, the Pittsylvania Regiment. Still more Pittsylvanians rallied to defend Virginia.

On June 28, the Pigg River Grays organized at Museville. Four more companies formed in July: the Henry and Pittsylvania County Rifles, the Ladies Guards, the Pittsylvania Life Guards, and the Galveston Tigers.

These five companies became Keen's Battalion under Major Elisha F. Keen of Cottage Hill.[244] The thirty-six-year-old Keen was a tobacco planter, slave owner, politician, secessionist, and descendant of local Revolutionary War figure Captain Elisha Keen.

Keen's Battalion left for Richmond in August. The victory at Manassas excited the new volunteers. Each craved a part in the drama. By then Camp Lee had reached capacity. The state posted Keen's men to Camp Belcher near the Fairfield Race Course.[245] Although many communities uniformed their companies, most of Keen's men arrived in civilian attire. Training progressed awkwardly, for they were ill-clad, ill-shod, and unarmed, and Keen had little, if any, military training.

Inexperience affected more than drill, for although the camp had ample fresh food, sanitation was deplorable. Many sickened with diarrhea. A few contracted typhoid.

Major Keen received five additional companies from other counties. On September 23, the ten companies became the 57th Virginia Volunteer Infantry Regiment. Fully half of the soldiers in the 57th Virginia were Pittsylvania men. The untrained, unequipped, unarmed, understaffed organization remained a diamond in the rough until appointment of a suitable colonel and lieutenant colonel.

On September 25, Lewis A. Armistead received promotion to colonel and given command of the 57th Virginia. Lt. Colonel George W. Carr was second in command.[246] Armistead had scarcely taken charge when called away to Upperville to bury his mother, who died September 30.

* * *

Lewis Addison Armistead (pronounced *UM-stead*)[247] was born in New Bern, North Carolina, to a prominent Virginia family of stellar military heritage.[248] His father, Major General Walker Keith Armistead, served in the War of 1812 with four brothers. He lost an arm and two brothers in that war.[249] He named his firstborn after brothers Lewis and Addison, who gave their lives for their country.

The general's third brother, John, served as a captain of dragoons. His fourth brother, Major George Armistead, commanded Fort McHenry during the 1814 bombardment, which inspired "The Star-Spangled Banner."

In early colonial Virginia, Judith Armistead of Hesse in Gloucester County married Robert "King" Carter. Lewis Armistead's line also branched from the Armistead family of Hesse. He was, therefore, an FFV related to Presidents Monroe, Harrison, Tyler, and other Virginia aristocrats, including the Lees.

Lewis Armistead grew up on the family plantation Ben Lomond near Upperville in Fauquier County.[250] In 1833, Lewis's father secured him appointment to West Point. Faced with failure, Lewis feigned illness and resigned before his first-year exams. He later reapplied and returned to struggle again with studies. Following an incident on the parade ground, Lewis vented anger in the mess hall by breaking a plate over the head of classmate Jubal A. Early.[251] Lewis withdrew from his 1836 term to avoid expulsion. The incident covered imminent dismissal for academic failure.

Three years later, General Walker Keith Armistead replaced General Zachary Taylor as army commander in the Second Seminole War. The new commanding general commissioned son Lewis second lieutenant in the 6th U.S. Infantry. Lewis served in his father's command at Fort Andrews, Florida. Ironically, Lewis received his commission about the same time his West Point classmates received theirs.

In the Mexican War, Armistead fought at Contreras, Churubusco, Molino del Rey, and Chapultepec. He was twice promoted for bravery: first to brevet captain and then brevet major.

Armistead was wounded at Chapultepec. The extent of his injury is not known. However, the army posted him to Louisville, Kentucky. There he suffered a severe case of erysipelas in his left arm, an infection likely related to his war wound.

Doctors feared for his life and surgically removed the affected tissue. The excision was sufficiently severe that one doctor suspected Armistead would "never recover the entire use of his left arm."[252] Recovery was painful and slow, but recover he did.

Armistead lagged his peers in advancement.[253] He finally received promotion to captain in 1855. However, his advancement came only after letters to the secretary of war called attention to past merits and his having held first lieutenancy longer than anyone in the U.S. Army.[254]

The rigors of army life on western outposts cost Armistead dearly. By the end of 1855, he had lost two wives and two children. One son, Keith, survived.

Armistead briefly commanded Fort Riley, Kansas, during the Cheyenne unrest in 1857. His performance there was lackluster at best.[255]

The 6th U.S. Infantry went to Utah to fight Mormons, but the ruckus ended before Armistead arrived. The unit remained in the West, where Armistead fought Indians. His first overall battlefield command occurred in August 1859, when his company of fifty muskets fought off two hundred Mojave Indians armed with bows and arrows. For reasons unknown, Armistead took leave afterward until late 1860.[256]

Lewis Addison Armistead, Captain, USA.
(Courtesy Library of Congress)

1861 opened with Armistead no longer in the field but assigned quartermaster duty in Los Angeles. There he served with his friend Winfield Scott Hancock.

Virginia's secession prompted Armistead's resignation. The parting scene recorded by Hancock's wife, Almira, is among the famous stories of the war.

Armistead gave her some personal effects for safekeeping. These included a prayer book with flyleaf inscribed "Trust in God and fear nothing."[257]

Armistead made his way to Texas with the Los Angeles Mounted Rifles along with Albert Sidney Johnston. Armistead continued east and arrived in Richmond by September 15. There he entered Confederate service as major. Within ten days he received colonelcy of the 57th Virginia.

* * *

After burying his mother, Armistead returned to Camp Belcher in mid-October. Lt. Colonel Carr had drilled the men well. The farm boys balked at strict discipline, but military science administered by professionals transformed the 57th Virginia into a proper regiment. They received uniforms, and the state arsenal armed them with percussion muskets converted from flintlocks. The regiment approached readiness.

Twice Armistead received orders for the 57th Virginia to join forces in western Virginia. Each was canceled. In December, the regiment marched the mile into Richmond and pitched winter camp in Howard's Grove.[258]

The duty was like no other they would experience. The hillside camp overlooked Richmond's Shockoe Valley. The capitol and the governor's and president's mansions stood on the opposite hill crest amid church spires. Provisions were plentiful and the citizens gracious. Treatment as heroes fired patriotic fervor like no other billet could have. The city provided whatever army life lacked.

City amenities, light duty, and healthy diet ended when Union forces invaded North Carolina. Federals captured Roanoke Island on February 8. Two days later, the U.S. Navy destroyed the Confederate mosquito fleet at Elizabeth City. Federal troops then occupied that town.[259]

The 57th Virginia exited winter quarters on February 15 and rushed to counter vulnerabilities at the North Carolina border.[260] The regiment broke camp and boarded railcars for Suffolk. They then marched south to Manney's Ferry at the confluence of the Blackwater and Nottoway rivers.[261] There they established Fort Dillard on thirty acres of cold, wet swampland. Water bordered the fort on three sides. One narrow road through marsh provided the only land access.[262] Water was bad, food was poor, and any rise in temperature bred swarms of mosquitoes.

A constant ration of salt beef and sweet potatoes gave the majority loose bowels. An unidentified malady spread throughout camp referred to simply as "the itch."[263] Life at Fort Dillard quenched much zeal brought from Richmond.

Governor Letcher's militia activation March 10 drafted former militiamen back to duty. Unless otherwise directed, those from Southside Virginia counties reported to General Huger, headquartered in Norfolk. Meanwhile, threats from neighboring North Carolina grew as New Bern fell to Union forces on March 14.

On March 22, the 57th Virginia welcomed forty-three drafted militiamen from Callands and Museville. Charles Oakes hated leaving his wife and children. He joined his militia chums bound for Company E. He enjoyed their camaraderie. Also, being a family man, the unit was a safer bet than joining his brothers in the 38th Virginia, already in harm's way.

* * *

On April 1, Lewis Armistead received promotion to brigadier general. Two weeks later he took command of the 14th Virginia, 57th Virginia, 3rd Georgia, and 22nd Georgia plus cavalry and artillery units deployed in the Suffolk area. Lt. Colonel Carr assumed command of the 57th Virginia. His tenure as colonel was short-lived.

George Watson Carr, like Armistead, was a native Virginian and an old army officer. He was reputed "a man of quick temper at all times."[264] In early 1861, he resigned from the 9th U.S. Infantry, having been fourteen years a first lieutenant. He immediately received majority in the Virginia militia.

The day Virginia seceded, former governor Henry Wise usurped authority and ordered Harpers Ferry seized. Major Carr entrained two University of Virginia companies (Southern Guards and Sons of Liberty), two militia companies (Monticello Guards and Albemarle Rifles), and a section of artillery. These departed Charlottesville for Harper's Ferry.[265] They bivouacked there four days. During their stay, Carr quelled a drunken brawl in camp with his sword by slashing and stabbing unruly soldiers into submission. Several required a surgeon's attention.[266]

Upon return to Charlottesville, the two university companies disbanded without entering state service. The two local militia companies became Company A and Company B in the 19th Virginia. Carr's career marked time five months until given lieutenant colonelcy in the 57th Virginia.

When Carr became colonel of the 57th Virginia, the North Carolina coast swarmed with Union activity. Naval and land forces invested Fort Macon. Sorties from Elizabeth City demanded action. Armistead ordered Carr and his men to Sandy Cross.[267] The forced march with full gear in cold and rain under the irascible Carr taxed morale. The 57th Virginia held the crossroad until relieved by the 14th Virginia, which had been transferred from the Peninsula to Armistead's command and marched from Suffolk.[268]

On the return trip, the 57th Virginia bivouacked at Gatesville. There General Armistead inspected the regiment.[269] Once back at Fort Dillard, mumps ravaged wearied participants. Although military necessity demanded the ten-day excursion in bad weather, Carr's demeanor sealed his fate with the rank and file.

On May 7, Colonel Carr fell victim to democracy. Upon everyone's forced reenlistment, the regiment voted the return of Elisha Keen to command.[270] Thus rejected, Carr resigned his commission and went home for the war.

* * *

Confederate forces on the Peninsula withdrew to Richmond as McClellan advanced beyond Williamsburg. Johnston ordered Norfolk abandoned. General Huger, in turn, ordered Armistead's brigade to Petersburg. The 57th Virginia abandoned Fort Dillard on May 12. Colonel Keen detailed men to obstruct river navigation to Franklin.

Company H boarded a steamboat, towed a schooner up the Blackwater River, and sank it. They continued upstream and rejoined their regiment in town. After burning the traffic and railroad bridges, the 57th Virginia resumed their retreat on foot. Rail transport was not an option, for Huger had already ordered the tracks to Petersburg demolished.

Citizens at Jerusalem (now Courtland) met passing troops with refreshments. John Tyler Jr. ordered his servants to fill soldiers' knapsacks with cornbread.

Armistead halted the 57th Virginia at Littletown (now Littleton) to await the rest of the brigade. Upon resuming the March, the Piedmonters acted as rearguard with the distasteful task of goading stragglers with bayonets. The regiment covered nineteen miles on May 15 and made camp midway between Petersburg and City Point (now Hopewell). Heavy guns thundered upstream on the James River as a

Union fleet attacked Drewry's Bluff. The brigade then worked feverishly to obstruct the Appomattox River at Point of Rocks. Camp conditions were poor. Many fell ill.

McClellan's threat to Richmond grew. On May 28, Armistead's brigade boarded railcars to join Huger's division at the city. However, the 57th Virginia detrained at Gregory's Crossing to reinforce Drewry's Bluff. The rest of the brigade reported to Huger in Richmond's inner defense line.

* * *

On May 31, in the hours immediately preceding the attack on Seven Pines, Huger replaced the two Georgia regiments under Armistead with the newly arrived 9th Virginia and 53rd Virginia.

The 9th Virginia was comprised exclusively of Tidewater companies. When ordered to abandon Norfolk and Portsmouth, some paid brief, last visits home and then rejoined their unit. Others deserted to care for their families abandoned to the enemy.

The 9th Virginia reached Richmond on May 30 and bivouacked on the capitol grounds. Next morning, they joined Armistead in the defense line. Until then, the Tidewater boys had only performed garrison duties. Their spiffy, clean uniforms attracted mocks and halloos from muddy veterans.[271]

The 53rd Virginia had organized at Grafton in December to consolidate Montague's Battalion, Tomlin's Battalion, and Captain Waddell's Company. All were among the first units deployed on the Peninsula. Montague's men included the Chatham Greys, which had fought at Big Bethel. These found themselves south of the James on May 8 when ordered to evacuate. The 5th Battalion Virginia Volunteer Infantry had also fled Tidewater. Huger attached them to the 53rd Virginia.

Huger's last-minute reshuffling of units in the wake of the horrific thunder storm the previous night added to the day's confusion. Armistead's brigade (9th Virginia, 14th Virginia, 53rd Virginia, and 5th Virginia Battalion) followed Huger down the Charles City road. Johnston had issued confusing orders to Huger and Longstreet. Consequently, Huger's command spent the first day of Seven Pines marking time on muddy roads blocked by Longstreet's misdirected columns.

After sundown, Huger's division relieved that of D. H. Hill. Armistead's brigade occupied the Union camp captured earlier that afternoon by Garland's brigade. Armistead's men had ample time to plunder the camp and found much of value. John Lewis in the 9th Virginia acquired a premium pair of boots.[272]

That evening General G. W. Smith assumed army command after Johnston's wounding. Smith planned to strike again the next morning with eight fresh brigades. He expected D. H. Hill to repeat his stellar performance of the first day; however, all of Hill's men were exhausted. Hill needed fresh troops. Smith placed three brigades from other divisions at Hill's disposal: Mahone's and Armistead's brigades from Huger's division and Pickett's from Longstreet's division. General Longstreet with his remaining five fresh brigades completed Smith's battle plan. Coordination was key to success.

Armistead was already short a regiment with his 57th Virginia at Drewry's Bluff. He lost yet another. During the night, Longstreet appropriated Armistead's 53rd Virginia to guard his headquarters. Armistead spent predawn hours protesting to Hill, who then ordered the 53rd Virginia released. This foreshadowed the confusions and personality conflicts that doomed the operation before it began.

At daybreak June 1, the sleep-deprived Armistead still had only his 9th Virginia and 14th Virginia. He ordered them assembled on the Williamsburg Road. The men quit their looting, stepped over the first day's carnage, and formed lines of battle. Pickett's brigade, on their right, still stood in column while Pickett rode to Hill for clarification of orders.

The attack began before the 53rd Virginia rejoined Armistead. About eight a.m., Mahone stepped off on the left with Armistead center. Pickett's brigade held fast, waiting for Pickett's return.

The assault blundered forward. Mahone's regiments became separated and disoriented in tangled brush and morass. Armistead also advanced without skirmishers, even though the location of the enemy was in doubt.

As Armistead's two spiffy, untried regiments moved away from Pickett's left into the woods, two officers, familiar to the reader, commented on the movement. Colonel Robert Withers of the 18th Virginia turned to Lt. Colonel Henry A. Carrington and asked, "Where do you suppose those troops are going in that direction?" Carrington replied, "I have no idea, but don't they look clean and nice?"[273]

The 3rd Alabama of Mahone's brigade stumbled upon the enemy posted behind the York River Railroad. Union volleys blasted them. Their rout precipitated panic. Mahone's whole brigade fell back to D. H. Hill's dismay. Mahone's retreating 41st Virginia ran headlong into Armistead's 53rd Virginia as it arrived on the field. The 53rd Virginia mistook the onrushing 41st Virginia for enemy and fired on them.[274]

Like Mahone's men, Armistead's two lead regiments blundered blindly through tangled, swampy woods. Upon reaching the railway, a devastating volley crashed into the flank of the 9th Virginia. Many fell. The color bearer went down. Colonel Godwin's horse fell dead and crushed him against a tree. The fusillade shot Armistead's horse from under him.

Thus shocked, the green, leaderless 9th Virginia panicked. One recalled, "Some of the boys just at that time seemed to have urgent business in Richmond."[275] The regiment broke and ran.

Armistead grabbed the colors and chased the fleeing 9th Virginia on foot. His voice boomed clear above the din of battle but with little effect.

As the men tore out of the woods, Pickett rode toward the origin of the rout and "found nothing between me and the railroad but the gallant Armistead himself with a regimental color and some thirty persons, mostly officers, with him."[276]

The stampede slowed when it ran into the 53rd Virginia, but the 9th Virginia left the field. The 14th Virginia exchanged galling fire with the enemy until they realized themselves alone. They then pulled back alongside the 53rd Virginia to reassess the situation. The regiments realigned and advanced.

The 53rd Virginia closed to within forty yards of the enemy. Union musketry drove them back. The 53rd Virginia rallied on their colors for another assault and ventured forward again. In the confusion of the pine thickets, the 14th Virginia mistook the 53rd Virginia for foe and fired on them from behind.

The 53rd Virginia withdrew again to shake off this latest shock and regrouped. In disjointed efforts, the 53rd Virginia and the 14th Virginia each charged again and drove the enemy back across the rail embankment.

Lt. Benjamin Farinholt of the 53rd Virginia wrote,

> The carnage from today and yesterday is terrible and every where we walk numerous dead men (killed in every conceivable way) and dead horses strew the ground and the wounded are still calling out

> for help on every side and they are still left in danger as bombs and Minnie balls are flying in every direction. Horses disemboweled and men with head and arms shot off are every where to be seen.[277]

By one p.m., D. H. Hill realized the five brigades promised from Longstreet were not coming and halted the action. Thus, ended the Battle of Seven Pines (Fair Oaks) and Lewis Armistead's first action as brigade general.

* * *

June 1 was a day for tarnished reputations. G. W. Smith had sidelined Huger in preference for the more capable D. H. Hill. Hill then engaged the enemy with three unfamiliar brigades borrowed from other commands. The attack amounted to a series of costly, uncoordinated musketry exchanges.

Hill redressed Mahone for pulling his brigade back prematurely. Mahone took offense and considered challenging Hill to a duel. His staff talked him out of it.

Hill cited Armistead for bravery under fire. Nevertheless, this could not mask the fact that he lost control of his troops. The 9th Virginia broke and ran away, his 53rd Virginia fired on Mahone's men, and his 14th Virginia fired on his 53rd Virginia.[278]

The self-aggrandizing Pickett boasted success touting that his brigade defeated several Federal lines behind an abatis. He further claimed that lack of reinforcement prevented his driving the enemy beyond the Chickahominy. As it happened, his men skirted the end of an abandoned position and charged into the weak juncture of two green brigades.

The main assault by the five brigades of Longstreet's division never happened. The many missteps at brigade levels in Hill's command diverted attentions away from Longstreet.

G. W. Smith's performance as army commander was worse than Johnston's the previous day. Jefferson Davis removed Smith and gave overall command of the army to General Robert E. Lee.

Danville's Colonel Robert Withers, 18th Virginia, an eyewitness, surmised, "I have always thought, and still believe the second day's fight at Seven Pines was the most useless sacrifice of life I have ever known."[279]

Seven Pines was a no-win situation for Lewis Armistead. His original regiment, the 57th Virginia, was posted away at Drewry's Bluff. Of his three regiments in the fight, the 14th Virginia had been under his command for less than a month, and the 9th Virginia and 53rd Virginia for only a day. Except for elements of the 53rd Virginia, like the Chatham Greys, which had participated at Big Bethel, Armistead's men had seen only garrison duty in Tidewater. The numbers of green and recently amalgamated units unaccustomed to their brigadier and each other were difficult to manage under ideal circumstances.

Prior to Seven Pines, Armistead had never led more than a company in a fight. He had never fought as a battalion or regiment commander. His ability to control a brigade in combat remained undemonstrated and doubtful.[280]

* * *

In the weeks after the battle, Armistead's brigade dug fortifications and served picket duty, as did most of the besieged army.

The 9th Virginia swallowed its pride, licked its wounds, and sought a new color bearer. One sergeant was asked if he would "take the colors and carry them to the death." He considered the end of the previous fellow and replied, "No; I'll be damned if I do."[281] Another accepted the honor.

The Confederate Army of the Potomac shed its title. General Lee renamed it the Army of Northern Virginia. Lee then brigaded regiments by state. Garland's brigade became exclusively North Carolina troops.[282]

On June 17, headquarters transferred the 38th Virginia to Mahone's brigade of Huger's division. This gave Mahone six regiments, Wright five, Armistead four. By end of the day, Huger reassigned the 38th Virginia to Armistead.[283] That same day the 57th Virginia rejoined the brigade. Armistead now commanded the 9th Virginia, 14th Virginia, 38th Virginia, 53rd Virginia (5th Virginia Battalion attached), and 57th Virginia. These regiments would be brigaded together for the rest of the war.

Seventy percent of all Pittsylvania County infantry sent to the war served in Armistead's brigade. Pittsylvanians comprised fourteen of its fifty companies. The 38th Virginia, the Pittsylvania Regiment, was the bellwether unit with seven of ten companies from that county. It was a county of tobacco farmers like the Oakes.

The Oakes name had landed at Yorktown in the late 1600s.[284] Nine Oakes from Pittsylvania County served in the 38th Virginia. Thomas Clement, John Kerr, and James Lafayette Oakes were brothers; the other six were cousins. A fourth Oakes brother, Charles Harmon, served in the 57th Virginia. Every regiment in Armistead's brigade listed at least one Oakes (or Oaks). They had many cousins with different surnames dispersed throughout the brigade. James Oakes's wife had five uncles surnamed Shellhorse in the 53rd Virginia.

One may make similar statements about their neighbors named Adkins, Fuller, or Gregory. The blood relationships within Armistead's brigade are too many and complex to enumerate.

Companies from the five tobacco counties adjacent to Pittsylvania comprised half of the brigade. Fully three quarters of the brigade were Piedmonters. Only five companies originated north of the James River. The brigade was overwhelmingly clansmen from the Dan River watershed.

They were lions of the Dan.

CHAPTER SEVEN

Malvern Hill

While McClellan's army invested Richmond by way of the Peninsula, the Union I Corps posted near Fredericksburg threatened the Confederate capital from the north. Lee ordered diversions in the Shenandoah Valley. The resulting victories by Stonewall Jackson's "foot cavalry" so unnerved Lincoln that he kept the I Corps and two other corps near Washington, thus denying them to McClellan.

Even so, the threat to the Confederate capital remained grim. Besiegers still outnumbered defenders three to one. Richmonders prayed for deliverance. Many despaired. Some prepared to evacuate. Lee prepared to strike.

* * *

Although the 38th Virginia had relinquished hard-fought ground and returned to their fortifications, their success against the enemy at Seven Pines instilled confidence. They had fought like lions and knew it.

For the first time since deployment, the Pittsylvania Regiment was brigaded exclusively with other Virginia units. The regiment had the most field service and the best reputation, and their flag bore the most battle honors of any in Armistead's brigade.

Their new assignment required adjustments. Although Colonel Edmonds grew up knowing the Armistead family and was good friends with his brother Frank, Lewis Armistead was very much an unknown quantity. Furthermore, General Huger, their gray-haired division commander, lacked the fire and presence of D. H. Hill.

Major General Benjamin Huger was fifty-seven years old, a South Carolina–born army officer who retained the Huguenot pronunciation of his name: *Oo-jay.*

Both his grandfathers were Revolutionary War patriots of note. Huger graduated eighth in his class from West Point in 1825. He served with distinction during the Mexican War as ordinance officer for General Winfield Scott.

Huger had commanded both the Harpers Ferry Arsenal and Fort Monroe. He resigned from the U.S. Army after Fort Sumter and was commissioned major general in the Confederate army. After Virginia and North Carolina seceded, the War Department assigned him defense of Norfolk and Eastern North Carolina.

Since the beginning of the year, the Confederacy had suffered one reversal after another. Huger received much bad press. The public blamed him for the loss of Roanoke Island, New Bern, and Norfolk and the scuttling of the CSS *Virginia.*

Abandonment of Norfolk thrust Huger into field command. The ordinance expert had never commanded infantry. Adverse circumstances prevented Huger from delivering his troops on the first day of Seven Pines. His lackluster performance prompted G. W. Smith to borrow Armistead's and Mahone's fresh brigades from Huger for D. H. Hill's use on the second day. As soon as Lee took command, he assigned Huger a defensive role and gave aggressive assignments to infantry commanders suited to the tasks.

* * *

The rank and file of the 38th Virginia thought the Union seemed content in holding their position. So much was the case that they speculated on being sent to join Jackson.[285] This changed the morning of June 25 when McClellan advanced to clear Rebel pickets from the woods.

Union infantry sallied forth from their fortifications at Seven Pines. McClellan kept advised by telegraph three miles away at Savage's Station. The Union's own abatis impeded their advance. The delay concerned McClellan. He halted the attack midmorning and resumed operations upon his personal arrival that afternoon.

The Southerners fought tenaciously, as if Richmond's fate depended upon them alone. Ambrose Wright's and Robert Ransom's brigades bore the brunt of the fight. The 9th Virginia and 53rd Virginia defended Armistead's front, supported by the 38th Virginia and 14th Virginia.

General Lee personally surveyed the action with keen interest, for he had already staged the bulk of his army north of the Chickahominy to strike McClellan there. Only Huger's and Magruder's divisions stood between McClellan and Richmond.[286]

Darkness ended the contest. McClellan had advanced his picket line six hundred yards at heavy cost. This was one of his last preparations before launching a general assault on Richmond. However, McClellan had waited too long. History reckons the day's action as the Battle of Oak Grove.[287] It was the first fight in what became known as the Seven Days Battles.

* * *

Throughout that night, Armistead's men noted unusual levels of hubbub and invectives coming from the new Union position. The commotion stopped before dawn. Daylight revealed McClellan's men had relinquished that part of the field. The reason was that they had entrenched into graves of rotting Seven Pines dead.

The Federals forsook their ghastly pits and withdrew to a more tenable position. The 38th Virginia and 14th Virginia moved forward on heightened alert. Late that afternoon, guns opened north of the Chickahominy as Lee attacked McClellan at Mechanicsville. The enemy, strongly entrenched behind Beaver Dam Creek, repulsed Lee's uncoordinated assaults.[288]

Gunfire reverberated in Richmond as if thunder. The incessant rumble excited Captain Raleigh Daniel. The young adjutant of the 5th Kentucky, on furlough seeking position with the 1st Virginia, could not remain idle in the crisis. Daniel proceeded to General Armistead's headquarters. Armistead directed Daniel, a relative of the Carringtons, to Colonel Edmonds, who gave Daniel command of Company F in place of Captain Jennings recuperating from wounds.

On June 27, McClellan abandoned his Beaver Dam Creek position and pulled back to high ground behind Boatswain's Creek near Gaines's Mill. Lee again hammered the enemy with piecemeal attacks throughout the afternoon. A coordinated assault at dusk broke the Union line. McClellan withdrew his battered forces south across the Chickahominy River. This required his army to change its supply base from the York River to the James River, a major undertaking.

South of the Chickahominy that day, Huger's and Magruder's divisions remained the only resistance between McClellan's Army and Richmond. Lee ordered Huger to hold his lines at bayonet point and to call for reserves from Drewry's Bluff as needed.

The order confused Huger. He requested clarification from the secretary of war and the Petersburg command. This generated more confusion and false alarms of a landing at Bermuda Hundred.[289]

McClellan launched a diversionary assault upon Huger to help cover his massive retreat in progress. Three companies of the 53rd Virginia on picket fell back under infantry and artillery fire. Huger's left wing advanced and repulsed the enemy.[290]

On June 28, Lee, unsure of McClellan's intent, ordered Huger's division forward on the Charles City Road. Huger advanced Armistead's and Mahone's brigades but held back Wright's. The column encountered no resistance. It rained that night.

On June 29, Armistead's brigade countermarched against the Union position at Seven Pines. Armistead's men pressed through swampy woods. Some tramped on or stumbled over Union dead partially submerged or hidden by grass and debris. They emerged into the clearing before the Union works. They dressed their lines and charged the same fortifications the 38th Virginia had taken a month before. This time there was no resistance. Some stopped their breath "to pass the bodies that lay in piles stenching."[291] A flag of truce met them at the works. The enemy had fled, leaving only their wounded and a few attendants. Meanwhile, Lee attacked McClellan's rearguard at Savages' Station three miles away.[292]

On June 30, Armistead's brigade counter-countermarched back to the Charles City Road. Huger's division advanced. Felled trees barred the road beyond Fisher's Ford. Rather than clear obstructions, the ever cautious Huger ordered a mile of new road cut. This slowed his column to a crawl.

At two thirty p.m. Huger probed Union strength near the Williams house. Longstreet misinterpreted the gunfire as Huger signaling his arrival. This prematurely initiated the Battle of Frayser's Farm (Glendale).[293] Huger held his division on the road to await orders. His halt aided McClellan's escape.

Retreating Federals consolidated behind massed artillery two miles to the south on a plateau known as Malvern Hill.[294] It was the perfect spot to make a stand. The plateau easily accommodated McClellan's entire army. A gentle slope bounded by steep bluffs funneled pursuing troops to the narrow access. The Union lined the approach with forty artillery pieces.

When gunfire subsided at Frayser's Farm, Huger had no clue to the outcome. He assumed the enemy was still in his front. They were not.

At three a.m. on July 1, the Pittsylvania Regiment took the lead as Huger sent Armistead's and Wright's brigades on a "flanking maneuver." The moon had set hours before. As day dawned, the men felt their way through dark, swampy woods and reached Long Bridge Road by sunup. There Armistead encountered General Lee.

The army commander had just conferred with Longstreet, A. P. Hill, and Magruder. Lee was frustrated over the uncoordinated attacks that allowed McClellan's army to escape. He was also physically drained from the week-long fighting. Lee managed his temper despite feeling unwell.[295]

Lee personally directed Armistead to move his brigade southwest along the "Quaker Road" (Willis Church Road) to contact the Federals. Armistead detached the 5th Virginia Battalion to guard his wagons. He then discovered the assigned road clogged with other troops, wagons, wreckage from the previous day's battle, and jetsam from the Union retreat. Armistead sent his men through the woods parallel to the road.[296]

The 38th Virginia led the way moving cautiously, wary of ambush. They advanced about a mile through tangled brush and briars. They forded Western Run and then a feeder branch. Beyond the wooded gulley skirting the Carter farm, they turned southeast onto an unnamed road (now Carters Mill Road). Less than two tenths of a mile brought them to the edge of the woods. Enemy pickets spanned the open clover field beyond.

Armistead deployed the 38th Virginia, 14th Virginia, and 53rd Virginia in lines of battle within the tree line and held the 9th Virginia and 57th Virginia in reserve. Ambrose Wright moved his brigade of Georgians to Armistead's right.

The 38th Virginia, 14th Virginia, and 53rd Virginia advanced skirmishers into the field. Major Cabell dismounted and led about fifty men from the 38th Virginia. They exchanged fire with the enemy pickets who retired.

Armistead and Edmonds spurred their horses up the nearby hill to reconnoiter the area with a spyglass. The high green clover pasture on which they stood was perfect for artillery. It sloped gently to an inflection point about two-thirds of the way then rose to the enemy's guns three-quarters of a mile distant. Halfway down the slope a fence line separated the clover from a ripened, partially harvested wheat field. The farthest portion stood in bundled shocks.

Clearly visible, less than a mile away, McClellan's main force waited in spectacular array. Artillery supported by infantry lined the ridge. Bright summer sun flashed off bayonets, rifle barrels, and bronze guns. Star-spangled banners streamed gallantly over determined blue mass.

Armistead's skirmish line reached the fence and halted. These kept an eye on the enemy while Edmonds sketched positions. Armistead carried the drawings to General Lee, headquartered at Smith's Shop on the Willis Church Road about a thousand yards to the southeast.

Lee's army had pushed the enemy for six days. The amount of equipment shed in retreat convinced Lee of a thoroughly demoralized foe. Armistead's report agreed with other intelligence. The Army of the Potomac had its back to the James River. This was their last stand. A successful assault would destroy McClellan's army. Lee prepared to attack.

Armistead trotted back to his men about noon and requested artillery. He and his officers sent their mounts to the rear, a lesson learned from Seven Pines.

About one o'clock, Grimes's Battery arrived for action. Only two of their guns were Parrott rifles with sufficient range. Union guns opened fire, killing one man, wounding three, and killing one horse and wounding two before Grimes even unlimbered.[297] Thus began a pathetic, lopsided duel. Moorman's Battery unlimbered near Grimes's. Guns from Purcell's Battery under William "Willie" Pegram went into battery on the Carter farm.

Lee also positioned guns to his far left on the Poindexter farm. In theory, the cross fire provided nominal support for an attack. Lee considered Armistead in best position to judge the effect of the bombardment. Lee issued written orders for a general assault to commence when Armistead's men "charged with a yell."[298] From about one thirty p.m. on, the Army of Northern Virginia awaited Armistead's signal.

General Longstreet appeared about three o'clock. He observed for himself that Confederate artillery arrived piecemeal and proved no match for the enemy's superior firepower. Armistead asked Longstreet for more and heavier guns. Longstreet agreed and departed.

Additional light artillery arrived as a matter of course but not the heavy pieces requested. For some reason, no one could locate Lee's chief of artillery reserve General Nelson Pendleton. Securing the quantity and caliber necessary to counter Union firepower was impossible without Pendleton.

The Union sent forth skirmishers in green uniforms. The distinctive color was that of the 1st U.S. Sharpshooters, Berdan's Rifles. The marksmen focused effectively on the gun crews while harassed by Armistead's skirmish line. Edmonds ordered Cabell to have his men throw down the fence rails and prepare to advance. Soon thereafter, Armistead ordered his skirmish line against the sharpshooters. Edmonds relayed the order. Cabell started his men forward.

In view of the green line's tenacity, Armistead reconsidered and escalated his response. He ordered Colonel James G. Hodges, 14th Virginia, his senior colonel, to advance the brigade. The order did not reach Edmonds directly. As soon as Edmonds sent Cabell and his skirmishers forward, he noticed the other regiments in motion. Edmonds turned to see Armistead behind him, waving his hat and shouting, "Go on!" Edmonds drew his sword and led the 38th Virginia forward with the other regiments.

Union artillery opened fire. A shell explosion wounded Colonel Hodges. This elevated Edmonds to senior colonel in command of the forward elements of the brigade. Command of the 38th Virginia defaulted to Lt. Colonel Powhatan Whittle.

Wright's brigade started forward upon seeing Edmonds's advance. Wright, returning from a brief reconnaissance, met his brigade exiting the woods. He immediately halted his men in the clover field and sought explanation. The shelling forced Wright and his men back into the trees.

Edmond's attack drove back the green-clad sharpshooters. Once Berdan's men reached the safety of their lines, Union guns peppered the approaching Rebels with canister. Edmonds judged it safer to push ahead into a depression rather than retrace their steps. The colonel hurried the men double quick into cover and ordered them to the ground.

The advance complicated the situation. The 38th Virginia, 14th Virginia, and 53rd Virginia lay pinned in the field without support. Grimes's Battery was silent. Moorman's and Purcell's batteries were badly damaged. Willie Pegram remained the last man standing in his unit and serviced his last gun alone.

Lacking specific targets, Union artillery shelled the woods. In a rare use of indirect fire, U.S. Navy gunboats *Galena* and *Mahaska* on the James River threw their heavy shells into Rebel positions. These streaked through the sky and exploded with extraordinary force. Men fell victims to cannon balls, shrapnel, chards, concussions, and falling timber.

The gulley where Armistead held his 9th Virginia and 57th Virginia in reserve became untenable. Armistead shuffled these sideways through the trees over beside Wright's men. Soldiers hugged the ground. Many took cover behind trees, as did Armistead. A Georgian of Wright's brigade shared a tree with Armistead and noted the general took a "long pull" on a brandy bottle.[299]

Edmonds's men, pinned under fire for nearly an hour, needed guidance. Major Cabell braved hazards and reported to Armistead. The general foresaw no opportunity to safely extract his units before nightfall. Cabell returned to Edmonds with orders to hold.[300]

Success depended on heavy artillery which never arrived. Prospects became so grim that about four p.m. Armistead ordered his few remaining guns silent.[301] Lee, too, had given up on attacking that day. However, the exhausted army commander had not canceled his written order with the signal to attack.

The men pinned in the swale took heart in the order to hold. The pluperfect hell before them declared a desperate foe. The Pittsylvanians saw themselves positioned as Lee's spearhead, as if chosen by God to be foremost in the final stroke.

* * *

Major General John B. Magruder arrived, having spent most of the day on the wrong road. Although his division was still en route, Magruder took command of Armistead's field and posted him back to his 9th Virginia and 57th Virginia.

Painful dyspepsia plagued Magruder. Morphine-laced medication dulled his judgment. He was hours late and peeved at his own confusion. In addition, the general still smarted from Lee's redress two days before for inaction at Savage's Station. Magruder had a reputation to redeem. The combination created a lethal mindset.

Magruder acted on Lee's outdated written instructions passed along to him. At five thirty p.m. he ordered Armistead and Wright forward.

Wright and his Georgians rose and charged with a yell. Armistead and his 9th Virginia and 57th Virginia followed. The rest of the army perceived the commotion as the long-awaited signal to attack. This initiated a general frontal assault with virtually no artillery support. Only the Letcher Artillery (four guns maximum) and the lone "Willie" Pegram with his one gun supported Magruder's front.[302]

Massed Union artillery roared. The cannonade shook the earth. The gunfire sounded in Williamsburg forty miles away.[303] Shells exploded all around the troops exiting the woods into the clover. Thick, sulfurous smoke enveloped the field. As the Rebels closed within five hundred yards, gunners switched to canister. Supporting infantry on the rise behind the guns volleyed.

Wright led his brigade forward into the fray, waving his hat in one hand and his sword flashing in the other. Colonel Edmonds's men cheered their approach. Edmonds ordered the 38th Virginia, 14th Virginia, and 53rd Virginia to their feet and dressed ranks. When the advancing gray line reached their position, Edmonds waved his sword forward and led his men up out of the swale and into the guns.

Cannons and muskets roared. Iron and lead filled the air. Dust erupted from canister ball impacts. Thuds! Groans! Men cringed as if walking into a storm. In Company B, 38th Virginia, Jimmy Dunn took a canister ball in the chest. Others fell. At the forefront, Edmonds cheered the brigade forward. To their right rear, Armistead maneuvered the 9th Virginia and 57th Virginia into the gap between Edmonds and Wright.

Cannons blazed! Muskets volleyed! Fire! Smoke! Shrieks! Confusion!

Color bearers waved their red battle flags. None was more zealous than Color Sergeant Luke Tarpley of the 38th Virginia. Tarpley carried the colors well ahead of the regiment. Lt. Colonel Whittle ordered the spirited youth to move slower.

The line halted two hundred yards from the guns, unleashed a volley and poured independent fire into the Union gunners. The 9th Virginia obliqued clear of units blocking their front and volleyed.

Color bearers attracted fire. The gallant Tarpley, waving the battle flag of the 38th Virginia, fell dead. Color Corporal Gilbert picked up the colors. He waved the cotton bunting proudly and fell mortally wounded with a bullet in his head. Color Corporal Chris Gregory grabbed the colors and fell seriously wounded, as did likewise Color Corporal John Burlington. Color Corporal Linnaeus Watkins seized the flag. Similar scenes occurred simultaneously in each regiment.

The attack dissolved before the massed artillery and musketry. Survivors withdrew and regrouped in the safety of the swale. Dead and wounded littered the field.

Magruder's division arrived piecemeal. The brigades of D. R. Jones and McLaws trickled in support. Wave after uncoordinated wave of fresh brigades emerged from the woods and advanced across the field. Five more times Armistead's brigade would rise to join reinforcements and charge Malvern Hell.

The advance of D. H. Hill's division on their left drew much fire off Armistead's men. Nevertheless, the roaring, fiery inferno was insurmountable. Enemy fire repulsed each assault.

Seeing messmates and kin blown to pieces all around them taxed the green 57th Virginia to its limit. Their position exposed them to volleys from infantry on the Union left. Bullets whizzed past heads like angry hornets. In the midst of their second attack, a well-aimed volley reaped a murderous harvest in the 57th Virginia, including two captains. Thus shocked, those companies broke and fled. The wounded standard bearer left with the colors. Panic ensued. The remainder of the 57th Virginia followed. They ran "...like the dickens...a perfect pell mell... Guns, hats, accoutrements strewn in our stampede in all directions."[304] To their credit, the 57th Virginia had already sustained the highest number of casualties of any of Armistead's regiments that day.

The moment the 57th Virginia bolted, the colors of 9th Virginia went down, its shaft shot in two. Captain Phillips rushed forward and saved the flag. Without their standard to rally upon, the 9th Virginia joined the 57th Virginia as they rushed past. Armistead struggled to rally the troops and pursued his fleeing men off the field. A few Paladins rallied and attached themselves to other units. They were the exceptions.

On the extreme Confederate left, Stonewall Jackson's men pressured the Union right and drew more attention away from Magruder's section of the field. Colonel Edmonds retained control of his three regiments and cheered the remnants of Armistead's brigade forward in each wave.

In the 38th Virginia, Watkins again carried the colors forward and fell seriously wounded. Private Parker took them up and was "killed almost instantly." Lt. Colonel Powhatan Whittle picked up the flag and advanced it prominently before the regiment. Sword in his right hand, standard in his left, Whittle's Washington-like persona electrified his battle line until a ball tore through his upper left arm. The flag dropped. The regiment faltered.

Powhatan Bolling Whittle, Lieutenant Colonel, 38th Virginia Infantry. (Courtesy H. George Carrison)

Captain Raleigh Daniel, the Kentucky volunteer leading Company F, ran forward, took the colors from Whittle and waved them defiantly. The men rallied and poured vengeful fire into the enemy. Three bullets pierced Daniel's body. He supported himself with the staff long enough to plant the colors upright and then sank to the ground.[305]

Colonel Edmonds ran over, grabbed the colors of the 38th Virginia, and held them high. Gallantry, honor, and conviction brought them within seventy-five yards of the Union guns.[306] At that range, muskets on both sides delivered telling effect. Gun crews dissolved. Infantry behind them volleyed and decimated the gray battle line. A bullet splintered the flag staff in Edmond's hand. Miraculously uninjured, he passed the limp flag to Color Corporal William Bohanon. The attack collapsed.

That last wave receded back into the safety of the swale at dusk. After nightfall, Colonel Edmonds and the battered brigade followed the sheltering contour across the road into the wooded gulley. The tattered colors of the 38th Virginia hung from Bohanon's bayonet and musket.

None on the field stood taller that day than the "little colonel" and his men. They had charged massed artillery and musketry not once, but six times! The flag of the 38th Virginia boasted fifty holes. The flag of the 14th Virginia had forty-seven holes.[307] The flag of the 53rd Virginia was similarly pierced. Each riddled battle flag presented less than twice the frontal area of the average soldier who followed it into the fray. Such daring! Such fortitude! Such courage!

They were lions of the Dan!

* * *

Desultory gunfire continued after dark, then stopped. Clouds rolled in. There was no moon. In blackest night, Confederates struggled to regroup. Calls to assemble mixed with cries of wounded. Lanterns and torches bobbed in the woods. The few luminaries amid McClellan's artillery and infantry disappeared as they withdrew.

Heavy rain fell. Wet soldiers shivered from the chill.

At dawn, only Union cavalry lined the ridge. They soon departed.

Daylight revealed a piteous scene. The rows of wheat shocks lay flat. Rain had washed away much red gore of the previous evening. Still, the carnage executed by massed artillery was especially grisly. Wounded, dead, and dying covered the field. Witnesses reported there were so many wounded moving that the field seemed to crawl.

Lewis Armistead searched for his command. He wandered about with a dozen or so men. Those with him were all he knew anything about except those lying in the field.[308]

Again Company B, 38th Virginia, the leftmost company in the line, suffered fewer casualties than most. They left Green Jones dead on the field. Jimmy Dunn died of wounds. Chris Gregory, Harrison Gibson, David Ules, Henry Adkins, John Arthur, and Lt. Warren were wounded. Henry C. Fuller was missing. Waddy Fuller grieved little brother Henry's unknown fate. Months later he would learn Henry died in Winder Hospital.

Armistead's brigade held the field for a week. Officers detailed able-bodied men to collect arms and ammunition and bury dead. Bullets had riddled every house, outbuilding, and slave cabin on the plateau. The Yankees left behind many seriously wounded at Malvern Manor. Most lay in the yard fully exposed, except for shade trees. All waited for either medical attention or the angel of death. The latter visited many.

Lee's army had saved Richmond. McClellan's army escaped to fight another day. That guaranteed continuation of the war.

* * *

The cost of the Seven Days Battles was staggering. Richmond was unprepared for the flood of casualties. The city was one great hospital. Losses in dead, wounded, and maimed attested to sincerest dedication. There was no shortage of heroes.

In his official report on the campaign, Lee wrote that "under ordinary circumstances the Federal Army should have been destroyed." There had been too many missteps by division commanders. Even Lee was new to his job.

The campaign provided measures by which Lee reorganized his army and leveraged proven leadership. The army soon conformed to Lee's purposes with generals Longstreet and Jackson each commanding a wing. Stuart commanded the cavalry.

On July 8, Armistead's brigade marched to Chaffin's Bluff and crossed the James River on a pontoon bridge. They camped with Huger's division on Falling Creek. On July 23, Lee replaced the slow acting Benjamin Huger with Major General Richard H. Anderson.

Twenty-two-year-old Major Joseph Cabell commanded the 38th Virginia in absence of both Colonel Edmonds and Lt. Colonel Whittle. Colonel Edmonds took sick after Malvern Hill and was hospitalized. Lt. Colonel Whittle recovered from his wound at his brother's home.

The ball that ripped through Whittle's upper left arm missed the bone. A makeshift tourniquet prevented his bleeding to death before reaching the field hospital. The regimental surgeon ligated the brachial artery and closed the wound. Upon regaining consciousness, Whittle suffered a merciless wagon jostling into Richmond. He boarded the train to Danville and from thence a painful buggy ride to his brother's home in Chatham.

Family friend and neighbor Dr. Rawley Martin visited Whittle. The captain in the Chatham Greys (Company I, 53rd Virginia) was himself home recovering from a wound received that same dreadful afternoon at Malvern Hill.

Eventually, Whittle's slapdash surgical repair hemorrhaged. A servant summoned Martin. He rushed to Whittle's aid and applied a tourniquet. It was apparent only amputation could save Whittle's life. Martin was in no condition to operate alone.

James Whittle raced to Dr. Robert E. Withers. The colonel of the 18th Virginia was home, having taken a bullet through a lung at Gaines's Mill. Weak and painfully sore, Withers was reluctant. He recommended other surgeons in the area. Nevertheless, Withers yielded to his friend's pleas and returned with him to find Powhatan in critical condition. Withers and Martin amputated Whittles's arm.[309] The stump healed. The indomitable Whittle resolved to return to duty. Indeed, he would.

In Company B, 38th Virginia news arrived that Seven Pines casualties John Stokes, Leo Grubbs, Dick and Nathan Gregory, and Dan Fuller had died. The six remaining Fuller brothers and cousins mourned Dan's death.

John R. Gregory had been detailed as a nurse since Seven Pines. He watched two of his brothers die from wounds. He sought to tend his remaining brother, Chris, after learning of his injury at Malvern Hill.

Combat losses required realignments. 38th Virginia, Company B promoted James Berger to 2nd Sgt. Tom Oakes replaced Berger as 3rd Sgt. John Oakes became 3rd Cpl. in place of Nathan Gregory killed.

Eldest brother Charles Oakes in the 57th Virginia also survived Malvern Hill unharmed. News arrived that their fourth brother, James, planned to join the 38th Virginia. Imminent conscription forced him to leave his wife and infant daughter. Enlistment assured service with his brothers rather than chance other assignment.

* * *

Each regiment in Armistead's brigade received bright, new, third-issue wool bunting flags to replace those destroyed in battle. Quartermasters stenciled white unit designations upon each, except for that of the Pittsylvania Regiment. The stylized black "38th" and "Va" painted on their shot-up cotton flag were carefully excised from the tatters and sewn onto their new flag. This made their flag unique in the Army of Northern Virginia. The appliqué was intrinsic battle honor and testament to their extraordinary courage at Malvern Hill.[310]

* * *

Armistead's brigade served duty in the fortifications at Drewry's Bluff. Food was plentiful again. The men worked on breastworks every other day.

An administrative transfer reduced the 38th Virginia to nine companies. Company I, 38th Virginia became Company G, 14th Virginia.[311]

Absences without leave reached epidemic proportions. Armistead prosecuted offenders to restore discipline. By mid-July, the brigade held over fifty men in the guard house. For most, Armistead stopped their pay for six months. Some received sentences of hard labor on fortifications with their ankle chained to a twelve-pound ball. Two or three had deserted multiple times and risked execution.[312] Armistead scheduled two to be shot for attempting to desert to the enemy.[313]

On August 1, gunboats thundered below them on the James River.[314] Nothing came of it. Colonel Edmonds returned to the 38th Virginia on August 3. The colonel looked very thin.

Some men secured substitutes. This did not sit well with either volunteers or those compelled to be there without means to buy one. The inequity of soldiers paid eleven dollars a month fighting beside a substitute hired for hundreds or thousands of dollars was intolerable.[315]

Substitutes were generally shirkers, bad for unit morale, and worthless in battle. One sub in the 38th Virginia disappeared the day after the man he replaced departed.[316] Afterward, Colonel Edmonds refused to accept substitutes in his regiment.

Ensign John Bohanon returned from the hospital. He had been ill since the retreat from Williamsburg. Consequently, he had missed the fights at Seven Pines and Malvern Hill. John found his cousin William the sole remnant of his color guard. It gave John cause to ponder his future.

* * *

Lewis Armistead entered the Peninsula Campaign a freshly promoted brigadier general. He survived the fights around Richmond with an image as shot up as any of his battle flags. Despite his bravery, there was talk of his ineptitude at Seven Pines and drinking at Malvern Hill. In fact, men in Wright's brigade who witnessed him imbibe while taking cover behind a poplar tree dubbed Armistead the Poplar General.[317]

While Edmonds led three regiments of the brigade throughout the fight, Armistead led two and left the field early to chase them when they broke. One soldier in the 9th Virginia wrote, "Armistead cares nothing for his men." He claimed Armistead led from behind prodding "go on boys," but never "come on" when entering a fight.[318]

Upper echelons never recorded perceptions of Armstead other than affirmations of courage and austerity. Gentlemen would not do otherwise.

Superiors and peers, no doubt, considered Armistead a West Point reject commissioned by special privilege. Coupled with his unexceptional U.S. Army career and shortcomings in Richmond battles, it is no surprise that from Malvern Hill forward, Lewis Armistead sucked hind teat in line for assignments. He always had.

CHAPTER EIGHT

The Second Manassas and Maryland Campaigns

Lee had defeated Lincoln's largest army. The Seven Days Battles cost nearly sixteen thousand Northern casualties, a third being captured or missing. Nevertheless, the Federal objective to preserve the Union remained fixed.

The South suffered double the North's numbers of killed and wounded. Pyrrhic victories consecrated the Southern cause with blood most dear.

An officer in Armistead's brigade expressed common sentiments when he wrote:

> The cry of the enemy is still for war, ours of necessity must be the same. I see but one way to end this war & that is to carry the war into the enemy's country. When they feel as we have done, I think that then and only then they will grant us Independence.[319]

Stonewall Jackson's Valley Campaign had made it clear to Lincoln that the disjointed commands of McDowell, Banks, and Sigel needed consolidation. On June 26, the day Lee first attacked McClellan, Abraham Lincoln summoned Major General John Pope from the West to lead the new Army of Virginia. This united the three corps under one commander.

Pope had first attracted Lincoln's attention by successfully protecting his person during that tumultuous trip to his inauguration. Pope's performance in the West commended his appointment. Unlike most of Lincoln's generals, who were Democrats, Pope was a Republican. For the first time, Lincoln and one of his army commanders shared political ideology.

McClellan never believed in waging war on the general population. In contrast, Pope issued orders suppressing all opposition to federal authority. Property and personal rights in occupied areas vanished. Vouchers for materials requisitioned from civilians promised payment at the end of the war but, then, only upon evidence of loyalty to the Union.

Pope held locals responsible for partisan activities. He endorsed reprisals and impressed civilians to make repairs. His men confiscated food, vandalized property, jailed Southern sympathizers, and held them hostage. Pope gave Virginians loyal to their state clear choice: flee or starve.[320]

Expanding the war beyond fields of honor affronted Cavalier sensibilities. By mid-July, Pope's depredations upon homes and families, sanctioned by Lincoln, fired demands for revenge throughout the South. True hatred for Yankee invaders supplanted resentments over conscription and dispelled reservations some had held about the war. Pope gave Virginians more reason to fight than ever.

Pope promised Lincoln swift victory. Units from McClellan's army reinforced Pope as they left the Peninsula.

Lee planned to expel Pope from Northern Virginia. Moreover, if presented opportunity to invade the North, Lee's men were eager to go.

* * *

Pope intended to first cut the Virginia Central Railroad at Gordonsville, thereby severing communication with the Shenandoah Valley. However, Pope's grand strategy went awry before taking that first step. Jackson's surprise attack at Cedar Mountain on August 9 routed Pope's II Corps (Banks) staged near the Rapidan River. Uneasiness in Washington arrested Pope's move on Gordonsville.

Lee seized initiative with a guarded eye, for McClellan still had forces on the Peninsula. Longstreet left Anderson's division outside Richmond to counter the threat posed by McClellan at Harrison's Landing. On August 13, the rest of Longstreet's men boarded trains to catch up with Jackson. When the last of McClellan's men sailed away on August 16, Anderson received orders to rejoin Longstreet.

That same day, the very day they marched, the 38th Virginia received new recruits. Company B added four new men: three from Callands and one from

Chatham. All were family men facing conscription. James Oakes joined his brothers Tom and John. John Mahan was a father of five from Chatham and a friend of the Oakeses. Mahan's little brother Alex had served in Company B until his death from typhoid the previous September.

Armistead's brigade marched at the rear of Anderson's column. The men boarded a train in Richmond for Louisa. There they detrained and bivouacked about a half mile outside of town. They had neither provisions nor cooking utensils.[321]

Anderson's division received supplies and equipment by August 19. That day they marched fifteen miles in oppressive heat to Orange Court House. As Lee prepared to advance, Pope completely abandoned his Rapidan River line and moved to more secure defenses behind the Rappahannock River.

August 20 marked the beginning of Lee's campaign. Jackson advanced his wing. Longstreet followed in support with Anderson's division rearmost.

Armistead's brigade arose at dawn and marched at the rear of Anderson's division. They bivouacked at dusk on the Rapidan near Clark's Mountain.

On August 21, Armistead's brigade marched to Stevensburg. On August 22, the brigade demonstrated along the Rappahannock. Captain Griggs, 38th Virginia, reported passing "over some fine land, now desolate from the ravages of war."[322] Griggs had viewed the landscape five months before. The destruction was the wanton work of Pope.

Those damned Yankees!

Stuart's cavalry screened Jackson's movements beyond Popes right. The gray riders struck the Federal supply base at Catlett's Station. The raid on his supply line rattled Pope.

Torrential rain fell as Pope prepared to attack Lee across the Rappahannock. The river rose quickly. High water prevented Pope's army from crossing.

On August 23, Longstreet's artillery dueled with Pope's on the opposite bank. The Union strongly held Kelly's Ford, Rappahannock Bridge,[323] and Beverly's Ford. The 38th Virginia awoke in the rain to the cannonade which rumbled throughout the day.

Next morning, Armistead's brigade marched to Jeffersonton as Anderson's division moved up river. They were the last of Longstreet's column. On August 25, the 38th Virginia performed picket duty on the banks opposite Fauquier White Sulphur Springs. They held the heights there with elements of Stephen D. Lee's artillery.[324] Veterans in the 38th Virginia remembered the site from their retreat in March.

Lee seized opportunity and split his army. On August 26, Longstreet pushed at the river fords while Jackson's wing marched around Pope's right. Longstreet's lead divisions filled the void left by Jackson and kept the Union occupied until late in the day. After sunset Longstreet marched after Jackson. Anderson's division remained behind facing the enemy.

That evening Jackson's "foot cavalry" destroyed two trains at Bristoe Station. Pope withdrew from his Rappahannock line to deal with that threat in his rear.

In the wee hours of August 27, Armistead's brigade marched at the end of Anderson's division. They crossed the Rappahannock at Waterloo as the sun rose. After several hours of rest, they plodded twenty miles in the heat through dust kicked up by lead units. They bivouacked at nightfall just west of Salem (now Marshall) on the Manassas Gap Railroad. Many straggled.

High drama developed as Jackson drew Pope's full attention by occupying the Federal supply depot at Manassas Junction. After fending off the first Union arrivals, Jackson's men sacked and burned the depot. Jackson then retired to strong positions along an unfinished railroad cut on the edge of the old Manassas battlefield. There he hoped to draw Pope into battle on ground of his own choosing and await reinforcement by Longstreet. Pope took the bait.

Late on August 28, fierce fighting erupted on the Warrenton Turnpike as Jackson attacked a Union column as they passed Brawner's farm. Pope arrayed his army to strike Jackson. Meanwhile, a dozen miles away, Longstreet routed resistance and pushed through Thoroughfare Gap.

On August 29, Pope attacked Jackson in earnest. Longstreet's wing arrived throughout the day. His lead units were in place by early afternoon. Pope repeatedly assaulted Jackson's position unaware of Longstreet's presence.

Anderson's division tramped to the rumble of distant guns as the first full day of the Second Battle of Manassas raged. Again, many straggled. Nevertheless, Anderson's men trudged through the night and arrived on the battlefield exhausted at three a.m. on August 30.

No staff officer met Anderson to guide his men into position. The exhausted, footsore troops halted along the Warrenton Turnpike and fell fast asleep. The Union dead along the road should have alerted Anderson to danger. His division had inadvertently marched onto the battlefield exposed to Union batteries. General Hood informed Anderson of the lethal situation in time to prevent disaster. Anderson roused his exhausted troops and pulled them back as day dawned.

The blunder proved serendipitous. Pope was already under the false impression he had beaten Jackson and expected Confederate withdrawal. At first light, Union observers saw the last of Anderson's division pulling back and reported seeing a large Confederate column leaving. This reinforced Pope's assumption that the Rebels were retreating.

Pope renewed his attacks, thinking he confronted Jackson's rearguard. Each assault met unexpectedly stiff resistance with staggering losses. Nevertheless, Pope believed he pursued a defeated enemy. Pope remained oblivious to Longstreet's presence and the fact that he faced Lee's entire army.

Longstreet staged his divisions for counterattack. Anderson's men slept at Brawner's farm for about an hour before forming lines of battle. Armistead and his men stood in reserve.

At four p.m. Longstreet launched the largest attack of his career. The objective was Henry Hill. Taking that high ground assured destruction of Pope's army.

Anderson's division moved forward in support of Longstreet's main advance. The Union fought tenaciously and received reinforcements at critical moments. The fighting on Chinn Ridge was intense and bloody. The advance took longer than expected. The Confederates pushed the Union off the ridge by six p.m. Federal troops frantically consolidated on Henry Hill.

Armistead's brigade halted briefly atop Chinn Ridge as the rest of Anderson's division obliqued right toward Hazel Plain.[325] the Chinn house. While Armistead's men waited in reserve, 1st Lt. Prichard, Company B, 38th Virginia, attended the mortally wounded Colonel Fletcher Webster, commander of the 12th Massachusetts, the only son of statesman Daniel Webster. Prichard accepted the dying man's personal items for safekeeping.[326]

Anderson's division pushed onward. Wright's and Mahone's brigades pressed the attack toward Henry Hill. Armistead's brigade continued around them over Bald Hill. Longstreet's attack stalled in the fading light. Anderson was unaware of the desperate weakness in the Union position and did not push further.

The regiments of Armistead's brigade wheeled left into line and halted on the extreme Confederate right astride Sudley Church Road facing the woods before

Henry Hill. Colonel Edmonds of the 38th Virginia stood once again on ancestral land. The site had become pivotal in his new nation's history for a second time. Near that very spot Kirby Smith, to whose brigade the 38th Virginia then belonged, had fought First Manassas while Edmonds and his regiment waited for a train to the battlefield. The moment presented so great irony to Edmonds as to suggest divine appointment.

General J. E. B. Stuart reinforced this feeling as he galloped up at the head of a patrol to report the enemy's flank exposed just beyond the trees. Being the last unengaged unit and poised at Lee's extreme right, Armistead's brigade was uniquely positioned to exploit the situation. An attack at that moment might very well have collapsed the Union line and carried Henry Hill.

Armistead, having personally experienced the shock of a flank attack, was keenly aware of its devastating potential. He had also experienced loss of control in a wood with friendly units firing at each other. The only two attacks he had personally led thus far had ended in routs. Impending darkness multiplied risks. The opportunity demanded immediate action. Armistead refused.[327]

Stuart lacked authority to order Armistead forward. By the time Stuart found Lee to recommend Armistead attack, Pope no longer had his flank exposed and had withdrawn under cover of darkness.[328] The Confederate line held fast. Thus, the Second Battle of Manassas ended with General Lewis A. Armistead and his men arguably at its high-water mark.

By eleven o'clock, Pope's army was well beyond Bull Run and taking refuge in the old Confederate earthworks at Centerville. It began to rain. Lee's soldiers remained at arms throughout the night.

The 38th Virginia had not been issued food for days. Colonel Edmonds detailed men to locate provisions. Edwin Penick, Company D, searched all night. At daylight, he guided a supply wagon back. Edmonds rewarded Penick by excusing him from duty the rest of the day. Penick spent his time ministering to the dying on both sides.[329]

Members of the 57th Virginia and others in Armistead's brigade replaced their old converted smoothbores with modern rifled muskets collected from the battlefield. The army gathered an estimated five thousand small arms. The 38th Virginia bivouacked in plain view of its winter quarters.[330]

Rain continued throughout August 31. Lee's army held their positions and dealt with supply issues. General Lee toured the field. He fell off his horse and sprained both wrists and broke bones in his right hand.[331] This restricted the general to travel by ambulance for several weeks.

* * *

Armistead's brigade reported two men killed and eighteen wounded, all victims of incidental fire.[332] One killed and three wounded belonged to the 38th Virginia.[333]

Armistead's was the only brigade in the Army of Northern Virginia not directly engaged in the fight. It reported the lowest number of casualties in the bloodiest battle of the war to date. Armistead's brigade marched last in the rearmost division throughout the campaign. They were last in order of battle. The situation was clear. Armistead's place was at the rear.

Only Pope's control of Henry Hill prevented the destruction of his army. Henry Hill would have likely fallen had Jackson advanced earlier to prevent Union reinforcement of Chinn Ridge—or had R. H. Anderson grasped Pope's weakness, or had Armistead launched the flank attack advised by Stuart. The destruction of Pope's Army of Virginia would have left little or no organized resistance between Lee's Army and Washington. One can only speculate on the result and its ultimate effect on the war.

Faint heart never filled a flush. At Second Manassas, Lewis Armistead likely folded his only winning hand.

* * *

On September 1, Lee moved to encircle Pope. Jackson's wing marched north around Centerville toward Fairfax. They clashed with Union troops in driving rain at Ox Hill (Chantilly).

The divisions of McLaws, D. H. Hill, and Walker arrived from Richmond. Thus reinforced, Lee intended to strike Pope the next day. However, Pope abandoned Centerville and retreated to Washington.

Lee had successfully outmaneuvered and beaten Pope. Lee, Jackson, Longstreet, and Stuart had established their unique synergy in a stellar campaign.

Lee had started with fifty-five thousand men. Battle losses amounted to nine thousand. Effective strength was depleted that much again by straggling.[334] The arrival of three fresh divisions brought Lee's army up to about fifty thousand effectives.

The area was divested of supplies and unable to support an army. Lee had to move forward or retreat. Return to Richmond would forfeit hard-won gains. Concurrently, British politicians debated support for the South. Lee's army appeared unstoppable. More and more Northerners wanted a quick end to the conflict.

Lee had neither the strength nor resources to attack Washington, which was defended by Pope's retreating army. With the federal government and its army off balance, the road north lay open. A successful invasion could win foreign support, sway Northern opinion, and seat sympathizers in the upcoming U.S. Congressional elections. Any of those possibilities might end the war. Lee ordered his men north while he weighed his options.[335]

* * *

Armistead's men knew nothing of grand strategy. They rested on the Manassas battlefield and cooked rations. On September 3, they marched eight miles to Frying Pan (now Floris).[336] Men in the 38th Virginia shot a hog and cooked it to the joy of all partakers.[337]

On September 4, they marched twelve miles and halted three miles shy of Leesburg. The army finally discharged Raleigh Fuller, Company B, and twelve others in the 38th Virginia for being over thirty-five years old. Rumors of invasion spread through the ranks. That day Lee committed to his plan to invade the North.

The following day, Armistead's brigade marched through Leesburg at the rear of Anderson's division. Cheering ladies lined the streets. Traffic clogged beyond the town. After three, slow moving miles they bivouacked at Big Spring about midnight. The large, spring-fed pool provided cool water for the troops staged for invasion.[338] Jackson's men had bivouacked there the previous night and had already crossed into Maryland.

As a final preparation, Lee appointed Lewis Armistead provost marshal for the Army of Northern Virginia. Provost duty normally involved detailing men to guard supplies, secure fords, and fill gaps as needed. In context of this campaign,

Armistead's primary task was to round up stragglers. Lee charged him to "punish summarily all depredators."[339]

Lee, a former West Point superintendent, must have discounted Armistead, the two-time dropout. Add to this Armistead's father-conferred commission, regular army record, reputation among peers, and dubious performance under Lee's own eye at Malvern Hill. There was also Armistead's recent risk aversion at Second Manassas. All totaled, Armistead had little to commend himself to the army commander. Even his promotion to brigadier general, dated April Fool's Day, hinted cosmic absurdity.

The army provost position Lee created was strangely unique to Lewis Armistead and the Maryland Campaign. Objectivity leaves little doubt that Armistead's appointment to provost marshal for the entire army was more pragmatic than honorary.[340] Lee, the quintessential gentleman, exercised decorum and tact by thus relegating his Jonah to an innocuous post.

* * *

Early afternoon September 6, Anderson's division waded across the Potomac into Maryland. The columns of infantry, trains of artillery, and wagons crossing the river inspired awe. Armistead forbade his men from removing shoes and clothing during the crossing.[341] The provost marshal halted his brigade on the opposite shore until assuming its place last in column.

On September 7, Armistead's brigade marched all day at the rear of the army. They waded across the Monocacy River twice and bivouacked near Buckeystown. On September 8, they forded the Monocacy River a third time. Although other brigades undressed to keep shoes and clothing dry, Armistead's men waded fully clothed and marched wet.

Straggling grew an increasingly desperate problem in Lee's army. Contrary to assertions by leadership, straggling involved more than shirkers. The army was largely exhausted. Thousands were barefoot and hungry.[342] Even the best soldier was susceptible to blistered feet, heat exhaustion, and dysentery. Hundreds were truly sick.[343]

Moreover, prime candidates for straggling included the untrained and unseasoned. Such were new enlistees like James Oakes and John Mahan in

Company B, 38th Virginia, who embarked on the campaign the instant they presented themselves for duty. These were ill prepared for hard marching and food deprivation. Mahan wrote his wife that he would have been "thankful for the victuals I have seen you throw out to the dogs."[344]

Armistead's assignment as provost marshal for the army proved exceedingly redundant since each brigade had its own provost guard to arrest stragglers and return them to their companies. Furthermore, water prematurely ruined irreplaceable shoes. Wet shoes stretched out of shape. They blistered feet. Leather stiffened when dried and chafed. The actions of the provost marshal exacerbated straggling within his own brigade. Armistead's assignment as straggler policeman was short lived.

Upon arrival in Frederick, Armistead moved into the building abandoned by the departed Union provost.[345] Armistead discovered Lee had appointed Colonel Bradley T. Johnson of the 1st Maryland regiment as civilian provost marshal.[346] Johnson, a native of that town, was the preferred liaison to local citizenry.

Lee then modified Armistead's mission to maintaining "good order and military discipline" and limiting "depredations on the community." Indeed, preserving the army's image was as strategic as any aspect of the campaign. Nevertheless, Armistead's modified assignment was as ambiguous as it had been redundant.

Days in Frederick afforded light duties and ample corn but little else in the way of food. One Piedmonter wrote that they ate corn until their bellies were "tighter than a drum."[347] Shrunken stomachs facilitated the condition. Armistead's brigade camped with the rest of their division at Monocacy Station between the railway and the river. The men rested, bathed, and washed clothes in the muddy stream.

* * *

Marylanders failed to welcome the Confederates as anticipated. Few enlistments and local resentments spurred Lee to act. Lee decided to move into Pennsylvania via Chambersburg. Citizens of Harrisburg already feared attack; some neared panic. Before moving farther north, Lee first needed to secure his supply line by neutralizing the Federal garrison at Harpers Ferry.

Lee's plan was risky. Walker's division, already in Virginia, would seize Loudoun Heights. Jackson's division would march, cross the Potomac at Shepherdstown, and attack from the west. Lee assigned McLaws the attack from the Maryland side with both his and Anderson's division. Lastly, Longstreet would march his men to Hagerstown to secure the invasion route north.

On September 10, Lee split his army. At one p.m. Armistead's brigade left Frederick at the tail end of Anderson's column. They marched until midnight and halted near Birkittsville.

Despite restful days in Frederick, poorly clothed, malnourished men without shoes on macadamized roads pushed limits of endurance. The steady diet of parched corn and green apples took its toll in diarrhea and dehydration. Scores fell by the wayside. Straggling in the Army of Northern Virginia reduced effective strengths of most infantry units to about half. Armistead's brigade was no exception. Sick, weak men struggled to keep up or yielded to capture. A few deserted. Most stopped, rested, and then pushed on to catch up with their unit by day's end.

On September 11, McLaws's and Anderson's divisions crossed South Mountain at Brownsville Pass into Pleasant Valley. Armistead's brigade, the rearguard, moved last.

The next day, Armistead's brigade marched to Weverton. The 38th Virginia skirmished with Union pickets. On September 13, Armistead detached the 38th Virginia to serve as skirmishers for McLaws's advance up Elk Ridge. McLaws took Maryland Heights by four thirty p.m. The 38th Virginia remained on the heights September 14, while the rest of Armistead's brigade guarded Sandy Hook Road.

McClellan's troops attacked Lee's forces guarding the three main South Mountain gaps. McLaws dispatched the remainder of Anderson's division to Crampton's Gap to counter the Union advance there. Confederate artillery atop Maryland Heights fired on Harpers Ferry. The 38th Virginia watched the bombardment from their well-earned perch. Gunfire from all actions reverberated up and down Pleasant Valley.

When Union troops took Crampton's Gap, it placed McLaws with his back against the Potomac with no route of escape. The surrender of Harpers Ferry on September 15 prevented the destruction of McLaws's force.

The situation proved too much for the color bearer in the 38th Virginia. Perhaps Ensign John Bohanon balked that he had not signed on to invade the North. Perhaps the month of hard marching with bloody, bare feet and an empty stomach taxed his limits. Perhaps the gore of Second Manassas and his looming fate as standard bearer illuminated Solomon's admonition that "a living dog is better than a dead lion."[348] For whatever reason, when the 38th Virginia assembled for roll call that morning, John was gone and never coming back.[349]

McLaws's task force crossed into Harpers Ferry September 16. Armistead's brigade received meager provisions, then marched three miles to Halltown. They rested briefly. At three p.m., orders came to march to Sharpsburg.

Armistead's men took their place last in Anderson's division, which followed McLaws's column. They bivouacked late evening. A courier from Lee urged McLaws to make haste as Lee desperately worked to reassemble his army to face McClellan. The men resumed their march after midnight.

Not all the 9th Virginia received word. The regiment marched and left a significant number of exhausted men fast asleep. Hours later, light rain awakened those left behind. They found themselves both literally and figuratively in a fog.

Armistead's brigade crossed the Potomac at Blackford's Ford.[350] First light illuminated the valley mist. Gunfire boomed in the distance. The Battle of Sharpsburg (Antietam) had begun.

McLaws's and Anderson's divisions reached Lee's headquarters about seven thirty a.m. The divisions stood in reserve formed in two columns. Lee sent McLaws to support Stonewall Jackson fighting in the West Woods. Lee requested an additional brigade from Anderson to support McLaws. Anderson sent Armistead.

As soon as Armistead formed his line of battle behind McLaws, Jackson rode up and told Armistead to have his men lie down until needed. Gunfire and musketry roared intensely before them. Overshot rounds posed the greatest threat to Armistead's men. Cannon balls bounced over the hill at them. Bill Allen, Company B, 38th Virginia, had fallen behind during the march. As he caught up to his unit, a cannon ball knocked him dead. Allen was Company B's only fatality that day.

A cannon ball rolled into Armistead's foot.[351] Thus injured, Armistead relinquished command to Colonel James G. Hodges, 14th Virginia, ranking colonel in the brigade.

Hodges reported Armistead's wounding to nearby General Jubal Early, who immediately directed Hodges to move his brigade to the front along the Hagerstown Turnpike.[352] Ironically, Armistead's brigade had lain in reserve until

Armistead's disablement. Only then did Early, Armistead's old West Point nemesis, send Armistead's men into action.

Hodges ordered the brigade up and forward. A shell exploded over Company D, 38th Virginia, and knocked Edwin Penick to the ground.[353] Another shell burst wounded Captain Griggs, Company K. General Jackson saw the advance at common time and ordered them at the double quick to minimize exposure to fire.[354] Shortly after the brigade took their place on the front line, the contest for the West Woods ended. Armistead's brigade (Hodges) held their position near the Dunker Church.

The fighting moved to the Confederate center. Lee moved Anderson's division in support of the Sunken Road. General R. H. Anderson was seriously wounded. Colonel Cadmus Wilcox assumed command of the division and was driven back with heavy loss. Fighting there subsided. The contest moved to the far Confederate right for the rest of the afternoon.

At sunset, the battle ended in stalemate. The carnage defied description. Armistead's brigade (Hodges) remained in place on the Hagerstown Turnpike through the night. On that bloodiest day of the war, when many commands were decimated, Armistead's brigade suffered the fewest casualties of any brigade in the Army of Northern Virginia: five dead and thirty wounded.[355]

Both armies remained static throughout the following day. Parties under flags of truce tended wounded. Confederate doctors at field hospitals returned any man to duty who could still walk.[356] Shortly after sunset, word spread that the army was moving back to Virginia. Armistead's brigade (Hodges) served as rearguard. They were the last infantry to quit the field.

The army withdrew through Sharpsburg along the Shepherdstown road and then down a farm lane to Blackford's Ford. Cavalry stood in the river with torches along both sides of the ford to guide the way. Lee's army crossed the Potomac throughout the night. Armistead's brigade (Hodges) crossed as the sun rose.

Lee's artillery reserve under General Nelson Pendleton protected the ford. Longstreet left Armistead's and Lawton's brigades with Pendleton to prevent Union troops from crossing. Lawton's brigade had lost half its men in the battle. Those present included many wounded without rifles. Straggling had severely reduced Armistead's brigade. The two units combined barely counted six hundred men.

Armistead's brigade (Hodges) manned positions along the ford. Initially, most of Lawton's battered brigade remained in reserve near the artillery. Pendleton soon dispatched those armed to reinforce Hodges.

Union artillery appeared on the bluffs on the opposite shore and commenced fire. Enemy infantry arrived. Colonel Hodges relayed the information to General Pendleton along with personal sightings of enemy skirmishers and signal flags on the mountains to his right. Captain Poindexter, Company H, 38th Virginia, reported additional enemy artillery at his position and sighted enemy infantry moving down river. Hodges then sent the 9th Virginia to cover another ford downstream. The 9th Virginia numbered no more than fifty or sixty men.

Of the forty-four guns under Pendleton, the terrain allowed thirty-three positioned. Only a few were rifled cannon with sufficient range to counter enemy fire. The rest were six-pound smoothbores, virtually useless under the circumstances. The enemy's numerous twenty-pound rifles outgunned Confederate batteries.

Colonel Hodges urgently messaged Pendleton:

> General: In obedience to your request that I would keep you posted, I have the honor to state that Colonel Edmonds, Thirty-eighth Virginia, reports that we have not a piece of artillery in position firing, and the enemy have, as far as he could ascertain, twenty-odd. There is nothing to prevent the enemy from crossing except the line of sharpshooters on the river.[357]

Resistance melted away. Pendleton received report that only three hundred soldiers remained at the ford. He asked Hodges to hold on for one more hour. The artillery reported low ammunition and requested permission to withdraw. Pendleton reached his wits' end.

At sunset, Union soldiers sprang from the dry canal bed on the opposite shore and advanced. The green-clad troops in front of the 38th Virginia were the 1st U.S. Sharpshooters, the same they had faced at Malvern Hill. Two regiments of infantry supported them.

The Piedmonters opened fire. The enemy's line waded forward with bullets skipping all around them. Wounded splashed into the Potomac. Rocks and shadows hid the Rebels. Only muzzle flashes suggested targets. Some attackers missed the ford, stepped into neck-deep water, and soaked their ammunition.

The overwhelmed, outgunned defenders evaporated. Men skedaddled up the steep road. At the top of the bluffs, they followed the last of their departing artillery in the direction of Martinsburg.

"Old Mother" Pendleton had already fled. The general outdistanced everyone. Pendleton stopped only upon reaching Lee to report the shocking loss of all forty-four of his guns. In reality, forty had been safely withdrawn.[358] Pendleton's ineptitude provoked Jackson to dispatch A. P. Hill to force the enemy back across the Potomac. This he did the following day at the Battle of Shepherdstown.[359]

Armistead's men retreated through the night and collected as exhausted rabble at Martinsburg. Wounded Southerners turned the town into a hospital.

Lee planned to regroup, recross the Potomac at Williamsport, and attack McClellan again. Subordinates convinced Lee of the spent condition of his army. In fact, not until Appomattox would the Army of Northern Virginia ever again be so weak.[360] Lee abandoned the idea.[361]

* * *

Armistead rejoined his brigade after it established camp. Supplies were scarce. Soldiers did what they could to supplement meager rations. On September 25, men of the 38th Virginia killed what they thought was a possum. It was a skunk. The camp reeked thereafter.[362]

A nearby house accidentally burned. Union troops assumed Rebels were burning supplies in retreat. Upon advancing, musketry convinced them otherwise. One noted, "The Yankees retreated more valiantly than they advanced."[363]

The enemy's attention encouraged the Southern command to move along. Armistead's brigade left Martinsburg on September 27. They tramped eighteen miles to Clearbrook and camped at Hopewell Meeting House.[364] The men camped there for the next month to refresh and refit as resources allowed.

They learned Lincoln promised to free all slaves in the rebelling states come New Year's Day. This was no surprise. The development was inevitable in a prolonged struggle.[365] Few had anticipated the length and ferocity of the war.

The men received rations of fresh beef and pork. They received no salt. Soldiers supplemented rations with produce from local farmers. Quakers drove hard bargains and were not always willing to sell. Some soldiers never caught the pacifists in the right mood.[366]

Veterans fared well. Recent conscripts sickened.[367] Revival meetings spiced camp life nearly every night that month. Many accepted Christ or rededicated themselves.

On October 2, Lee praised his men in General Order 116.

> Since Malvern Hill the Army of Northern Virginia defeated the enemy at Cedar Mountain; expelled him from his Rappahannock line; in a three day fight repulsed him from Manassas; forced him into fortifications around Washington; without halting crossed the Potomac; stormed the heights of Harpers Ferry capturing 11,000 prisoners, 75 guns and much small arms and munitions of war; resisted the enemy at Sharpsburg from dawn to dark with less than a third his number; stood next day ready to resume the fight on the same ground; and retired intact across the Potomac.[368]

Lee's soldiers that summer displayed exceptional fortitude and valor. Every unit did its duty.

Conspicuously, throughout each phase, General Lewis Armistead's place was at the rear.

CHAPTER NINE

Pickett's Division and Fredericksburg

The Army of Northern Virginia licked its wounds. Summer-like temperatures persisted well into October. Weather facilitated resupply and refitting. There was little rain. Water sources slowed to trickles and tasted earthy. Heat desiccated and muted autumn foliage to a cheerless yellow-brown. Camps were hot and dry. Dust was "ankle deep" according to Pvt. John Mahan, Company B, 38th Virginia.[369]

Mahan had faced conscription and enlisted in August. After enduring the ordeals of Lee's late summer campaigns, Mahan begged his father to find him a substitute. A couple of men in the 57th Virginia had just provided subs and departed. One proxy deserted after his first day and placed the released man in jeopardy of recall.

For such reasons, Colonel Edmonds refused substitutes in the 38th Virginia. Nevertheless, Mahan, husband and father of five, finagled arrangement with fellow company members Tom, John, and James Oakes. The trio persuaded brother Charles in Company E, 57th Virginia to swap places with Mahan whenever he found a sub. The mercenary could then replace Mahan in the 57th Virginia. Colonel Edmonds approved the shuffle. All Mahan needed was a substitute.[370]

Three days later, Mahan's heart broke to learn that his four little girls had all died of scarlet fever within a week. He requested furlough home. Armistead denied it, claiming he needed every man. Captain John Cabell and Colonel Edmonds interceded for Mahan without success.[371]

Fall temperatures arrived on October 11. On that date, the Confederate Congress passed the Twenty Slave Law. Prompted by concerns over servile unrest due to Lincoln's proclamation, provisions exempted owners and overseers of twenty or more slaves from military service. The law applied to less than 1 percent of white Virginia. Few claimed the exemption. Most of those eligible were already in uniform. They were leaders with much at stake in the outcome and remained at their posts. Few in the ranks qualified. It fueled recrudescent feelings that the war was a rich man's war and a poor man's fight.

* * *

On October 13, Longstreet reviewed his troops with two members of British Parliament. Placing his best foot forward, the corps commander forbade men without shoes at parade. Armistead left about a third of his men in camp.

Scarcities affected more than appearances. They also affected fitness and morale. Three days later, Colonel Edmonds approached Armistead on behalf of his men about the ongoing salt shortage. No salt had been issued for weeks. Armistead tolerated pressure from superiors; he refused demands from subordinates. Armistead took offense and placed Edmonds under arrest.[372]

Generals Lee, Longstreet, and Wilcox reviewed the men again on October 20. Fewer participated as even fewer had shoes. Prospects for footwear remained dismal. An unshod army is a crippled force. Cold weather magnified challenges faced by shoeless soldiers. A north wind blew in the first frost that night.

Ten days later, Anderson's division (Wilcox) left their camps at Bunker Hill and Clear Brook. Armistead's brigade marched twenty-five miles in freezing weather. Barefoot men fell out of ranks along the frigid road with painfully cold, bruised, bleeding feet. They stopped on the banks of the Shenandoah River three miles short of Front Royal.[373]

The next day, October 31, the men forded the river with a half inch of ice.[374] They trudged across the mountains at Chester Gap and halted at Flint Hill. The fourteen-mile mountain trek gave few barefoot stragglers time to catch up. The next day the brigade marched fifteen undulating, winding miles between mountains to Gaines Cross Roads (now Ben Venue).

On November 2, the brigade went into camp three miles north of Culpeper Court House. The long march created even more shoeless soldiers. Cold, hungry, footsore stragglers limped into camp over the next several days. It was a memorable ordeal and their last march as members of Anderson's division.

* * *

After reaching Culpeper, veteran Indian fighter Lewis Armistead implemented what he believed was the ideal, short-term solution to the shoe shortage. Moccasins!

Army slaughter pens produced plenty of fresh cowhides. Armistead requisitioned sufficient for his regiments. Each man received two strips of hide with orders to fashion moccasins with the pelage inward. The hides were fresh with residual meat. The men fleshed the hides and sewed them together as best they could. Those less skilled simply wrapped and tied the skins to their feet.

The rawhide did not wear well. The pelage provided little comfort to bare skin. The rawhide shrank and stiffened as it dried. Stiff hide cut, chafed, and promoted infection. Once dried, "there was no getting them off without cutting them."[375] The untanned, unpreserved skins became slimy, gelatinous when wet. They stretched out of shape, and the stitching tore loose. Wet rawhide putrefied, drew flies, attracted vermin, bred maggots, and stank. Some men carried switches to shoo flies away. The men loathed them.

The concept had merit, but proper moccasins required arts the soldiers lacked. Indeed, the desperate practice surfaced spontaneously throughout Confederate armies in bitterly cold weather. However, Armistead's implementation appears unique in scale and forced compliance. Given a choice, which they were not, most men preferred less problematic solutions, like wrapping feet in rags or straw or simply going barefoot.

* * *

Lee reorganized the Army of Northern Virginia after Sharpsburg. Longstreet's wing became the I Corps. The corps created a new division needing a commander. Timing coincided with George Pickett's return to duty after a three-month convalescence following his wounding at Gaines's Mill. Longstreet advocated for his friend to command the new unit. The changes took effect November 6, 1862.

Pickett graduated last in his West Point class of 1846 with 195 demerits, five short of expulsion.[376] He distinguished himself in the Mexican War at Chapultepec by seizing the colors from the wounded James Longstreet and carrying them to the top of the citadel.

After the war, Pickett served in the 9th U.S. Infantry on the Texas frontier. He married his first wife in 1851. She died in childbirth that same year. Five years later, his unit posted to the Washington Territory. There he married a Native American. In 1858, his second wife died weeks after their union produced a son. In 1859, Pickett recklessly exceeded his authority in a northwestern boundary dispute called the Pig War. Lieutenant General Winfield Scott had to travel from Washington, DC, to defuse the situation and personally redressed Pickett for nearly provoking armed conflict with Great Britain.

Upon secession, Pickett resigned his captaincy, left his son in the care of friends, and returned to Virginia.[377] As colonel in the Confederate army, Pickett's defense of the Rappahannock River line failed to earn promotion recommendation from his superior Theophilus Holmes. Pickett brazenly bypassed his commanding officer and went directly to the War Department. His arrival coincided with the suicide of Brigadier General Phillip St. George Cocke.[378] The overstressed department welcomed the convenience and gave Pickett the vacated generalship.

At Gaines's Mill, a bullet pierced Pickett's shoulder and knocked him off his horse. Pickett assumed himself mortally wounded. Staff officer John Haskell found Pickett in a hollow "bewailing himself" and calling for stretcher bearers. Haskell examined Pickett, determined "he was able to take care of himself," and rode away.[379]

Pickett had his wound dressed at a field hospital and walked out. As he departed, Pickett encountered the critically wounded Colonel Robert E. Withers, 18th Virginia being carried in on a stretcher. The Danville doctor was one of Pickett's own officers. Pickett ordered Withers taken directly to Richmond.[380] The ambulatory, thirty-seven-year-old Pickett then left for a three-month convalescence, nursed by his nineteen-year-old love interest LaSalle "Sallie" Corbell.[381]

Shortly after returning to duty, Pickett received promotion to major general. Pickett's new division consisted of his old brigade under Richard Garnett, plus Armistead's brigade and those of Montgomery Corse, Micah Jenkins, and James Kemper.

Although Pickett had performed competently as brigade commander under Longstreet at Williamsburg, Seven Pines, and Gaines's Mill, he was no Hill, nor

Garland, nor Early. When Major General George Pickett assumed his new post, he was damaged, distracted by love, and in a new job requiring greater focus and fitness than his previous post.

* * *

The transfer of Armistead's brigade to Pickett's division was seamless. November 8–10, the 38th Virginia performed picket duty on the northern approach to Culpeper. Sporadic gunfire sounded in the distance. On November 20, Armistead's brigade began a two-day march to Fredericksburg in freezing rain along muddy roads. The rain drenched those lacking oilcloths or captured gum blankets. That mattered little. Fording the frigid Rappahannock and the Rapidan rivers soaked everyone.

The brigade bivouacked November 23 two miles below Fredericksburg. They dug earthworks on high ground overlooking the river plain. The regiments rotated picket duty on the banks of the Rappahannock within plain view of the enemy on the opposite bank.

Armistead's camps were spartan. They had no tents, only improvised shelters. Food was poor. The daily ration was one pound of meat, fourteen ounces of flour, and a little salt. Only nominal calorie intake and mess fires fended off the cold. Eventually firewood grew scarce.[382]

When his brigade was not on picket duty or digging, Armistead drilled and inspected his men. Superfluous parades under dire circumstances dampened morale. The situation grated staff as well.

Colonel Harrison Ball Tomlin of the 53rd Virginia was a University of Virginia graduate and a former delegate in the Virginia General Assembly. Tomlin had organized one of the first battalions deployed on the Peninsula. Tomlin's and Montague's battalions merged to form the 53rd Virginia. Tomlin had held colonelcy in the regiment since November 1861. Tomlin kept his dissatisfactions with Armistead to himself, but he submitted resignation November 29 to be effective after the present campaign season.

Furloughs had always been few and far between, but the Union army, now under General Ambrose Burnside, posed imminent threat. The need for able bodies was so desperate that the army denied furloughs to men with dying wives.[383]

December 5 found Armistead's brigade still without tents, little fire, and meager rations. Bitter cold and five inches of snow on December 7 added to miseries.[384] No picket had benefit of fire. Activity in Union camps prompted alerts. All proved false alarms.

Captain John Cabell, Company B, 38th Virginia, resigned. The physician sickened with exposure to raw weather as he had on the Peninsula. He opted to return home to recuperate and care for his five motherless children.[385] 1st Lt. William Prichard assumed command of Company B with promotion to captain.

William Bond Prichard, Captain, Company B, 38th Virginia Infantry. (Courtesy Virginia Military Institute)

Union delays gave Lee's army time to prepare. Longstreet posted McLaws's division on his left and Hood's on his right. Pickett, the least experienced division commander, held the center in reserve. Gunfire early December 11 announced Union construction of a pontoon bridge to the town. Mississippi sharpshooters at the docks drove off Union engineers. General Burnside responded by shelling Fredericksburg. This allowed completion of the bridge. Union soldiers crossed that night and sacked the city the next day. Meanwhile, the 38th Virginia performed picket duty in view of the activity.

Troops awoke to dense fog the morning of December 13. When the fog lifted at ten a.m., Burnside launched his attack against Marye's Heights. Armistead's brigade watched wholesale slaughter of blue-clad troops. For six hours, wave after wave fell in futile assaults. The cost was staggering: 7,500 Union casualties. Another heavy action occurred simultaneously to their right with assaults upon Jackson's II Corps.

Lee expected Burnside to renew his attack the next day. Skirmishing occurred but no assault. Lee granted Burnside truce to retrieve his wounded. Intermittent cannonades and skirmishes sounded through December 15 as Burnside withdrew his last units. Fredericksburg was yet another great victory to which Armistead's men were spectators.

Rotations between camp and picket duties resumed. On December 19, reports of another Union advance circulated. Armistead's brigade received orders to stand at arms and be ready to march at moment's notice. The alert was unfounded. The regiments resumed routines with more drilling and inspections. Captain Griggs, 38th Virginia, Company K recorded being on picket duty at the river on December 23 and observed Union troops cross in a boat to exchange coffee for tobacco and newspapers.[386]

Christmas Day marked a reprieve from drilling and inspections, not from picket duty. The weather was unseasonably warm and pleasant. Conditions made for a remarkably dull holiday and fueled homesickness. Christmas normally fostered unexcused absences and arrests but not this time. There was little merriment locally, for the battle and persistent threats forced all but the most recalcitrant locals to flee. The sights of displaced families in winter wrenched hearts. Soldiers offered homeless women and children temporary refuge around their campfires.[387]

Those damned Yankees!

On December 27, the brigade marched down Telegraph Road. They halted in a pine barren along the RF&P Railroad three miles short of Guinea Station. There they began constructing winter shelters. Work stopped next day for Sunday observance and a dress parade. The brigade drilled the following day. Work on shelters progressed. On New Year's Eve, the brigade mustered for inspection in bitter cold and freshly fallen snow.

Eighteen sixty-two had been a year of real war waged by real armies. Setbacks and retreats had darkened hopes until Lee took command. Lee emerged a second Washington.[388] He had out-generaled McClellan, Pope, and Burnside. Victories brought encouragement. Northern depredations firmed resolves to resist subjugation.

The Pittsylvania Regiment had proved its mettle at Seven Pines and at Malvern Hill. No regimental commander was braver, more capable, or more beloved than Colonel Edmonds. No regiment had finer field officers and company commanders.

These lions of the Dan must have thought it odd to have been repeatedly held in reserve at Second Manassas, Sharpsburg, and Fredericksburg. Whether they realized it or not, the reason was Lewis Armistead.

* * *

Military culture refines leaders. It also shelters misfits. Lewis Armistead was more the latter than the former. Professional soldier was his identity. The uniform spoke for its wearer. Rank declared station. The army was refuge from the less structured civilian world, which demanded interpersonal skills Armistead lacked.

Lewis Armistead was heir to his family's military renown. This was both proud tradition and brutal personal measure. Armistead could boast significant heritage but few personal accomplishments. Much of the clout he enjoyed as a young man died with his father.

Armistead was reserved, honest, and candid. The latter qualities were awkward in Southern society unless one possessed finesse. Armistead lacked finesse. Brusque and uncongenial, he had many acquaintances but few friends. He was so shy with women that colleagues nicknamed him "Lo," short for "Lothario." The epithet was more mockery than jest.

Armistead was no scholar and never noted for wit. Facts infer a personality as bland as a hardtack cracker.

Armistead's role as "strict disciplinarian" compensated for inadequacies. Academic failures and a legendary West Point tantrum haunted his past. His army commission, conferred by his papa, gained him unearned entrance into that fraternity of merit. There was no bleach for those stains. Superiors tolerated Lewis Armistead with decorum due an FFV, but he was forever consigned to the bottom of that social stratum. Fellow officers received Armistead with propriety due his rank and class but also detachment as toward an uninvited guest.

By the time Virginia seceded, frustrations, tragedies, and disappointments had made Armistead ripe for immersion in the cause. The war afforded great opportunities for advancement. Dire circumstances rapidly promoted the unexceptional army captain to brigadier general. Dedication, hard work, and bravery sufficed in junior officer rolls, but the prosaic Armistead lacked imagination and boldness necessary to excel as a general officer.[389] Armistead's wartime rank pushed his abilities to their limits and beyond.

Born leaders inspire and motivate. For such, gold braid and epaulettes are mere trappings. In contrast, Armistead lacked command presence. He led simply by demanding unquestioned obedience. Galvanized civilians who served as officers under Armistead forever perceived him as abrupt and abrasive. Eventually, most found him intolerable.[390]

* * *

Armistead's brigade began 1863 in the doldrums. Winter quarters lacked dynamic immediacies of campaigns. Monotonous drills, inspections, and parades in midst of hardships and scarcities intensified personality clashes, none more so than those between Armistead and his subordinates.

Colonel Tomlin's November resignation took effect January 7. Tomlin's second in command, John G. Grammer, succeeded him as colonel of the 53rd Virginia. Tomlin was the first of four big changes in Armistead's command that season.

Friction between Armistead and Colonel David Dyer of the 57th Virginia came to a head. Dyer had led the 57th Virginia five months, including the Second Manassas and Maryland campaigns. Dyer was a farmer, a galvanized civilian elected captain, later major, by popular vote, a promotion route inconceivable for Armistead.

In fact, if Armistead had not received promotion to brigadier when he did, popular vote in the 57th Virginia may well have ousted him from command. The election that past May had indeed booted out Armistead's like-minded successor, professional soldier George W. Carr. The election that replaced Colonel Carr with Keen also elevated Waddy James to lieutenant colonel and David Dyer to major.

Colonel Keen resigned in the weeks following Malvern Hill, reportedly due to health. Strangely, Lt. Colonel James resigned three days before, as if to avoid reporting directly to Armistead.[391] Major Dyer had served under Armistead as a company commander. Upon resignations of the regiment's two top field officers, Armistead readily promoted Dyer two ranks from major to colonel.

Armistead grew to regard Dyer as if a clodhopper with no military training who had won a popularity contest. Ultimately, Armistead considered Dyer "entirely unqualified" to command a regiment, especially Armistead's old regiment.[392] Armistead insisted Dyer face a board of review. Dyer could no longer tolerate Armistead and resigned January 12.

Dyer's second in command was twenty-three-year-old John Bowie Magruder, nephew of Major General John Bankhead Magruder. He was an alumnus of the Albemarle Military Academy, University of Virginia, and Virginia Military Institute. Armistead deemed Magruder a better fit and promoted him to colonel of the 57th Virginia.

Winter quarters provided opportunity for smallpox vaccinations. At least one officer noted that his did not take effect.[393]

Unseasonably warm weather stirred Burnside to action. On January 20, he marched his army upstream to cross the Rappahannock River and flank Lee. Heavy rains turned roads into quagmires. The Mud March proved an exercise in futility. Lincoln replaced Burnside with General Joseph Hooker on January 26.

The next day, Pickett's division marched twelve miles to a section of unfinished railroad on the Plank Road near Salem Church to build fortifications. The weather worsened. Thirteen inches of snow halted work. The men marched back to their camps in bitter cold on January 29. More snow fell the next day.

In playful relief of boredom, Armistead's, Corse's, and Toombs's brigades mustered on January 31. Instead of the usual drill, they maneuvered and clashed in epic snowball fights. Battle flags waved in glaring sun and bright snow amid frenzied charges and volleys of snowballs. Brigades boasted glories measured in black eyes and bloody noses.

A minstrel troop formed in the division. These talents put on nightly shows when duties and weather permitted.

By February 10, Armistead's brigade marched back to Salem Church and resumed digging. Meanwhile, intelligence reported the Union IX Corps under Burnside departed Hooker's army and boarded ships on the Potomac. Their destination was unknown. Lee ordered Longstreet's Corps below Richmond as precaution.[394]

Armistead's brigade marched piecemeal. The 38th Virginia led the way on February 14. The 57th Virginia started three days later in deep snow. Cold, muddy slogs and bivouacs in snowy, wet woods promoted sickness and straggling. Many struggled to keep up or rejoin their units by evening. Some saw little need for heroics outside of campaign season and sought refuge at civilian firesides.

Sustained exposure to raw weather took constant toll. On February 17, Richmond's Chimborazo Hospital admitted James L. Oakes, Company B, 38th Virginia with "contagious fever."[395] Recovery would take months. That day, the 38th Virginia arrived at Chester Station with significantly fewer men than when they started.

The 14th Virginia and 53rd Virginia arrived over the next several days. The 57th Virginia halted at Falling Creek near Drewry's Bluff. The 9th Virginia bivouacked below Petersburg. A fifteen-inch snowstorm forced men to improvise shelters.[396]

The men received pay on February 28. The next day the brigade converged at Fort Powhatan on the James River thirteen miles below City Point. There they worked improving fortifications. Many missed roll calls. Laggards wandered into camps for days.

The prodigious straggling infuriated Armistead. He brushed hardships aside and convened court-martials. The general emphasized "no compromise" in dealing with absentees. Proven sickness was the only exception.[397]

Armistead's conduct alienated yet another subordinate. Command of the 53rd Virginia changed a second time in as many months.

Colonel John Grammer was a civilian physician in uniform. He had recently replaced Colonel Tomlin, who had resigned. Grammer served two months as a direct report to Armistead. He too reached his limit with the brigadier.

Grammer declared, "On every occasion Brigadier General Armistead's manner and tone are so offensive and insulting that I can but believe he…wishes to force me to resign." Grammer feared he would be "cashiered for insubordination." Armistead countered, "I have felt obliged to speak to him [Grammer] as one military man would to another and as I have passed nearly all my life in camps my manner may not be understood or appreciated by one who has been all his life a civilian."[398] Grammer resigned March 5.[399]

Grammer's second in command, Lt. Colonel William Roane Aylett, assumed command of the 53rd Virginia. Aylett was a University of Virginia graduate, an attorney, and proven leader with command presence. During the secession crisis, Aylett organized the Taylor Grays which mustered into state service April 15, 1861. The unit served in Tomlin's Battalion and became Company D, 53rd Virginia. Before the war, Aylett practiced law and managed Montville, his ancestral plantation. He acquired his military bearing from his father, an attorney, a War of 1812 veteran, and brigadier general in the Virginia Militia. Aylett was an FFV with blood ties to the Washington, Lee, and Dandridge families.[400] Aylett's great-grandfathers William Aylett and Patrick Henry served together in the House of Burgesses. Being a descendant of Patrick Henry afforded Aylett unique regard in this third fight for independence.

On March 11, Armistead finally sent a detail to retrieve the brigade's tents and baggage. He also proposed sending fifteen to twenty absentee cases to division and corps courts. These were above and beyond the scores already handled at brigade level.[401]

The vernal equinox brought another heavy snow. On March 21, the regiments engaged in another snowball battle. Colonel Aylett led his first attack as head of the 53rd Virginia against the other regiments in the brigade. The rank and file reaped a fresh crop of black eyes and bloody noses.

On paper, Lt. Colonel James Skelton Gilliam had led the 9th Virginia since Colonel Godwin's disablement at Seven Pines. Unlike Godwin, who had served as prewar colonel of the 3rd Virginia Militia and lieutenant colonel in the 14th Virginia before commanding the 9th Virginia, Gilliam had little to commend himself but social position. He was chronically ill and only an occasional presence in camp. Armistead would not recommend Gilliam for colonelcy and convened a board to review his fitness.[402] Nevertheless, Gilliam refused to resign.[403]

Armistead promoted Captain James J. Phillips to major and acting colonel in Gilliam's absence. Phillips, a VMI graduate, joined the war at the outset and organized the Chuckatuck Light Artillery. Upon evacuating Tidewater, Phillips and his men converted to infantry as Company F, 9th Virginia. Even as captain, Phillips had often commanded the regiment, most notably at Sharpsburg. As for gallantry, it was Phillips who saved the 9th Virginia's colors at Malvern Hill.

On March 25, Armistead asked Inspector General Cooper to transfer his son Lt. Walker Keith Armistead, 6th Virginia Cavalry, to his headquarters as his aide-de-camp.[404] The youth had been at the general's side since mid-February.[405]

By April 1, regimental leadership within Armistead's brigade was unquestionably qualified, competent, and among the finest in the army. Whether the result was skillful management or serendipitous outcomes of personality clashes, credit for the changes belonged to Armistead.

April Fool's Day also marked the first anniversary of Armistead's promotion to brigadier general. It had been an eventful year with Seven Pines, Malvern Hill, Second Manassas, Sharpsburg, and Fredericksburg. Each battle demonstrated the South's unshakeable resolve.

For Lewis Armistead personally, those battles yielded embarrassments and marginalization. Armistead ranked lower in the army's social and political pecking orders than he ever had. Furthermore, Armistead now reported directly to Major General George Pickett, the army's newest division commander. Pickett had observed Armistead in battle once. The image of Armistead amid that hapless rout at Seven Pines surely left an impression.

One postwar comment proposed Armistead needed "fit opportunity to prove himself the hero he was."[406] Armistead had shunned one such opportunity at the climax of Second Manassas. He needed another.

Lewis Addison Armistead was a brave professional soldier with personality and abilities best suited to supportive roles. Although he was no champion in any classic sense, he commanded men who were.

CHAPTER TEN

The Siege of Suffolk

General Robert E. Lee spent the first months of 1863 countering threats along the Rappahannock River and the North Carolina coast. In mid-March, Longstreet sent D. H. Hill to attack New Bern. The three-day fight failed to retake the town. On March 21, Longstreet detached Kemper's and Garnett's brigades from Pickett to support Hill in a siege of Washington, North Carolina. Lee then approved Longstreet's investment of Suffolk with Hood's and Pickett's divisions. Those moves would contain the Yankee garrisons and allow the Rebels to gather food and forage in that region. A threat to Suffolk would also pin the Union forces at Newport News.

Jenkins's brigade was already on the Blackwater River along with Davis's brigade temporarily assigned to Pickett.[407] Corse's brigade was near Petersburg, and Armistead's was at Fort Powhatan. On March 23, Pickett ordered Corse's brigade to Ivor. He summoned Armistead last. The 38th Virginia marched on March 26 and reached Ivor on March 28. The 57th Virginia arrived April 2.

Winter had passed. Spring was "the time when kings go forth to battle."[408] Troop concentration alerted the rank and file to imminent action. Joseph Payne, Company C, 38th Virginia wrote from Ivor April 3 that he was not likely to get a substitute in time.[409] Payne had just returned from the hospital in Petersburg. Cost of a substitute there exceeded $2,500.[410] The issue was moot, for Colonel Edmonds banned substitutes. Perhaps Payne had a prearrangement with the colonel like the months-old, pending swap of Mahan for the Oakes brother. Even so, there were no candidates with credentials acceptable to company commanders.[411] Qualified substitutes themselves had become subject to conscription.

John Mahan, Company B, 38th Virginia, and others seeking substitutes realized their prospects were nil. Even if an agent secured a replacement, it was too late to avoid the next campaign. Tom Oakes wrote most letters for Mahan. However, Mahan personally scribbled a note to his wife despairing of his "servitude" and imminent dangers.[412]

Armistead's brigade camped at Ivor until the morning of April 9. An unseasonably hot, dusty trek took them through Jerusalem and Franklin to Pickett's staging area on the west bank of the Blackwater River at South Quay.[413] Armistead's men spent the next day cooking rations and refreshing ammunition.

The Suffolk Campaign began April 11 at six o'clock in the morning. Cavalry preceded Pickett's men across the pontoon bridge. The structure consisted of nine boats spaced fifteen feet apart and planked.[414] Inadequate bridging necessitated leaving behind the baggage wagons and the sick.

Jenkins's brigade advanced by the most direct route. Corse's and Armistead's brigades turned off the South Quay Road to approach Suffolk from the south. While Pickett's division invested the town south of the Nansemond River, Hood's division crossed the Blackwater at Franklin and marched to the north bank of the Nansemond.

The weather was clear and cool. The roads were good and movement unimpeded. Jenkins's brigade overran Union picket lines, vedettes, and signal towers. Silenced communications, fleeing pickets, and contrabands alerted the town. The Union commander ordered fortifications manned. He telegraphed for reinforcements and ordered women and children evacuated. By four o'clock that afternoon when Jenkins's men reached Suffolk, the town "resembled an anthill that had just been kicked."[415]

Jenkins's brigade halted before armed and ready bastions and began digging in. Two hours later, Hood's division appeared north of town. The Union then blew up the drawbridge spanning the Nansemond at the foot of Main Street.

By nightfall, Jenkins's brigade was the only one of Pickett's units in position. Corse's brigade halted beyond Leesville.[416] Armistead's men bivouacked just shy of that village. Kemper's brigade, released from D. H. Hill's siege of Washington, arrived in Franklin and marched to rejoin Pickett.

Before daylight next day, Corse's brigade reached the Dismal Swamp and advanced up White Marsh Road. Union pickets retreated and torched every farm house along their route.[417] Families fled their burning farms with only the clothes on their backs.

Those damned Yankees!

Armistead's brigade advanced up the dusty Somerton Road (U.S. Rt. 13). The 38th Virginia led the way. Abatis and other obstructions slowed progress. By noon, the 38th Virginia was within a mile of the enemy's picket line. Armistead ordered the 38th Virginia forward for a reconnaissance in force. Colonel Edmonds advanced his battle line. The Pittsylvanians drove the Union pickets through woods and into open ground. The 38th Virginia swept past the Smith house, occupied by George Robinson Smith; his wife, Judith; and their seven children.

As they pushed the enemy into his works, Edmonds and his men stepped into converging fire from three forts.[418] Armistead recalled the 38th Virginia. They fell back and rejoined the rest of the brigade in the woods before the Smith house. Armistead posted sharpshooters atop Smith's outbuildings.

Corse's brigade arrived on Armistead's right. Both brigades dug in. Heavy rain fell that evening and turned rifle pits into mud holes. Armistead summoned Dearing's Battery in preparation to renew action.

Steady rain continued April 13. Armistead's brigade advanced again upon the Smith farm, this time supported by artillery. There they again engaged enemy pickets.

The terrified Smith family huddled together on the ground floor of their frame house as fighting raged around them. A cannonball ripped through their home and showered the Smiths with splinters. The family ran for their lives into the rain. They fled "like a brood of partridges" desperate to reach the woods.[419] Forty-one-year-old Judith Smith ran with her babe in her arms across their muddy, plowed field until a bullet struck her square in the head.[420] George Smith rescued his baby from his dead wife's embrace. He and their panic-stricken children scattered in the trees.

The rain stopped by noon. Armistead drove the Union pickets into their works. Major Cabell anticipated taking the town, but no such order came.[421] Union cavalry sallied forth to probe their line. Well-placed volleys sent them back into their defenses. Union infantry then advanced over their works in a dense skirmish line and pushed Armistead's men back beyond Smith's farm. The Rebels withdrew past their initial position and established a line before the Brothers house. There they held fast.

Union infantry fired Smith's house and outbuildings. They pushed forward and retook their original picket line. That line would hold for the remainder of the siege. After shooting ceased, George Smith returned to his smoldering farm with a wagon under flag of truce and recovered Judith's muddy, rain-soaked body. Several of their children, dispersed by their flight, stayed cowered in the woods for days.[422]

After April 13, siege efforts concentrated north of town with artillery and gunboat actions on the Nansemond River. Pickett's division defended their lines to the south. A member of the 38th Virginia noted constant expectation of battle.[423] They harassed the enemy with sharpshooters from atop the Brothers house and repelled each attempt by the enemy to destroy that structure. Pickett's men reconnoitered their right for enemy weaknesses and opportunity to destroy the railway into Suffolk. Colonel Edmonds sent Captain Griggs with Company K to scout the edge of the Dismal Swamp. Enemy pickets thwarted their efforts.

Union sorties from Suffolk torched more civilian homes which obstructed fields of fire or served as Rebel sharpshooter perches and observation posts. Armistead endorsed hanging any incendiaries captured.[424]

On April 23, Yankees probed Armistead's defenses across the swampy White Marsh Road. The 57th Virginia manned a forward position a mile and a half in advance. The 38th Virginia held the main line and endured an artillery barrage. The men of the 57th Virginia killed one Yankee and wounded several others.[425] The next day the 38th Virginia moved single file through swamp to reinforce the 57th Virginia. Colonel Edmonds had his men dig in to the right of the Everett house. There they fended off yet another probe, killing four attackers wounding about as many. One Yankee fell within twenty-five paces of their line.[426]

Enemy action ceased on their front. Both sides remained idle but vigilant. An officer in the 38th Virginia wrote, "I do not believe that it is the intention of Gen. Longstreet to attack Suffolk and I don't think the Yankees are bold enough to attack us."[427] There they remained entrenched through at least April 29.[428] On that date, Lt. Colonel Whittle rejoined the regiment. He was as fit as ever despite missing his left arm.[429]

It was well the sector quieted, for General Pickett spent significant time away on self-indulgent furloughs. He skirted the siege nightly to spend time with his love, Sallie Corbell.[430] Pickett had never been a model officer. He was even less focused since his wounding at Gaines's Mill.[431]

* * *

May opened with General Joseph Hooker moving against Lee at Chancellorsville. The Siege of Suffolk had successfully contained the enemy while Longstreet's Corps gathered supplies from the region. Lee summoned Longstreet to rejoin the main army fighting Hooker.

The 38th Virginia broke camp the evening of May 3 and led the brigade in a wet, muddy, twenty-seven-mile march to Franklin. They arrived exhausted at midday May 4. They marched again next day. Cool, wet weather impeded progress. They trudged eight miles to Jerusalem. The following day it rained heavily. They waded ten miles up the much-flooded Jerusalem Plank Road. Many went barefoot to save their shoes. They marched another twenty miles on May 7. They passed through Petersburg late on May 8 and bivouacked two miles beyond town.

Lee's stellar victory at Chancellorsville canceled the immediate need for Longstreet's Corps. The 38th Virginia halted along Falling Creek May 9 after having marched every day for one week.[432] Meanwhile, Lee argued strongly against the War Department's intentions to send Pickett's division west to reinforce Vicksburg.[433]

Stonewall Jackson died at Guinea Station on May 10 from wounds at Chancellorsville. Jackson's death forced Lee to hastily reorganize the Army of Northern Virginia.[434] On May 11, some of Armistead's men obtained twelve hour passes to Richmond to pay their respects to the fallen leader at the capitol.

The next day, James Oakes returned from the Danville General Hospital to rejoin his brothers in Company B. He had been ill since February. On May 13, the 38th Virginia shifted to its old camp on Falling Creek nearer Drewry's Bluff. For two days Union prisoners captured at Chancellorsville passed by on their way to exchange at City Point.

On May 15, Armistead's brigade marched. The 38th Virginia led the way and bivouacked within a mile of Richmond. They passed through the city the next day and continued ten miles up Brook Turnpike (U.S. Rt. 1). They bivouacked about halfway to Ashland. Another ten-mile march on May 17 brought the brigade to camp on the Little River at Taylorsville, two miles south of Hanover Junction. There they camped for the next sixteen days.

Routine activities resumed. Wood, water and cooking details, drills, and inspections filled the day. There was no entrenching work except for individuals assigned punishment to dig sinks.

Here the brigade received new shoes in anticipation of a campaign. Purchasing agents abroad had never marched anywhere. These acquired certain German-made footwear. They were light, flimsy, russet leather, low-quarter styles. The shoes were fine for artisans and clerks, not soldiers. The uppers softened and stretched when wet. The soles did, too.[435]

Some in Company B, 38th Virginia, received food parcels from home. John Mahan wrote his wife how he enjoyed the cakes and peaches she sent. He wanted more pickled eggs as received in the past. He also sent home his heavy socks and comforter for safekeeping until the fall.[436]

Pickett reviewed Armistead's brigade on May 29. Three days of camp routine followed. Rumors of enemy cavalry in the vicinity prompted Pickett to send Armistead's brigade on a reconnaissance in force.

The brigade marched early June 2 to Hanover Court House. Colonel Edmonds detailed Captain Griggs and his Company K to guard the bridge over the Pamunkey River. On June 3, the brigade marched northeast all day over hot, dusty roads. There was no sign of the enemy.

They resumed marching next day. Much of the way was full sun on dusty roads bordering slave-cultivated fields. Occasional stretches tunneled through forests and wooded ravines. Men welcomed the shade.

They crossed the Mattaponi River and bivouacked in woods two miles before Newtown. The next day they marched and countermarched. Still, there was no sign of the enemy.

On June 5, they marched west to Reedy Mills. The following day they recrossed the river and proceeded eastward to within five miles of Aylett when ordered back to Hanover Junction. The 38th Virginia reached the railroad early in the afternoon June 6.

The 53rd Virginia remained behind a day. Their proximity to Aylett afforded Colonel Aylett a brief visit with his wife at Montville.[437] As the 53rd Virginia returned to Hanover Junction, the 38th Virginia marched back to Hanover Court

House, where Captain Griggs and Company K still guarded the Pamunkey River crossing.

Armistead's brigade had completed a week-long, dusty trek in mid-eighty-degree heat with no sign of the enemy. Parrying cavalry with infantry was necessary at times. It was largely a fool's errand, like sending pawns to chase knights across a chessboard. Pickett sent Armistead rather than Corse, Garnett, or Kemper.

On June 8, Lee ordered Pickett's division to Culpeper Court House. Pickett had orders to leave Jenkins's brigade near Richmond and Corse's brigade at Hanover Junction to protect the capital. Pickett's other three brigades prepared to move. The Army of Northern Virginia headed north again.

With little rest between marches, Armistead's brigade took its place at the end of Pickett's column. Once again, the lions of the Dan marched last as they embarked on their most noted campaign. Since Malvern Hill, the year-long, last-in-line, bottom-rung association with Lewis Armistead had given his brigade a reputation throughout the Army of Northern Virginia as being more a troop of tagalongs than fighters.

The 38th Virginia followed last of the last having to rush from Hanover Court House to catch up with the brigade. They would once again prove themselves among the best troops in Lee's army and mirror the biblical expression "The last shall be first."[438]

CHAPTER ELEVEN

Gettysburg

On June 10, after three days marching, Armistead's brigade crossed the Rapidan River at Sommerville Ford and halted for the night. They marched five miles closer to Culpeper and then rested four days. A member of the 38th Virginia reported being "very much worn down by hard marching."[439]

Sunday was their last rest day. Rev. Ransel Cridlin held his first worship service with the regiment. The 38th Virginia had installed its new chaplain as it departed Hanover Court House.[440] He replaced his predecessor noted for "prolonged absence." Cridlin lived what he preached and would abide with the regiment to the end of the war.

On June 15, the brigade departed with three days of rations in haversacks and ten days of rations in wagons. Notoriously brutal Virginia heat sapped strength. Their pace slowed to a crawl. Men broke ranks for any trickle of water. The column had moved only six miles by day's end. They bivouacked three miles past Culpeper on the Flint Hill Road (Rt. 729).

Daytime temperatures hovered in the mid-nineties for the next three days. June 16 was very hot. The 38th Virginia served as rearguard on the march to Gaines Cross Roads. Steep, rolling terrain exacerbated conditions. Men fainted from heat and dehydration. The next day was hotter.

The brigade passed through Barbee's Cross Roads (now Hume). A physician in the 57th Virginia wrote that heat overcame a great many men. He observed one sunstroke victim left [dead] on the side of the road.[441] James Oakes, Company B, 38th Virginia, reported similar scenes.[442] Eight men in Company K collapsed. The regiment bivouacked two miles short of Piedmont Depot.[443]

On June 18, the 38th Virginia marched eight miles to Paris. Armistead's brigade bivouacked in the Paris/Upperville area, boyhood homes to both General Armistead and Colonel Edmonds. The two refreshed themselves at Edmonds's uncle's Belle Grove plantation. Longstreet and Pickett also enjoyed Lewis Edmonds's hospitality.[444] A thunderstorm brought the soldiers welcome relief from the heat.

On June 19, Lewis Armistead and Ned Edmonds departed the neighborhood of their youths for the last time. Armistead's brigade marched ten crooked miles to Snickers Gap, while their cavalry screen clashed to the east with Union troopers at Aldie. The 38th Virginia also skirmished with Union cavalry patrols while the rest of the brigade trudged the mountain pass to Castleman's Ferry (Snickers Ford). High water delayed crossing the Shenandoah River until late afternoon on June 20. The men crossed in groups of four. Some locked arms to prevent being swept off their feet by swift water. The brigade camped that evening near Berryville.

Confederate cavalry clashed daily with Union probes. Southern horsemen yielded at Upperville on June 21. By then the last of Lee's men were through the passes.

Armistead's brigade rested until roused an hour before dawn on June 24. They drew three days rations and marched to Bunker Hill. On June 25, the brigade marched at first light under overcast sky. They tramped through Martinsburg under threatening clouds.

The brigade crossed the Potomac at Williamsport. They marched in wet drizzle and bivouacked two miles beyond the town. Some had misgivings about crossing the Potomac again. Joseph Payne, Company C, 38th Virginia, wrote that General Lee assured them "if we follow him there, he will bring us out with him."[445] So, they followed.

Lee ordered his men to respect private property. Despite orders, the temptation for many Virginians to repay visitation in kind was irresistible. Colonel Aylett, 53rd Virginia, issued matches to his men for that purpose, "orders or no orders."[446]

The brigade marched again at four a.m. It rained all day. They slogged twenty-two miles on muddy roads and crossed into Pennsylvania. Men joked about having "rejoined the Union" as they continued through Greencastle.

Rain stopped June 27. Advance columns had churned the wet roads into mire. Armistead's men sidestepped the impedance and tread down wheat fields bordering the way. The 38th Virginia passed through Chambersburg late in the day. Sundry discards strewn about the streets testified to vandalism by preceding troops.

The men found stores open and fell out to shop. Some paid with Confederate notes. Others simply took what they wanted. Frightened store owners dared not resist. The men carried away chickens, bacon, vegetables, honey, butter, virtually anything edible.[447] The 38th Virginia bivouacked with the brigade two miles north of the town on the York Road.

The next day, Armistead's brigade marched along the Cumberland Valley Railroad to Scotland. Impromptu Sunday services reestablished the day of the week for those prone to lose track.

On June 29, Longstreet ordered Pickett to garrison Chambersburg until relieved by Imboden's cavalry. Armistead's brigade countermarched through the town and camped in woods to the south. Armistead detailed men to tear up the railroad. They stacked cross ties and laid rails across them. When fired, the rails heated red hot and bent under their own weight, rendering them useless. Those not assigned work or guard duty spent hours drilling in camp.

Regiments mustered for pay the next day. Railway destruction continued.

The Army of Northern Virginia gathered supplies from the bountiful Pennsylvania countryside. Commissaries requisitioned livestock and the contents of "Dutch" barns. Patrols arrested free blacks and sent them south for enslavement. Despite orders prohibiting looting, some exacted retribution for Yankee outrages back home. Officers posted guards to protect private residences.

James Booker, Company D, 38th Virginia, received board while guarding one household. The terrified hosts patronized their guest. Thus, Booker noted local citizens recognized Southerners fought for rights and abolitionists for money.[448] However, black Pennsylvanians en route to Virginia would have surely disagreed.

July 1 was like previous days. Armistead composed a response to Major Charles Pickett, brother and staff officer to the general. General Pickett alleged "a majority" of Armistead's men were seen "committing depredations in the neighborhood." Armistead asserted, "No cases of plundering by them have come to my knowledge." He reported, "Previous to the receipt of your note I had ordered three daily drills with the view of keeping the men in camp."[449] Thus, the disciplinarian penned his last missive.

Dr. Charles Lippit, surgeon in the 57th Virginia, noted July 1 was remarkably peaceful.[450] The good doctor contrasted that same date a year before at Malvern Hill. Ironically, as he did so, the Battle of Gettysburg had begun in full fury.

* * *

Shortly after midnight July 2, Pickett received orders to march to Gettysburg without delay. His men were up and on the road at two a.m. Armstead's brigade marched at the end of the division. One historian attributes Armistead's place in column to "luck of the draw."[451] This was no accident. Lewis Armistead marched last in every march with Lee's army. Forever posted hindermost bolstered the general opinion within and without the organization that Armistead's brigade "was not worth a cent" and would not fight.[452]

Bushwhackers harassed Pickett's column along the way, particularly as it crossed South Mountain at Cashtown Gap. Those captured in the act were either executed or consigned to Libby Prison for the duration of the war.

Pickett's division passed through Cashtown, crossed Marsh Creek, and turned right. They continued past Black Horse Tavern (Francis Bream), where Hood's division's hospital bustled in preparation for casualties. Pickett's men marched two miles past Bream's Mill. After twenty-two arduous miles, they halted about three thirty p.m.[453]

Kemper's brigade bivouacked on Fitzer's Run. Garnett's and Armistead's men planted themselves along Marsh Creek near Sachs Bridge. There, about three miles from Gettysburg, Lee rested and watered Pickett's men for duty next day.[454] Pickett's wagon park extended from the Curren farm back to Bream's Mill, where Pickett established his division's field hospital.[455]

At four thirty p.m. guns thundered nearby as the balance of Longstreet's Corp launched assaults in echelon upon the Union left. Dust clouds rose from roads as a two-way stream of ammunition chests, wagons, and ambulances rumbled past Pickett's camps. Hood's and McLaws's attacks on Little Round Top, the Wheat Field, the Peach Orchard, and Cemetery Ridge pushed Union defenses to their limits.

In the final, critical moments, as Early's division simultaneously pressed from the opposite direction up Cemetery Hill, attacks on Cemetery Ridge by Posey's and Mahone's brigades would have, with reasonable certainty, tipped the scales to Confederate victory.[456] Oddly, those brigades stood fast and failed to support.

By seven p.m. the bloodiest day of the bloodiest battle of the war ended. Lee's army had battered Union lines to the very breaking point, but they held.

* * *

Lee planned to renew attacks at daylight July 3. He had every reason to believe that if they delivered "one determined and united blow," the Union line would collapse.[457] He planned to strike both flanks simultaneously while assaulting the center with Pickett's fresh division.

However, five miles of exterior lines ensured poor communications within Lee's command. Furthermore, General Longstreet opposed the plan and argued against moving Hood's and McLaws's divisions already engaged on the right flank. In the predawn hours, Ewell's Corps readied itself on the left at Culp's Hill. The reluctant Longstreet had not yet summoned Pickett.[458]

Pickett received orders at three a.m. to move his division forward. It took hours for Pickett to get his division up and moving. At four thirty a.m. gunfire erupted in the distance. As it happened, the Union initiated the action. The ominous booming lasted fifteen minutes, and then ceased. At five thirty a.m., the artillery reopened in earnest. The fight for Culp's Hill had begun.

The coordinated strikes Lee envisioned that day were then impossible. To best recover from the boondoggle in progress, Lee modified his plan to a general assault upon the Union center by Pickett's, Pettigrew's, and Trimble's divisions, preceded by a massive cannonade. Longstreet balked at the plan and asserted that no fifteen thousand men ever assembled could carry such a position. Although Longstreet's argument was sound, Wright's brigade had, in fact, nearly carried that ridge the previous evening. In addition to the assault force, Lee had yet another eleven thousand men in reserve to follow up the attack. The cost would be unavoidably high, but the odds appeared favorable.

Lee accepted the risk and rescheduled the attack for ten a.m. However, exigencies created ever more delays.

* * *

Pickett's column advanced in the direction of the previous evening's action. It then turned onto the road behind Seminary Ridge. Armistead's brigade brought up the rear.

It must have seemed to Armistead's men as if they marched toward the guns, for they moved in the direction of the current contest. They halted after a couple of miles. The rank and file knew only that a fight was somewhere beyond the trees.

A brief rain cooled the men.

Longstreet prescribed the battle array. Pickett executed deployment. Kemper led his men up wooded Spangler's Lane. Garnett moved next. Armistead followed last. After one hundred yards, the lane exited the trees at the base of an open, grassy ridge. Directly ahead near the top of the rise was the smoking ruin of Henry Spangler's barn. Artillery had fired it the day before. Pickett's troops moved low on the ridge below the line of Confederate artillery posted along the ridge crest. Kemper deployed to the right of the burned barn, Garnett to the left. Pickett directed Armistead behind Garnett's brigade.

By ten o'clock, the time Lee had specified for the assault, Pickett's men lay in place on blankets as preparations continued. The 38th Virginia on the far left of the brigade had halted in the protruding portion of Spangler's woodlot. Theirs was the only regiment afforded shade. The rest baked in full sun.

The distant gunfire, which had rumbled steadily that morning, slowed to desultory booms. Listeners wondered the outcome and meaning. The ill-timed strike on the Union right was over. Culp's Hill was the first bloody disaster of the day.

The ridge blocked Pickett's men's view. The growing line of cannon arrayed before them testified to strong enemy beyond.

Musket rattling erupted to their left. They could not see the action. Smoke billowed from that direction. A Union sortie had torched the Bliss house and barn.

More artillery and ammunition chests pulled onto the field and into line. An attack was imminent. Air temperature soon reached eighty-seven degrees, the highest temperature recorded for all that July.[459] Some sickened from the heat and mounting tension. Chaplains prayed with their regiments.

Armistead realized himself part of a momentous assault with his command posted behind Garnett's. He was in the rear again! Always in the rear!

Thus provoked, Armistead mounted his horse and galloped off to find Pickett. Unable to locate the general, Armistead chanced upon Major Walter Harrison of Pickett's staff. Armistead insisted his brigade be moved to the fore with the rest of the division. There was, after all, nothing to the left of Garnett to prevent it. Harrison rode off to find Pickett. Armistead trotted back to his brigade.

Unable to locate Pickett, Harrison approached General Longstreet with the matter. The corps commander curtly dismissed Armistead's pettiness, "General Pickett will attend to that, sir!" As Harrison turned to ride away, Longstreet apologetically shouted, "Never mind, Colonel [*sic*], you can tell General Armistead to remain where he is at present, and he can make up the distance when the advance is made."[460]

Lee had committed Pickett's fresh division and the divisions of Pettigrew and Trimble to the attack. The latter two had already suffered heavily on July 1. The division commanders met and assigned Archer's brigade (Fry), Pettigrew's rightmost unit, as the brigade of direction. Their mission was clear: take the high ground and break the enemy's line.

Pickett delivered instructions to his brigadiers and ordered them to lead on foot. Armistead dismounted and sent his horse to the rear. However, Garnett (unable to walk) and Kemper (feeling ill) both remained mounted.

At 1:07 p.m., one of two signal guns fired. A dud friction primer delayed the second report.[461] Confederate artillery opened fire. From right to left, the chain of muzzle blasts moved north along the ridge. The cannonade unleashed by seventy-five guns stretching from the Peach Orchard to Spangler's Woods targeted Cemetery Ridge. About as many additional guns in flanking areas pounded enemy positions.[462] Union batteries replied in kind.

Hundreds of roaring cannons and shell bursts shook the earth. The noise deafened. Ears rang. Smoke obscured views. Captain Poindexter, Company H, 38th Virginia reported, "We lay quiet and (some of us) hugged the ground."[463] One had to lay quiet or scream to be heard. The incessant roar was horrific.

Two days of fighting had consumed most of Lee's long-range ammunition. The cannonade consumed virtually all the rest. To further complicate matters, Lee's artillery lacked precision and accuracy under best conditions, for shortages prevented adequate target practice before the campaign.[464] Once bombardment began, the smoke obscured the gunners' views. In addition, Confederate ammunition was notoriously problematic. Powder quality varied. Poorly manufactured fuses exploded shells prematurely or not at all.

Longstreet assigned artillerist Colonel Porter Alexander responsibility to judge effectiveness of the barrage and determine when to send Pickett forward. It was hard to judge the effect. Alexander could not discern Confederate aims trended high and pounded rear areas rather than the front line.

Union return fire remained steady. Cannon balls careened across the field. Some crashed into trees, knocked down limbs, and showered splinters and debris. Some shot rolled into or bounced onto men, smashing bones. Shells exploded, killed, and maimed. In 38th Virginia, Company D the shelling killed Tap Eanes and wounded Joe Robertson and Flem Gregory.[465]

A shell fragment hit Colonel William Aylett, 53rd Virginia, in the chest and knocked him off his feet. His blanket roll saved him. Aylett was stunned and bleeding from his mouth and nose.[466] Orderlies carried Aylett from the field on a litter. Lt. Colonel Rawley Martin of Chatham took command of the 53rd Virginia.

Colonel Edmonds, 38th Virginia, summoned Commissary Sgt. Blackwell, a relative. He gave Blackwell his watch, pipe, sewing kit, and silver fruit knife for safekeeping with instructions to forward those to his young wife if he was killed.[467]

Armistead and his staff shaded themselves in the trees with the 38th Virginia. A shell cut through a hickory tree and exploded near Armistead, wounding several men. One noted Armistead always seemed in the best mood when under fire. To the men shifting positions to avoid missiles, Armistead quipped, "No safe place near here, boys!"[468]

Perils liberated Armistead from social angst. Pretenses vanished amid lethal hazards. His brandy flask helped.

After twenty-five minutes, Confederate ammunition ran low. There was no time to resupply. Alexander dashed off a note to Pickett that he must advance now or the artillery could not support him.

Pickett rode to Longstreet for confirmation. Longstreet, dead set against the attack but following orders, affirmed with a nod. Pickett galloped off in high spirits for his long-awaited opportunity to lead his division into battle. Pickett required another forty-five minutes to get his assault moving.

The Confederate barrage stopped. Fewer than twenty guns had ammunition left.

Union fire slackened. Guns along the ridge loaded canister with orders to hold their fire until the Rebels reached the Emmitsburg Road.[469]

Pickett cantered up before his prostrate division. His sweaty locks bounced beneath his kepi. He halted before the mounted Garnett, who commanded Pickett's old brigade. Garnett asked instructions. Pickett advised him to get his men across the valley quickly. "It's a hell of an ugly looking place over yonder!"[470]

General Pickett beamed Cavalier aura as he encouraged his brigades. At that moment, he embodied every fancied ideal of the proverbial Virginia Cavalier. Pickett jauntily exhorted, "Up men, and to your posts! Don't forget today that you are from Old Virginia!"[471]

The quixotic image inspired a nobleness of purpose throughout his rank and file. The great irony lost upon his Southside Virginians was that the majority of them were descendants of religious dissenters, refugees from the colony, and non-English immigrants—the very off-scourings of Old Virginia.

Armistead ordered his men to their feet. The men complied in fine spirits. Men rerolled blankets and donned accouterments. Wounded and sunstroke victims stayed down. There were few shirkers. Regiments formed lines of battle with the brigade arrayed north to south, the 38th Virginia, 57th Virginia, 53rd Virginia, 9th Virginia, and 14th Virginia.

Successive commands echoed throughout the division. Actions spiked adrenaline.

"Load!" Leather cartridge boxes flapped and ramrods clattered. Loaded weapons came to shoulder arms.

"Fix bayonets!" Arms shifted to order. Smartly unsheathed spear points slid over muzzles. Locking rings clicked. Muskets returned to shoulder arms.

Armistead drew his sword to carry and took his position twenty yards front and center of his brigade. In his clear, strong voice Armistead bellowed, "Remember, men, what you are fighting for. Remember your homes and your firesides, your mothers and wives and sisters and your sweethearts."

Armistead boomed, "Attention!"

Officers repeated the command. Muskets rose in unison to right shoulder shift. Pickett's division bristled with five thousand bayonets.

The entire division stood ready to advance. Lt. Farinholt, 53rd Virginia, described it as "the greatest and most imposing sight I ever witnessed."[472]

If reality had not struck yet, it did then. Brothers, cousins, and friends exchanged glances. Some waved and shouted farewells.

Armistead approached Color Sgt. Blackburn of the 53rd Virginia, pointed his sword toward their yet-to-be-seen objective and challenged, "Sergeant. Are you going to plant those colors on the enemy's works over yonder?"

Blackburn replied, "Yes, General. If mortal man can do it, I will!"

Armistead returned his sword to its scabbard, produced his brandy flask, uncapped it, and offered it to Blackburn. The color bearer took a big swig and returned it. Armistead returned the flask to his pocket and redrew his sword to carry.

Garnett's and Kemper's brigades stepped off and moved forward.

Armistead resumed his position before the brigade and exhorted his men one last time to follow their colors and remember the words of Sgt. Blackburn. Then loudly, clearly Armistead ordered, "Attention, second battalion!...Battalion of direction forward,...guides center...March!"[473]

Color guards at the forefront of each regiment bore high their red battle flags. The bright devices with star studded crosses floated before the dressed ranks of flashing bayonets that moved as waves toward the shore. Garnett's and Kemper's men guided around the artillery. When Armistead's men neared the top of the artillery ridge, most glimpsed the Union line for the first time. Massed blue troops, burnished guns and colorful flags crowned the distant high ground. It was Malvern Hill again, only worse!

The two armies embodied the rare spectacle to which King Solomon repeatedly referred to "as awesome as an army with banners."[474]

Thousands anticipated these as their last moments. The tension was too much for some. One man of the 14th Virginia dove into a ditch manned by the 5th Florida. Another of the same unit broke and ran down the lines of the 57th Virginia, followed by a file closer with cocked weapon.[475]

The lines moved in silence up and then down the artillery ridge into a sheltering depression. There units paused to dress their lines.

Company B, 38th Virginia with forty-eight men was the leftmost company of the leftmost regiment of Armistead's brigade. Since Armistead's line jutted beyond Garnett's and progressively more so as they advanced, Company B, 38th Virginia, the Pittsylvania Vindicators from Callands, was the leftmost company in all of Pickett's division. Their line of march undulated least. Theirs was the most constant, starkest, most terrifying view of the enemy atop Cemetery Ridge.

Almost immediately, the brigades left obliqued to close on Pettigrew's division. Pickett and his staff rode between Garnett and Armistead for a few minutes. Once his division cleared their artillery, Pickett galloped to the Sherfy orchard and then galloped back to observe Pettigrew's advance.

Pickett had formed his line four hundred yards from Pettigrew. Archer's brigade (Fry), Pettigrew's rightmost, was the brigade of direction.[476] Yet, Garnett's men did not align with Fry's men as planned. This exposed Fry's right flank throughout his advance, especially as they approached the Angle. From the moment Pettigrew's men stepped off, they faced a solid wall of fire.[477] Pickett returned to his staff distressed that Pettigrew was already in trouble. Pickett intensified efforts to close onto Pettigrew's division which had a head start and less distance to traverse.

Armistead's men followed 150 yards behind Garnett's. Armistead ordered his brigade to move by the left flank to close on Pettigrew, but farm fences posed an immense problem. Major Cabell, 38th Virginia estimated "not less than from five to seven fences" intersected their line of march.[478] Indeed, if there had ever been intention for Armistead make up the distance and align with Garnett, such as Longstreet proposed, chances of completing the maneuver were dismal.[479] The gap between Pettigrew's and Pickett's divisions persisted.

Union artillery reigned supreme as it had at Malvern Hill. McGilvery's batteries on Cemetery Ridge and the enfilade pieces on Little Round Top belched shot and shell. Iron balls cut swaths through ranks of all three divisions, Pickett's especially. Shells blew gaping holes in formations. One explosion leveled an entire company in the 53rd Virginia.

Major Cabell, 38th Virginia described it as "a most terrific fire."[480] Three fist-sized holes in the center of the 38th Virginia's battle flag soon testified to the fact. Nevertheless, the lines dressed and moved onward.

The catawampus march put Kemper at the Emmitsburg Road first and within musket range. Men fell at every step.

Sturdy, five-foot-high fences lined both sides of the road. Much of the fence in Kemper's path had come down in the previous day's assault. Shot hit standing rails and threw them "spinning through the air as a man would throw a drumstick."[481]

Garnett's and Kemper's troops advanced up the swale before the Codori farm. Kemper passed to the right of the Codori house and barn, Garnett to the left. Garnett's brigade incurred considerable casualties while climbing fences. Once past the double fences bordering the road, his battle line re-formed, dressed, and resumed its march. One Union observer described the advance as "an irresistible machine which nothing could stop."[482]

Armistead's men ascended the last swale two hundred yards from the Emmitsburg Road. The sturdy, five-rail fences, hidden from their view until that moment, rose up before them. Union musketry then added to their woes. Junior officers and file closers encouraged their men, "Forward. Steady. Close it up."

The fences loomed large. Officers shouted, "Pass obstruction!" Men struggled up and over. Some gravitated to the breaches opened by artillery. These easy ways through attracted musket fire and proved deadly bottlenecks.

Garnett's men swept down from the road and moved up Cemetery Ridge, taking frightful casualties. The murderous fire to the right of Codori's farm slowed Kemper's advance and pressed his files to the left. His leftmost units now marched behind Garnett.

As Armistead's brigade re-formed past the road and dressed lines, Kemper galloped over to Armistead. He reined to a stop and shouted, "Armistead! Hurry up! My men can stand no more! I'm going to charge those heights, and I want you to support me!"[483]

Armistead replied, "I'll do it!" He proudly pointed with his sword, "Look at my line! It never looked better on dress parade!"

Kemper had no time for Armistead's twaddle. He dug in his spurs and galloped back.

One hundred yards from the wall, Kemper and Garnett committed the great taboo of bayonet charges: they stopped to fire.[484] Their volleys had little effect. Both brigades loosed their Rebel yells and charged, but they had emptied their muskets and forfeited momentum.

Armistead copied the folly. He halted his men and stepped into the ranks to give clear field of fire. The brigade volleyed over Garnett's men. Armistead ran back in front of the 53rd Virginia, placed his black slouch hat on his sword, extended it high toward the enemy's breastworks, and shouted, "Colonel! Double quick!" The brigade surged forward as the order spread along the line.

At the beginning of the charge, the Angle was weakly defended.[485] As the Rebels' direction became clear, reinforcements rushed to meet them. Now the Union line unleashed murderous blasts of double canister and musket volleys. Kemper and his men practically vanished.

Fusillades blasted Garnett's men into disarray. The colors of the 18th Virginia dropped. Their commander, Lt. Colonel Henry A. Carrington, a lion of the Dan, picked up the battle flag to rally his men. As soon as Carrington raised it, he fell seriously wounded.[486] His regiment, three of its companies from Pittsylvania County, disintegrated with the rest of the brigade. Some of Garnett's men reached the stone wall; others receded toward Armistead. Garnett's horse bolted away, riderless.

Armistead's brigade became the predominant target. Captain Poindexter, 38th Virginia, Company H noted, "The guns on Cemetery Ridge blazed in our faces, and every regiment of Armistead's brigade dressed on its own colors…The battle raged with double fury."[487] Bullets and canister balls filled the air with hissings. The thud, crack, ping, impacts on flesh, bone, and accoutrements were as incessant as hailstones on a barn roof.

Casualties mounted. In Company B, 38th Virginia, James Oakes dropped with a bullet through his left shoulder. He struggled to his feet and started for the rear. His brother Sgt. Tom Oakes fell with a bullet shattered thigh. Third brother Cpl. John Oakes took Tom's place as file closer. Musketry killed John R. Gregory outright.

Forty yards from the stone wall, Armistead's sword tip worked through his hat and slid down the blade. He pushed it back up and yelled, "Charge!" The command spread electrically. The war-whooping mass rushed the stone wall. The defenders rose, fired, and pulled back while reloading in a frantic fumbling of cartridges and ramrods.

Thirty paces from the wall, the 38th Virginia had lost two-thirds of its number.[488] Yet, on they rushed.

Division timing had gone awry from the start. Pettigrew's attack on their left was already spent and falling back before Armistead charged. The 38th Virginia extended beyond the Angle where the last of Archer's brigade (Fry) had been repulsed.

Union forces seized opportunity and exploited the void. The 1st Delaware and others crossed their breastworks and moved into the field. Elements of the 8th Ohio started down the Emmitsburg Road.

Colonel Edmonds reacted to the threat on his exposed flank and worked frantically to refuse his left and return fire. The 14th Connecticut directed its fire from its stonewall perch above and beyond the Angle down onto the 38th Virginia. Edmonds ordered his men down. The terrain rose just enough there to shelter them from that fire. A few New Englanders armed with Sharps repeating rifles stopped to cool their overheated barrels with water from canteens.[489]

Edmonds dashed over to his right-wing commanders, Captains Herndon, Company D, and Townes, Company A. As he spoke, a bullet slammed into Edmond's head.[490] He died almost instantly.

Lt. Colonel Whittle was down, hit in the thigh. The one-armed Whittle, seed of Powhatan, raised himself with his right arm, his only arm, and was shot twice more in the shoulder and good arm.[491] Men rolled Whittle onto a blanket and dragged him away.[492] Major Cabell, yet another descendant of the great Powhatan, took command of the 38th Virginia.

Concurrently, Armistead crouched behind the stone wall beside Lt. Colonel Rawley Martin, 53rd Virginia. Yes, that same doctor, once junior officer of the Chatham Greys, wounded at Malvern Hill, who had helped amputate Whittle's arm.

As his men loaded and fired over the wall, Armistead turned to Martin, "Colonel! We cannot stay here!"

Martin shouted, "Forward with the colors!"

Color bearers pushed their way to the front. Lt. Carter bore the colors of the 53rd Virginia. Color Sgt. Blackburn and the rest of his color guard had been shot down. The moment the flags reached the wall, Armistead rose with hat raised on his sword and boomed, "Follow me boys! Give them the cold steel!"

Those near Armistead rose with a yell and scrambled with him over the wall. Major John Timberlake, 53rd Virginia, mounted the wall in Armstead's footsteps and cried out, "Look at your general! Follow him!"[493]

The battle flags of the 9th Virginia, 14th Virginia, and 57th Virginia waved defiantly with that of the 53rd Virginia and with the four remaining flags from

Garnett's and Kemper's brigades.[494] Between one and four hundred determined men followed Armistead.

In the excitement and confusion, the color bearer of the 38th Virginia at the Angle sprang over the wall. A few of the 38th Virginia beside him must have done likewise. The color bearer realized himself separated from his regiment. He climbed back over the wall with his flag and rejoined his unit. Some later recalled that it looked as if he just turned and walked away.[495]

The butternut flood pushed the enemy with sufficient vigor to capture those of the 69th Pennsylvania who had not acted fast enough when pulled back. The 69th Pennsylvania rallied higher on the ridge and fought back tenaciously.

The Southside Virginia tide engulfed the orphaned guns of Cushing's Battery.[496] Colonel Magruder, 57th Virginia, exclaimed, "They are ours!" Two bullets then struck him dead in the chest. Armistead, beside a cannon, shouted, "The day is ours men, come turn this artillery upon them!"[497]

Those at hand wrestled to turn the gun. However, artillery required teamwork. Few grasped their role. Those with a clue, scrambled for scattered tools.

The 72nd Pennsylvania crested the ridge and volleyed. Bullets hit Armistead in the flesh of his right arm and left leg below the knee.[498] He staggered and fell beside a gun wheel.

Lt. Colonel Rawley Martin struggled to man the gun with befuddled assistance of riflemen. Another volley wounded Martin, who sank to the ground. Sgt. Tredway rushed to Martin's aid and fell shot in the chest across Martin, pinning him under his body.[499] In face of enemy counterattack, Major Timberlake, "not being an artillerist myself," ordered his men back behind the wall.[500]

The Rebel flags inside the Angle went down. The men who followed them there suddenly faced death or capture. Timberlake, the ranking officer among those trapped at the wall, ordered his men to cease fire and surrender.

Brigadier General Lewis Addison Armistead and his men at the climax of Pickett's Charge; this sketch by war correspondent Alfred Waud is the only known depiction by a possible eyewitness to the event. (Courtesy Wallach Division Picture Collection, New York Public Library)

Meanwhile, Major Cabell had fully refused the 38th Virginia with Company A anchored at the wall.[501] Most lay flat and rose only to fire over the ground swell. While Captain Herndon conferred with Captain Townes, Townes fell dead, "shot through from side to side."[502] Herndon walked up and down his line shooting his pistol and feeling "the hand of Providence." No sooner did he slide his empty pistol back into its holster than a rifle ball smashed it.[503] Herndon remained unhurt. Cabell, Herndon, and the unnamed color bearer carried on as if divinely shielded from harm.

Blue-clad units had advanced beyond the Bryan farm. Some gathered prisoners from Pettigrew's command. Others fired on Armistead's flank, where the prostrate 38th Virginia remained the last cohesive regiment in Armistead's command. The 8th Ohio continued its advance along Emmitsburg Road on a vector behind the 38th Virginia, threatening their retreat. Major Cabell realized it impossible to hold their position.

At the Codori farm, Pickett looked on the contest in shock and disbelief, as one helplessly watching family massacred. His support? Where was his support? Pickett could see their battle lines. They were not advancing.

Longstreet considered the day lost and issued no order to advance. He had, however, left the option open to Pickett's discretion. Pickett sent riders to beg them to hurry. When the riders reached Wilcox, he started two brigades forward, but it was too little, too late.[504] The Confederate tide receded from its high-water mark down the ridge as a wave from a beach.

Cabell ordered his men to their feet. Several, no doubt, remained down. Reduced to about a quarter their initial number, the 38th Virginia withdrew while returning fire. The remnants of the brigade under Lt. Colonel White, 14th Virginia, passed behind them. White went down. Brigade command conveyed to the twenty-three-year-old Cabell.

At the Emmitsburg Road, Cabell rallied the men for a last stand under the colors of the 38th Virginia. Wounded men nearby waved white handkerchief flags. Cabell ordered them down, but they rose again.[505] The 8th Ohio rushed in from the left rear and engaged hand to hand. Once again, the fence proved a daunting obstruction. Those skirting the melee scrambled over, around, or through.

The tattered colors of the 38th Virginia dropped to rise no more. A Yankee had them![506] Organization collapsed. Confusion turned to chaos.

Surrender or flee? No time to think! Every man for himself! One either dropped his weapon and threw up his hands or bolted away. The fight was over.

Lee considered his men invincible.[507] They had won his past gambles. This time they lost.

Closeup of the 38th Virginia Infantry's battle flag captured at Gettysburg; battle damage restored by conservators is digitally highlighted. Note the faded cotton unit designation salvaged from the Malvern Hill flag. (Photo by Author)

CHAPTER TWELVE

The Aftermath of Gettysburg

At the stone wall, desultory fire, jumbled commands, and cries of wounded replaced the din of battle. Victors herded prisoners and gathered battle flags. A group of blue uniforms shouted, "Fredericksburg! Fredericksburg!" at the retiring Rebels, a declaration of retribution for similar slaughter seven months before.

All over the field, friend mixed with foe in smoke and confusion. This limited fire from both sides. The bloody, shaken remnants of Pickett's, Pettigrew's, and Trimble's divisions retired to Seminary Ridge. Walking, limping, few dared to stop until back within their artillery line. Many supported injured. Some carried or dragged them on blankets.

Lee met Pickett's Virginians with assurances that the failure was his fault, not theirs. There were no flags to rally upon, no chain of command, and no guidance from their stupefied division commander.

Pickett rode back in tears, stunned and unequal to his duty at hand. Rather than rally troops as did Lee, Pickett gave no thought to re-forming. He came upon Captain Henry T. Owen in the process of rallying the 18th Virginia. He told Owen not to stop his men but to let them go to the rear, to their initial camp.[508] So, on to camp they went. Armistead's few fit survivors filtered through the woods and fields back to Marsh Creek.

Pickett's bloody, wounded majority collected themselves along the ridge. Many desperately sought transport to the division hospital at Bream's Mill. Those able to walk suffered to make their own way.

Lee approached Pickett and directed him to ready his division to repel counterattack. Pickett replied, "General Lee. I have no division now."[509] Pickett then followed his remnants to the rear and left the Confederate center devoid of infantry.[510]

Pickett had to first pull himself together before he could re-form his command. His division was his identity. It was smashed. Pickett's Cavalier aura vanished with the smoke that day. He would never get that back. Never.

Lee tasked Longstreet to organize a defense. Lee's counterpart Meade assessed pursuit with exhausted troops needing resupply. No counterstroke materialized. The two exhausted armies faced each other across bloody fields littered with dead, dying, and seriously wounded. The sun set to the piteous moans and cries for water. Darkness masked the carnage. Fireflies swarmed. Lanterns and torches dotted the field. A bright moon arose.

* * *

The Pickett-Pettigrew-Trimble assault had swept the high-water mark of the campaign. Lee's army sat at slack tide before ebb. Able-bodied men on both sides focused on immediacies. Independence Day dawned on much distraction.

One soldier in the 38th Virginia noted Pickett's division looked like one or two regiments. "Only a few hundred answer to the rolls where thousands answered a few days ago."[511] Of all the field officers in Armistead's brigade, only Major Joseph R. Cabell escaped unhurt. Young Cabell stood a marvel, a miraculous deliverance from death and injury. Cabell was, in fact, the only field-grade officer in Pickett's division to return from the charge unhurt.[512]

Cabell must have been dumbfounded by the sudden responsibility. The twenty-three-year-old major, unfamiliar to many outside the 38th Virginia, now commanded Armistead's brigade. Confusion reigned. Units sorted themselves out and reconsolidated.

While brigade recovery consumed Cabell's attentions, a captain commanded the Pittsylvania Regiment. Of ten company commanders, the 38th Virginia lost six: one killed, four wounded, and one missing.[513] Captain Griggs was seriously wounded in the thigh. Captain Jennings took a spent canister ball in the face, breaking his upper jaw. Captain Lee was shot in the arm. This left Captain Grubbs, Company C senior captain, in command.

Three hundred and fifty effectives in the 38th Virginia made the charge. Seventy-three answered roll. The severely wounded Powhatan Whittle declared, "My poor regiment is ruined."[514] It would be months before Whittle could return as its colonel, if ever.

Of the forty-eight men in Company B, only seven answered roll. Four of those were slightly wounded. Cpl. John Oakes was one of three unhurt. Oakes, no doubt, wondered about his brothers. He saw James and Tom shot down. James got up. Tom refused aid and lay where he fell. He knew nothing of brother Charles in the 57th Virginia.

* * *

The biggest challenge facing Lee was getting his battered army back to Virginia. Under cover of darkness July 4, the main force withdrew via the Fairfield Road and through Monterey Pass. Pickett's shattered division was among the first to move. They were in no condition to fight. Lee assigned them escort duty for the nearly four thousand Union prisoners.[515] Many in the division, George Pickett particularly, considered the task demeaning, but the duty matched their capabilities.[516] They marched for Williamsport while the main army checked pursuit.

The ambulance train departed via Cashtown Pass escorted by Imboden's cavalry. The wagon loads of wounded stretched seventeen miles. Company B, 38th Virginia, members James Oakes, Coleman Reynolds, and Ferdinand Allen and over eight thousand other injured soldiers began their excruciating, two-day, forty-five-mile wagon jostle to the Potomac.

The army left behind four thousand unfit for travel. Among those from Company B, 38th Virginia, were leg amputees James Allen Oakes and Suter Blair. Brittain Fuller and several others remained as hospital aides to face inevitable capture.

Rain fell in torrents that night. Roads turned to mud.

Cries, moans, oaths, and appeals to heaven sounded from lurching wagons. Discarded dead littered the muddy roadside. Details hastily buried them on the spot. Some wounded, unable to bear the harsh, jarring torture any longer, lay on the roadside in the rain per their piteous pleas to await death or capture.

On July 7, the seemingly endless ambulance train meandered into Williamsport via Potomac Street and proceeded through town to the Potomac River. The wagon loads of hurting, hungry, thirsty wounded crowded the flat between the river and the C&O Canal to await their turn on the ferry. The sick and wounded unable to continue filled makeshift hospitals in the town. The army eventually left them behind.[517]

Engineers jury-rigged a second ferry. The army also pressed canal boats and additional ferries into service. The wagon loads of injured conveyed across the Potomac was one of the great feats of the campaign.

Pickett's men herded their prisoners near the canal and waited. On July 8, they stood queued to cross on the improvised ferry. This broke and the prisoners resumed their wait. The army repaired the ferry. Prisoners then crossed with their escorts.[518]

Pickett designated Armistead's brigade (Cabell) provost guard for the town. The 38th Virginia turned their prisoners over to Imboden's cavalry and assumed provost duties.[519]

By July 10, mail delivery brought news that Vicksburg had surrendered.[520] Colonel William Aylett returned to duty and assumed brigade command from Major Cabell.[521] Aylett's week-long disablement, staggering losses, and defeat deeply affected Aylett, who hated Yankees anyway. A letter from Aylett's wife reported Union cavalry had terrorized his family and ransacked his beloved Montville. The raiders had also sacked the village of Aylett and burned several homes in the vicinity.[522] This proved too much for Aylett, who ordered twelve of his eighty remaining prisoners "shot on the spot" in retaliation.[523] Quick action by a staff officer stopped the executions in the nick of time.

Provost duty for the 38th Virginia ended next day. Armistead's brigade (Aylett) forded the Potomac. They were the last of Pickett's division to leave Williamsport.[524] Two days later, on July 14, the very last of Lee's troops crossed at Falling Waters just hours before General Meade planned an all-out attack.

History ignores the numbers of enslaved wagoners, cooks, and body servants who accompanied the Army of Northern Virginia into Pennsylvania. The figure is unsearchable but known to have been considerable. Those looking to get free surely took advantage of opportunities to sneak away. One assumes significantly fewer returned to Virginia.

On that July 14, Cpl. John Oakes, Company B, 38th Virginia, camped with his unit at Bunker Hill as did his brother Charles, Company E, 57th Virginia. The Virginia Central Railroad had delivered their brother James to the receiving hospital in Richmond the day before.[525] James would soon be transferred to the general hospital in Danville.

Back at Bream's Mill, recent amputee cousin James Allen Oakes suffered his last full day before being unceremoniously ditched in a mass grave. Fellow Company B amputee Suter Blair died the same day as Oakes.

James Allen Oakes, Private, Company B, 38th Virginia Infantry. (Courtesy Joe R. Gibson)

Sgt. Thomas Oakes, the fourth Oakes brother from Callands, languished at the Union II Corps hospital. Left on the field, he had lain near the Angle with a bullet-shattered thigh until transported. Many lay for days unattended. Once transported to one of the overwhelmed field hospitals, casualties lay on open ground to await treatment only to be returned outside to recover with scant attention. Union soldiers received priority. Most of them, too, lay exposed to the elements.

Summer sun blistered! Thunder storms soaked! Wet wounds festered! Poor sanitation! Flies! Mosquitoes! The living hell rivaled anything in Dante's *Inferno*!

Agonies! Miseries! Pain! Thirst! Hunger! Pests!

Oh, that precious sip of water! Oh, that rare taste of broth! Oh, that blessed shade from a makeshift canopy!

Tom Oakes lingered until August 2. Local physician Dr. John W. C. O'Neil, a Virginian living in Gettysburg, recorded his burial between the Schwartz and Bushman farms.[526] Oakes's descendants would not learn his fate until over a century later.

James Oakes's wife had two uncles in the 53rd Virginia who made the charge, descendants of a Hessian surrendered at Yorktown.[527] One returned. One was wounded and captured. The many, many interpersonal relationships in Armistead's brigade compounded grief.[528] It was truly family tragedy on grand scale.

* * *

Attendants removed wounded Brigadier General Lewis Armistead from the field. He conveyed his personal effects to Union Captain Henry H. Bingham. Armistead requested the fellow Mason deliver them to his friend Major General Winfield Scott Hancock, commander of the Union II Corps at the Angle. Armistead added, "Say to General Hancock for me, that I have done him, and you all, a grievous injury, which I shall always regret."[529]

Armistead's captors transported him to the XI Corps hospital at the George Spangler farm. Surgeons dressed his wounds and bedded him in the farm's detached kitchen. They deemed his injuries serious but not life threatening. However, on July 5 his condition deteriorated. A doctor called attention to corn kernels fallen from his pocket. Armistead boasted, "Men who can subsist on raw corn can never be whipped."[530] Thus were his last recorded words before his heart stopped.

Some historians reject Armistead's death from relatively minor wounds to invent a third wound to his chest. However, Dr. Daniel G. Brinton, who attended the general, established the fact that Armistead had only two bullet wounds: one in the flesh of his right arm and another similarly in the left leg below the knee. No bones were broken. Brinton considered neither wound "of serious nature."[531]

Holistic consideration adds the possibility of occult coronary damage from his prior severe erysipelas infection. Such condition aggravated by blood loss, dehydration, and exhaustion would have been life threatening. Perhaps a blood clot moved to his lung. In any event, Lewis Addison Armistead, a man of sorrows and mediocrity, died a brave soldier without any notion he would become an icon of heroism in art and legend.

* * *

News of Armistead's death filtered through channels. Brigade officers favored Colonel Edmonds to replace Armistead. This was despite the fact that Cabell, Herndon, and others witnessed the colonel killed. Nevertheless, every officer in the brigade signed a petition to the Secretary of War requesting Edmonds be given command as soon as exchanged. By mid-August official reports confirmed Edmonds dead. His officers resolved the following:

> In the qualities of a good commander in camp, uniform kindness of disposition, rigid impartiality, sound discretion in the administration of discipline, and an anxious and unceasing attention to the welfare of his men distinguished him. As a good leader in action, keen penetration, correct views of the matter in hand, a courage and self-possession that resembled ignorance of danger, gave him absolute control of his men. In the virtues of his private life, sterling integrity, unvarying politeness, ardent interest (without ambition) in all that affected society, a keen relish for the society of a few chosen friends, together with an unaffected modesty and a childlike simplicity, were specially noticeable. Few colonels were more gifted than he whom we delighted to honor and love to remember.[532]

Ned Edmonds was twenty-eight. The fact that there was never an Edmonds's brigade was most assuredly the army's loss.

* * *

No participant in Lee's invasion of Pennsylvania escaped ordeal. Each faced tribulation in one form or another. Captives faced hardships as great as any faced by anyone.

Armistead's uninjured men captured in the Pickett-Pettigrew-Trimble assault were rounded up, crowded into railcars, and sent to Fort McHenry. Ironically, Lewis Armistead's uncle Major George Armistead commanded that fort during the 1814 bombardment that inspired "The Star-Spangled Banner."

Crowded confinement in pens outside Fort McHenry was short-lived. Within days, the captives boarded steamboats. Most assumed their return to Virginia for exchange. However, their cruise down the Chesapeake Bay proceeded up the Atlantic coast and Delaware River. After three hundred nautical miles and two miserable days confined shipboard, they landed at Fort Delaware.[533]

Prisoners crowded barracks to more than three times designed capacity. Trigger-happy guards stood watch. Unsanitary conditions on Pea Patch Island promoted typhoid and smallpox. Scant plain rations caused scurvy. Some survived by eating rats. Several from Company B, 38th Virginia, died within months: Berryman Fuller, Allen Stokes, and John Mahan.

Conscription had forced Mahan to enlist the year before. He had already lost a brother to the war. Home occupied his thoughts. The husband and father of five desperately sought a substitute. Meanwhile, his four little girls died. He never found a substitute. He never received a furlough. He served reluctantly but faithfully. He never saw his wife and infant son again.

Overcrowding by the flood of Gettysburg captives moved federal authorities to establish another prison camp at Point Lookout, Maryland. By November, the fourteen remaining prisoners of Company B, 38th Virginia, boarded crowded steamboats. Again, they expected exchange in Virginia. Their two-day transport retraced the route of their first cruise and delivered them to their new camp.

Point Lookout had no prisoner barracks, only tents. Conditions on that cold, windswept, sandy spit in the Chesapeake Bay were as bad or worse than

Fort Delaware. Again, some survived by eating rats. Long-term uncertainty fed despondency and surrender to disease. By New Year's Day 1864, Sgt. Josiah Fuller, Richard Adkins, Tom Bradner, and Bolling Foust died from typhoid, smallpox, or scurvy.

Brittain Fuller and Harrison Gibson reached their limits. In January, they took the oath of allegiance and entered U.S. service.[534] Isaac Grant, Joseph Reynolds, and James Woodall were exchanged in failed health, too sick to ever fight again.

Sgt. Edward Hodges, Henry B. Fuller, Henry Adkins, Jordan Bates, and George Blair, the remaining Gettysburg prisoners from Company B, 38th Virginia, endured captivity until February 1865. They were then exchanged. All five refused customary furlough and returned to duty.

The number of killed, wounded, and missing at Gettysburg was high. Aggregate losses for Company B, 38th Virginia topped 85 percent. Indeed, the Pittsylvania Regiment had suffered heavy losses in killed and wounded at Seven Pines and Malvern Hill. In those battles, they had held the field as victors. Gettysburg was different. Grim roll calls tallied many men missing. The ensuing deaths and disablements of captives crowned defeat at Gettysburg as a true disaster.[535]

CHAPTER THIRTEEN

Pickett Descends on New Bern

Southern fortunes declined precipitously. Lee had met disaster at Gettysburg. Vicksburg had fallen. Union forces defeated Bragg's army in Tennessee. Bragg retreated to Chattanooga. Lincoln's Anaconda Plan strangled resources.

Southern independence had been an all-or-nothing wager from the beginning. Lincoln matched their bet. The will to resist federal subjugation remained strong, for militarized Southern honor was a life or death mindset, a baptized bushido.

Ordeals brought individuals to their knees. In a letter dated September 6, Chaplain Cridlin, 38th Virginia, requested help from fellow clergy. Cridlin had taken sick and was unable to minister amid a spiritual revival in Armistead's brigade. The chaplain wrote, "We have many proofs that it is a genuine and mighty work of grace."[536]

* * *

On September 8, Pickett's division marched toward Richmond. Rumors circulated that Longstreet's Corps had received orders west. However, Pickett marched south. They did not ride the Virginia Central Railroad as on past occasions. Locomotives and rolling stock concentrated at Gordonsville and Orange Court House to load Hood's and McLaws's divisions. Those departed next day to reinforce Bragg, who was then abandoning Chattanooga and retreating into Georgia.

On September 11, Armistead's brigade (Aylett) bivouacked in Hanover County along the South Anna River and Taylor's Creek. There they learned Pickett's division had been detached from Longstreet's Corps. Pickett's men had been sorely battered at Gettysburg, but so had Hood's and McLaws's, and to much the same extent. No doubt the inclination to trust Virginia's defense to Virginians was a prime consideration in Pickett's new assignment. Even so, detachment implied indefinite separation.

Pickett's men marched next day to Hanover Junction. There they boarded flat cars destined for Petersburg to transport Longstreet's artillery to Georgia.[537] The men detrained and camped outside that city. On September 15, Pickett married Sallie Corbell in Petersburg.

News arrived the following week of Longstreet's great victory at Chickamauga. On September 23, the War Department placed Pickett in command of the Department of North Carolina. This officially severed his division from Longstreet's Corps.

On October 6, Armistead's brigade (Aylett) broke camp and boarded trains for Kinston, North Carolina. Pickett reinforced the town as a forward position and protection for the new Confederate ram CSS *Neuse* being outfitted there.[538] The movement required two days and multiple trains. One officer noted it a thirty-six-hour trip.[539] Those arriving after sundown bivouacked at the depot until daylight allowed march to a camp site.

* * *

In the wake of Gettysburg, Lt. Walker Keith Armistead, aide-de-camp to his late father, returned to duty with the 6th Virginia Cavalry to serve out the war with his uncles. Captain William B. Edmonds, commissary for the 38th Virginia and brother of the late colonel, transferred to division staff.

Senior Colonel William Aylett anticipated permanent command of Armistead's brigade. However, Aylett's campaign indiscretions, which included enabling incendiaries, attempted prisoner executions, and controversy over his "bloody nose" before Pickett's Charge, nearly cost him his commission.[540] These issues biased present and future considerations for his promotion to brigadier general. On October 9, Aylett resumed command of the 53rd Virginia and relinquished the brigade to Brigadier General Seth Maxwell Barton. Armistead's legacy became Barton's brigade.

Barton was a recently exchanged prisoner of war. He was intelligent, levelheaded, a native Virginian, and a seasoned combat commander. Barton was born and raised in Fredericksburg. His father was a prominent attorney.[541] Barton graduated from West Point. He resigned his captaincy in the U.S. Army and entered Confederate service as lieutenant colonel of the 3rd Arkansas. Barton fought under Robert E. Lee at Cheat Mountain and Greenbrier River.

Seth Maxwell Barton, Brigadier General, CSA. (From the Collections of the Confederate Memorial Literary Society managed by the Virginia Historical Society)

Barton served as chief engineer for Jackson's Romney campaign. He impressed Jackson sufficiently to receive his endorsement for promotion to brigadier general to command the famed "Stonewall Brigade."[542] However, Joseph E. Johnston denied Barton's two-rank advancement. Barton received a colonelcy shortly before his division moved to the western theater. He quickly advanced to brigadier general and served gallantly until surrendered at Vicksburg. There was none better qualified to command the veteran Virginia brigade. Nevertheless, Barton arrived a stranger to his men.

The brigade initially camped about three miles southeast of Kinston and set up a defensive perimeter. Aylett described the area as "very lonesome, lacking and uninviting…level as the sea with nothing to meet the eye but farm country and pine woods."[543] Within days they established their base camp west of town on what was generously considered high ground. There they constructed cabins from the abundant pines. It was the earliest in the season the men had ever entered winter quarters.

The post suited most. The sector was quiet and removed from the major armies. It was sharp contrast to Virginia where Lee had just tangled again with Meade at Bristoe Station.[544] The small town of Kinston thrived before the war. Union raiders had ransacked it the previous December. Citizens welcomed protection.

Kinston boasted a rail spur and a hardtack factory. The Neuse River provided natural salient. Once outfitted, the guns of the new ironclad could be brought to bear if needed. Unfortunately, shortages already placed the ship a year behind schedule. Neither guns nor machinery had been installed.

An anticipated attack on the railroad prompted action. On November 1, Barton's brigade left behind the 53rd Virginia and moved by rail to Weldon. After that threat subsided, the brigade boarded trains to Petersburg. The 38th Virginia continued to Hanover Junction to counter yet another threat. Tensions relaxed by November 11, and the brigade returned to Kinston.

Lt. Colonel Joseph Cabell commanded the 38th Virginia while Colonel Powhatan Whittle recovered from Gettysburg wounds. George Griggs was then major. Their promotions were retroactive to July 3. However, the indominable Whittle was too shot up to ever return to field service and too dedicated to resign. On November 15, Whittle reported to duty as a judge on General A. P. Hill's staff.[545] Young Cabell received promotion to full colonel with command of the 38th Virginia. George Griggs became lieutenant colonel. Henderson Lee, commander of Company G, received a promotion to major. Lee was on furlough recuperating from his Gettysburg wound.[546]

A number of Gettysburg casualties returned as doctors declared them fit. James Oakes rejoined brother John in Company B. A bullet through his shoulder early in the war might have earned him discharge but not in late 1863.[547]

Barton detached the 57th Virginia just before Christmas to man a fort at Greenville. The move interposed additional soldiers between the important rail junction at Goldsboro and Union raiding parties from the coast. An enemy force advanced upon them from Washington, North Carolina. The Federals ambushed a cavalry patrol, approached within five miles of the fort, and then inexplicably returned to base. Fresh troops relieved the 57th Virginia. They marched back to Kinston in cold, blustery weather and rejoined their brigade in time to flip calendars to 1864.

In Kinston, soldiers with means paid or bartered to supplement meager rations. However, many soldiers did not have wherewithal to pay or trade. Despite attentions to discipline, hungry men stole edibles, everything from potatoes to hogs.[548] One woman confronted Barton after men ran off with her "skillet of soup."[549] The loss of precious fare was bad enough, but it paled in significance to the iron pot essential to her living. She demanded its return. Such incidents strained civilian relations.

Not all theft was petty. Men of the brigade stole $18,000 from the quartermaster. Barton called his men "rags and thieves."[550] This did not sit well with those who felt as James Booker, Company D, 38th Virginia, that "it is not healthy for him [Barton] to give honest people such a bad name because some men do wrong."[551]

Drills, picket duties, foraging, and work details kept men busy. As more and more shortages plagued the Confederacy, soldiers worried increasingly about their families. Unauthorized absences increased. Officers minimized picket duty to limit opportunities for those tempted to slip away home.

* * *

Three thousand Union troops held the town of New Bern thirty miles away. Federal forces stockpiled considerable goods there. Lee proposed retaking New Bern to regain control of the region and seize much needed supplies. A three-day attack on the town the previous year had failed, but Brigadier General Robert F. Hoke devised a better plan. Lee recommended Hoke lead the expedition. President Davis countered that the size of the operation required oversight by a major general. On January 20, Lee assigned the operation to the department head George Pickett. It was the first Pickett learned of the plan.[552]

New Bern was situated at the confluence of the Neuse and Trent rivers. The region had always been a valuable source of naval stores. The Union seized the town in 1862 for its strategic importance and fortified all approaches with forts and earthworks. Hoke's strategy called for a four-pronged attack. Pickett planned his operation accordingly.

Barton with his brigade, Kemper's (Mayo), and three regiments of Matt Ransom's North Carolinians along with eight rifled guns, six smooth bores, and six hundred cavalry would attack New Bern from the south. Colonel James Dearing would lead his three hundred cavalry backed by three infantry regiments and three artillery pieces against Fort Anderson on the north bank of the Neuse River.

Pickett assigned Hoke the main assault. Hoke's, Corse's, and Clingman's brigades would take the earthworks on the south bank of Batchelder's Creek.[553] There they would await the sound of Barton's guns. That was Hoke's signal to attack Fort Rowan, pierce the defenses, and take the town.

A flotilla would descend the Neuse River and neutralize enemy gun boats. These were known to be "small and indifferent and do not keep up a head of steam."[554] As added measure, General Whiting in Wilmington would demonstrate against Swansboro to prevent Union reinforcements from Moorehead City.

Pickett massed thirteen thousand men at Kinston. Fourteen navy cutters and crews arrived by rail from Petersburg and Charleston. The unfinished CSS *Neuse* was no help.

Barton's column left Kinston on January 30 with four days of cooked rations. Colonel Aylett led Barton's brigade. To maintain secrecy, Barton deployed his cavalry screen to the south and east. They arrested sundry slaves and other potential informants wandering the roads.

The soldiers marched all day, covering eighteen miles over flat land. The topography was foreign to Piedmonters. The terrain was as flat as a table top. One seldom saw beyond immediate ranks. A monotonous scene of pine forests and farmland in full winter drab persisted on both flanks.

The column bivouacked in the muddy fields around Chinquapin Chapel.[555] The troops arose at three a.m. and marched again at first light. They tramped the day, treated to more flat land and dull scenery. The column proceeded east through Pollocksville.

The region produced much pine pitch essential for wooden ships. Pine trees boxed to collect turpentine gum added their scents to the salt marsh air. The sap did not flow freely in winter as it did in summer. Still, the aromatic gum oozed from cuts in cool weather.[556]

Terrain became increasingly swamp-like. The chilling sea breeze increased as they neared the coast. The procession kneaded trail-like roads into mud. After marching twenty miles, the column halted for the night eight miles from their objective. Proximity to the enemy forbade campfires. Clouds hid the quarter moon, which did not rise until after midnight. Darkness, wind, cold, and damp ensured a cheerless night. Messmates pooled blankets and huddled together for warmth in four- to six-man bundles.

The men rose at three a.m. and marched the remaining distance. Cavalry seized several outposts and a blockhouse. The surprised captives proved Barton had successfully concealed his approach. The column reached Brice's Creek at eight a.m. Fortifications, ship masts, and church spires confirmed to all that their mission was to retake New Bern.

Barton advanced skirmishers to the creek bank. The Rebels' sudden appearance south of the town caught Union defenders off guard. However, of all those involved, Barton was the most surprised.

Union engineers had cleared the banks of Brice's Creek to provide an expansive, unobstructed field of fire. Barton, an experienced military engineer, expected this. Remarkably, Pickett, his thoroughly Piedmont staff, and the mountain-raised Hoke, who devised the plan, had totally misjudged a major topographic feature.

To Piedmonters, the word *creek* meant something completely different than its homograph: a channel through coastal marsh. Brice's Creek was nothing like Falling Creek, Beaverdam Creek, or Antietam Creek. It was no branch, brook, or mill stream. To the contrary, it was a navigable river! Tidal salt water! Deep! Eighty yards wide!

Barton ordered his artillery into position while he, Colonel Aylett, and General Ransom reconnoitered the scene. Tide was at low ebb. Even so, the creek was unfordable and snaked south for miles through marshland.

There was one dry route across. A single bridge stretched to a narrow spit of land where the creek circled around to its mouth at the Trent River. Immediately past the bridge was a blockhouse supported by earthworks at the far end of the spit. Beyond that was a fort on the Trent River with ten guns. Across the open expanse were additional, heavier fortifications directly opposite the town.

Barton had no pontoon bridging.[557] He considered marching several miles south and crossing at Evan's Mill. The movement around impassable water would take the better part of a day and only position exhausted men for headlong assault across wide, open fields against massive fortifications with guns manned by waiting enemy.[558] Any such attack would be suicide. Subordinates agreed.

Obstacles were great. Options were few. The situation was insurmountable. Barton dispatched a courier to inform Pickett that he could only demonstrate, not attack.

Pickett waited north of the town with Hoke ready to attack at the sound of Barton's guns. Hoke's men had fought a sharp action the night before. They successfully carried the south bank of Batchelder's Creek as planned and took many prisoners. Hours passed with Hoke's men poised for action.

Late that morning, Pickett received Barton's dispatch detailing his stymied attack. About the same time, another courier reported that Colonel Dearing had aborted his attack north of the Neuse River. The four-pronged attack suddenly lost two tines.

Pickett had no planned contingency. He canceled Hoke's assault to rethink the situation. Barton's guns opened fire shortly after noon. The cannonade was diversion, not the attack counted upon. The thundering piqued the thoroughly frustrated general as he brooded over limited options.

Barton's guns probed. Union artillery returned fire. Some shells exploded close to Rebel infantry lying on the cold, wet ground.

Barton sent cavalry around Evan's Mill twice to cut the Atlantic & North Carolina Railroad. The tracks were well defended. Each attempt failed. Barton had no way to know that the rail line to New Bern had already been cut. General

Whiting's diversion twenty miles south had routed the enemy and destroyed the rail bridges from Morehead City.

Barton's force held fast and awaited further orders. Artillery dueled. Rain set in.

In the early hours of February 2, the bombardment held the garrison's attention while Confederate sailors and marines rowed fourteen cutters down the Neuse River. They expected three warships in New Bern harbor. They found only the gunboat *Underwriter*. The raiders took the ship by surprise and fought the crew to submission. Shouts and small arms popping alerted shore batteries, which then opened fire.

The four-gun sidewheeler had no steam, and there was no time to fire the boiler. The raiders took the crew captive, set their prize ablaze, and rowed away.

Flames licked skyward and silhouetted the town until the ship exploded. Three miles away, Barton's infantry took no notice. They lay wet, shivering, sleepless, clustered beneath oilcloths and blankets and rattled by cannon blasts and shell bursts. Several were killed and about two score wounded.

Pickett decided to concentrate his four-to-one numerical advantage for a general assault on the town. This required Barton to disengage and cross the Trent River upstream at Trenton, normally a day's march.[559]

The withdrawal from Brice's Creek late that day lacked scale of the war's more famous mud marches, but few columns experienced worse. The soggy, wintry route preconditioned by the army's kneading days before had since collected rain in wheel ruts and countless foot- and hoofprints. The muddy road inbound became a vast quagmire on the way out, "about the consistency of batter," one testified.[560] No doubt, veterans in the 38th Virginia recalled their retreat from Yorktown.

The cold slime was ankle-deep and deeper. Viscosity varied. Mud swamped shoes and sucked them off. Men stuck fast in places and had to be pulled out. Horses sank well past fetlocks. Here and there a wagon abandoned, a horse or mule shot. The column slogged forward. Sounds of gunfire in the rear prodded troops forward and minimized straggling. Gray daylight faded. Nightfall threatened blindness.

One by one, lanterns and torches bobbed along the struggling column to counter imminent blackness. Some thinking man ignited the flammable gum on a boxed turpentine tree. Soon scores of these sooty, resinous fires blazed along the way. Foggy mist diffused the orange light. The roadway glowed hellishly surreal.

The struggling column looked as eerie as it was miserable. The ordeal pushed men's limits. The 38th Virginia noted six soldiers from various companies slipped away in the confusion to surrender. Other regiments experienced similar losses.[561] A few were seasoned veterans who had simply had enough.

Pickett anxiously awaited word of Barton's crossing at Trenton. Instead, the general learned Barton had only reached Pollocksville. Thoroughly exasperated, Pickett abandoned New Bern and issued orders to return to Kinston. Barton's men retraced their initial route. They bivouacked again at Chinquapin Chapel on February 4 and arrived at Kinston at sundown February 5.

Pickett refused responsibility for his failure and sought a scapegoat. He blamed Barton for "want of cooperation."[562] Barton demanded a formal investigation to refute allegations. Pickett ignored the request.[563] Lee, on the other hand, supported Barton and recommended review.[564] Pickett tabled the matter. Nevertheless, the New Bern expedition won Barton the respect of his subordinates and confidence of his men.

Lee had emphasized to Pickett the importance of secrecy, expediency, and boldness as crucial to success. Lee's handholding stopped short of battlefield topography. New Bern was Pickett's first offensive as head of a department.[565] It was also his last.

* * *

Kinston continued to offer comforts superior to any previous winter quarters. Many cabins had floors and fireplaces. Nevertheless, the cold, damp, gray weather on the inner banks of North Carolina was most dreary. The war was almost three years old with no end in sight. Gettysburg haunted survivors. Men longed for the homes for which they fought. Letters from loved ones detailed hardships. Men sat idle in Kinston while families desperately needed them at home. Many grew restless.

Long awaited furloughs began but only at the rate of one per every twenty men. Some soldiers who had not been home since first muster in 1861 still had to wait their turn. Necessity drove some to elect French leave with intention of returning before winter quarters ended. Always risky, absences without leave grew ever more so under the increasingly petulant George Pickett.

Hoke's men had netted 179 prisoners at New Bern. An officer recognized two members of the Second North Carolina Union Volunteers as former Confederates.[566] Pickett ordered them executed.[567] He considered the men traitors and insisted they be hanged rather than shot. Barton's brigade witnessed the double hanging on February 7.[568]

The tragedy deepened as news of the sentencings filtered through Union lines. Major General John J. Peck threatened Pickett with reprisals on Confederate prisoners.[569]

Peck did not know the names of the men convicted and was unaware of completed executions. Peck's intercession supplied the names of fifty-three men who had switched sides. Pickett thereby identified an additional twenty "turncoats" in custody. Questionable proceedings found each guilty. Pickett ordered them all hanged in Kinston before his brigades. Seven met their fate on February 13, thirteen on February 15.

Among attending townsfolk were wives, children, and relatives of the condemned. As if the events were not sufficiently revolting, the bodies were stripped naked and left beside the scaffold for devastated families to claim. Hangmen threw unclaimed corpses into a common grave beneath the gallows.

The irascible Pickett notified Peck of the hangings and countered with threat to execute ten Union prisoners for each Confederate Peck might execute in reprisal.[570] Pickett's behavior at Kinston would haunt him after the war.[571]

* * *

The campaign season loomed amid the drama at Kinston. Union preparations again threatened the capital. Richmond demanded troops. Pickett's New Bern fiasco left him no leverage to resist. He used the opportunity to rid himself of Barton.

On February 12, Pickett ordered Barton's brigade to Richmond. They marched next day to the Kinston depot. The 38th Virginia and 53rd Virginia waited until the next day to board. Thus, Barton's men exited their most comfortable winter quarters early. As a result, Barton's brigade missed the bulk of the "turncoat" hangings. However, members returning from French leave also missed their troop movement. It was no time to trifle with Pickett.

On March 7, ship fitters in Kinston finally installed the two 6.4-inch Brook rifles on the ironclad *Neuse*. The progress instilled a measure of hope, but the ship still had no engine. That same day Pickett convened a general court-martial in town to try men of Barton's brigade for unauthorized absences.[572]

Of the enlisted men charged, four were of the 38th Virginia, four of the 57th Virginia, eleven of the 53rd Virginia, and twenty of the 14th Virginia. Convictions ranged from absence without leave to desertion.

Penalties for being AWOL varied from policing camp to loss of pay, furlough forfeiture, wearing placards, guardhouse confinement, cutting wood, and digging sinks. Those convicted of desertion generally received sentence to have the letter *D* branded on their left thigh and six months of hard labor on government fortifications with a twelve-pound ball attached to their left ankle by a three-foot chain.

Moses Hoofman, Company D, 38th Virginia, had his head shaved and his thigh branded and was given twelve months of hard labor.[573] Thomas Quinn, also of Company D, received the harshest sentence. Quinn had deserted once before at Malvern Hill. He was apprehended, disciplined, and returned to his unit. This time, Quinn had not only deserted but encouraged others to do so. The court sentenced Quinn to death by musketry. Fortunately for Quinn, his officers interceded and saved him from being shot.

* * *

The 38th Virginia and 53rd Virginia departed Kinston February 14. The train ride was cold, slow, and wearisome, and it snowed. They arrived in Richmond on February 15 and tread fresh snowfall on Nine Mile Road to fortifications near the York River Railroad. Snow fell on them again February 17.[574] They remained there until February 23, when they moved to guard New Bridge on the Chickahominy River. The 57th Virginia and 9th Virginia served picket duty and improved fortifications downstream at Bottoms Bridge.

The 1861 enlistments, extended to three years, neared expiration. On February 26, the 38th Virginia formed ranks for an address by Governor William "Extra Billy" Smith, who encouraged the troops to reenlist "for the war." Everyone knew reenlistment was mere formality since conscription laws already bound them to service. The government hoped a report of massed reenlistments might send a message of unfaltering resistance to the North. The effort stank of political sham.

Young Colonel Cabell assumed everyone in the Pittsylvania Regiment would respond favorably to the governor. Cabell enthusiastically advanced the colors and urged all those willing to be free to step forward and reenlist. Those willing to be slaves to the enemy needed only to stand fast. A third stepped forward. The rest held back, to Cabell's dismay.

It was not so much that the majority desired freedom less nor that any wished to be a slave. They simply believed themselves good fighters, whether reenlisted or not. Many feared stepping forward might encourage leaders to prolong the war unnecessarily.[575] Despite their overwhelmingly negative response, most eventually complied upon learning that refusal to reenlist eliminated any chance for furlough.

On March 1, Barton's brigade marched to Hanover Junction in response to Dahlgren's cavalry raid. The 38th Virginia remained behind to guard the bridges over the Chickahominy River. The brigade returned to the river crossings a few days later.

The men performed picket duty in three-day stints on meager rations. Since leaving Kinston, the men lived mostly off cornmeal and molasses. One soldier in the 38th Virginia recorded a pound and a half of cornmeal per day, next to nothing in the way of sugar and coffee, sometimes a few peas or a little rice, and occasionally a slice of beef.[576] The men reported feeling fit, but the food was inadequate for cold-weather duty. Light snow fell March 15. Daytime temperatures remained seasonal for the remainder of the month.[577]

The first day of spring arrived. Days later the men gave Easter a nod. The campaign season was upon them again. Unlike previous years, everyone knew an offensive on their part was unthinkable. Nevertheless, they knew they could still inflict frightful losses on invaders.

On March 31, at Lee's request, the War Department tasked Lieutenant General P. G. T. Beauregard with defense of all areas between the James River and Cape Fear. The assignment removed Pickett as head of the Department of North Carolina. Pickett and his men remained within Beauregard's jurisdiction but transferred to the Department of Richmond under Major General Arnold Elzey. The two-step demotion to Area Coordinator of Petersburg District reduced Pickett to little more than an observer.[578]

CHAPTER FOURTEEN

Chester Station, Drewry's Bluff, and the Howlett Line

Major General George Pickett submitted plans to retake Plymouth, North Carolina. General Braxton Bragg, the new military advisor to President Davis, studied Pickett's proposal and approved the operation. However, by then Pickett had been relieved as department head and transferred to Petersburg.

In an ironic reversal of roles, Pickett planned the attack, but Beauregard assigned Brigadier General Robert Hoke to lead the operation.[579] To Pickett's further chagrin, Beauregard placed the bulk of Pickett's men at Hoke's disposal. This left Pickett in command of a paltry two thousand regulars, militia, and civilian irregulars.[580]

Hoke handily captured Plymouth on April 20. This earned him immediate promotion to major general. On April 26, Beauregard received official appointment to the expanded coastal defense department, much of which had recently been Pickett's. The thoroughly debased Pickett requested transfer back to Longstreet's Corps.

* * *

Barton's brigade remained detached outside Richmond, guarding the bridges over the Chickahominy River. Camp routines and picket duties in wet, raw weather bred homesickness and dissatisfaction. Scarcity aggravated misery and frustration. In the snowy, rainy gloom of April 2, a disgruntled soldier in the 38th Virginia threw a bayonet into another's arm.[581]

Morale would have dropped further had the men known their chances for furlough were practically nil. On April 5, the quartermaster general recommended no leave be given soldiers to reserve railcar space for supplies. Moreover, the commissary general eliminated all passenger rail service to conserve irreplaceable rolling stock that was wearing out.[582]

The weather broke near the end of the month. Spring-like temperatures, songbirds, blooming dogwoods, and other resurrections of nature lifted spirits. Little else injected cheer. On April 25, the 38th Virginia received a new Company I, comprising heavy artillerymen converted to infantry under Captain George A. Martin. The regiment counted 303 effectives.

By May 2, Union activity along the Rapidan River moved Lee to action. The 38th Virginia broke camp May 3. Barton's brigade marched north to Brook Turnpike and bivouacked. The next day, they completed the twenty-five-mile march to camp two miles short of Hanover Junction.[583]

A major attack loomed as Grant and the Army of the Potomac converged on Wilderness Tavern. Lee also anticipated Grant sending a fleet up the James River with another army, but the Confederate high command dismissed that possibility.

Pickett received his anxiously awaited orders to rejoin Longstreet's Corps to be effective upon Beauregard's arrival. He then also received a telegram stating Beauregard was sick. The delay held Pickett in Petersburg.[584]

On May 5, the 38th Virginia guarded the railway bridge across the South Anna River. The Battle of the Wilderness erupted thirty-five miles away. A second threat to Richmond developed as the Union XVIII Corps splashed ashore at Bermuda Hundred. Pickett frantically pleaded for reinforcements. The War Department ignored Pickett and discounted his report as exaggeration.

The next day, the Union X Corps reinforced Bermuda Hundred. The amphibious landing was a remarkable success.[585] Major General Benjamin Butler had brought his entire Army of the James ashore unopposed. Butler's intelligence was accurate. The southern approach to Richmond was undefended. Nevertheless, Butler dawdled and squandered the opportunity.

General D. H. Hill, assigned to assist Beauregard, arrived in Petersburg. Hill helped Pickett cobble together resistance just as Butler ventured forward.

The 38th Virginia reunited with Barton's brigade at Taylorsville in preparation to move north to reinforce Lee in the Wilderness. However, in the wee hours of

May 7, Barton's brigade boarded trains and headed south to meet the emergency below the capital.

Upon arrival in Richmond, the brigade marched to Rockett's Landing and boarded steamers to Drewry's Bluff. General Robert Ransom deployed Barton and his men in breastworks across the Richmond-Petersburg Turnpike.[586] Ransom had just replaced Elzey as head of the Department of Richmond. This placed Pickett's detached brigade at his disposal.[587]

Chaplain Cridlin encouraged the men in the 38th Virginia. Most trusted Christ. Colonel Cabell was no church member nor had he ever made public profession of faith. Nevertheless, Cabell assured Cridlin that "he felt prepared."[588]

On May 9, Butler's forces probed toward Petersburg and halted at Swift Creek. A lesser force pushed to the rail line south of Chester Station, where they tore up much track and cut the telegraph. This disrupted communications with Petersburg.

President Davis met Ransom at Drewry's Bluff that evening to assess the situation.[589] Locals reported Federals camped five miles away near Chester Station at Winfree's farm.[590] There the Petersburg Turnpike (U.S. Rt. 1) intersected Bermuda Hundred Road (Rt. 10). Ransom agreed to a reconnaissance in force.

Ransom summoned Seth Barton and Archibald Gracie[591] to plan the advance. In "loud, imperious tones" Ransom ordered each to assign an entire regiment as skirmishers.[592] The tactic was unfamiliar to the brigadiers.[593]

Barton chose the 14th Virginia. Companies D and I were from Chesterfield County and acquainted with the terrain. The skirmishers deployed a mile in advance of their earthworks. Per Ransom's orders, Barton's skirmish line extended from the turnpike to the Richmond & Petersburg Railroad. In like fashion, Gracie's skirmishers stretched from the turnpike to the James River.

At dawn May 10, Barton and Gracie led their skirmish lines forward. The morning was a dry, summer-like seventy degrees. The temperature rose rapidly.

The main body followed about a mile behind with Ransom in command. From the turnpike to the railroad Barton arrayed the 38th Virginia, 9th Virginia, 53rd Virginia, and 57th Virginia. Time did not allow recall of men from picket duty. This reduced each regiment by about 20 percent of their already understrength numbers. The 38th Virginia fielded eight companies rather than ten.[594] Barton attached Donovant's Dismounted Cavalry to the 57th Virginia. Colonel Shingler's regiment of South Carolina cavalry secured Barton's right flank and scouted ahead.

Past the Half-Way House,[595] Barton's skirmishers guided around the morass at Proctor's Creek. Gracie's skirmish line compensated by extending right of the turnpike. Beyond the morass, Barton's men redeployed to the road. However, Gracie's skirmishers continued to overlap Barton's front.

The turnpike and railroad diverged. Dressing on the road drew Barton's right off the tracks. The railway remained in sight. Colonel Shingler reported the gap to Ransom. The general dispatched orders to halt the skirmish line and await the main body. Upon arrival, Ransom ordered Barton to fill the gap to the railroad. Since the understrength 14th Virginia was inadequate to cover the distance, Barton ordered two companies of the 57th Virginia forward at the double quick.

Five minutes later, Barton reported the gap covered. Strong prejudice surfaced. Ransom noticed the movement still in progress and berated Barton for insubordination. No doubt, Pickett's vengeful taint had colored his new boss's opinion of Barton.

Cavalry confirmed enemy infantry supported by artillery at the crossroads. Their line extended from Winfree's house in a crescent encompassing the crossroads. General Ransom ordered Barton deployed along Osborne Road in conformance to the enemy line.

Barton obliqued the 38th Virginia across the turnpike in line of battle. The 9th Virginia formed alongside the 38th Virginia and straddled the turnpike. The 9th Virginia's right connected with 53rd Virginia which diverged from the Osborne Road into the Purdue property. Ransom charged his adjutant-general Colonel R. H. Chilton to take command of the 57th Virginia, move it down the Chester Road to Bermuda Hundred Road, and form his battle line on the Union's left flank.[596]

Although Gracie's brigade had receded well east of the turnpike, his skirmish line still encroached on Barton's front. One of Gracie's staff reported the overlap to Ransom. The thoroughly rankled Ransom demanded Barton correct the situation immediately. This consumed even more time as Barton ushered Gracie's skirmishers to the left and ordered skirmishers forward from the 38th Virginia and 9th Virginia. The 14th Virginia remained deployed in front of the 53rd Virginia at the Purdue house.[597]

The Purdue House in 1978, looking northeast, over-the-shoulder from 53rd Virginia's initial line; the house was later razed for new development. The Purdue family cemetery, beyond left of view, remains. (Photo by Author)

Ransom grew ever more aggravated with what he perceived as sluggish deployment in face of the enemy. The angry commander exchanged more sharp words with Barton.[598]

Perdue's spring drained through a broad ravine perpendicular to the turnpike. The enemy occupied the high ground on the far side. Barton's men needed to advance downhill, cross the spring branch, and ascend the moderate slope covered with hardwood trees and tangled undergrowth. There was fallen timber where the railroad harvested fuel. The enemy had begun an abatis and was digging in. On the turnpike were two Napoleons. Their polished bronze barrels shone bright in the sun.[599] A line of infantry supported them.

Aggravated with Barton to distraction, Ransom overlooked the gap between his two brigades. Gracie's right had drifted hundreds of yards from the turnpike. Nevertheless, about nine a.m. Ransom ordered the attack. Barton was still positioning skirmishers when the signal gun fired.

Barton's brigade advanced. Skirmishers engaged enemy pickets.

On the far right, the 57th Virginia pressed the Union left at Winfree's. In the center, the 14th Virginia exited the woods beyond the spring and advanced into open fields toward the crossroads. The 53rd Virginia stepped off from Purdue's house in support of the 14th Virginia. To their left the 9th Virginia and 38th Virginia likewise moved down the hill, crossed the spring branch, and pushed up the wooded slope. The 38th Virginia engaged the battle line of the 169th New York. Smoldering cartridge papers from Springfields ignited dry leaves.

The Napoleons on the turnpike spewed canister. Each gun fired about once per minute. Every blast launched twenty-four deadly inch-and-a-half-diameter iron balls. Each bounced multiple times with powerful impacts.

Color bearers clutched flags against staffs to avoid snags as Barton's regiments picked their ways through brush and briars and drove the enemy back. Barton wrote:

> An advance of 100 yards brought us in contact with the enemy, whom we drove steadily before us, keeping as strict lines as the nature of the ground would permit. It was impossible to see more than a few paces; a captain could rarely see his whole company, a colonel never his whole regiment, at one glance. To add to these difficulties the woods were fired early in the action, and the smoke and flames driving into our line blinded us and deranged the precision of movements. I believe the distance between the combatants rarely exceeded 50 paces, often not 20.[600]

The gunfire upset Barton's distinctly colored horse. Barton swapped his unmanageable steed for another ridden by staffer J. D. Darden.[601] Barton rode back into the fray.

The irregular terrain had forced Gracie too far away to support Barton's left. The 38th Virginia advanced four hundred yards. Its unprotected left flank crept along the edge of a steep slope. The enemy directly before them broke and withdrew deeper in the woods. Some Yankees moved aside. These rallied beneath the brow of the wooded hill. They moved back up into position and fired on the flank and rear of the 38th Virginia. Colonel Cabell refused his two left companies, B and G. The Pittsylvanians volleyed several times and repulsed the threat. By then Barton had dispatched Captain Thom[602] on horseback to inform Ransom that his flank was turned.

All the while, the Napoleons on the turnpike blasted the smoky woods. Canister hail kicked up dust, chopped branches, pruned men, and showered debris.

In Company B, a canister ball ricocheted off a tree into James Oakes's right leg.[603] Another blast killed his cousin Christopher Oakes in Company D.

The 9th Virginia had a clearer field of fire. Their musketry whittled down the gun crews and killed five horses, more than enough to disable one caisson.

One crew limbered its gun as the Rebels closed within fifty yards. Colonel Cabell ordered a quick right oblique and captured one gun as the other pulled away. Barton reached the position and cheered his line forward.

With the enemy's right broken, Union artillery at Ware's Bottom Church lobbed shells and spherical case into the woods full of Pittsylvanians. The shelling fired more tinder dry brush. A breeze drove the flames.

The advance continued. The 38th Virginia and 9th Virginia gained significant ground. The 169th NY re-formed beyond the woods along the Bermuda Hundred Road (Rt. 10). The withdrawn Napoleon redeployed there. Union reinforcements arrived. When the 38th Virginia reached the edge of the woods, they encountered a triple line of battle. Muskets blazed. The lone Napoleon belched canister.

The 38th Virginia had orders not to advance beyond the Bermuda Hundred Road. They had reached their objective. They halted and fired from the tree line. The lively exchange continued.

In Company B, a bullet clipped one of Captain Prichard's fingers. Another hit him in the thigh. 1st Lt. Whitmell Adkins assumed company command. John Tatum took a bullet in the leg. Another ripped through Joe Reynolds's right arm.

Not since Seven Pines had the men of the 38th Virginia fired so many rounds in a fight. Barrels heated too hot to touch. In Company B, recent enlistee Tolbert Barker primed before loading. The hammer slipped and blew the ramrod through his hand. It doomed Barker to lethal infection.[604]

Sustained fire fouled rifles. Men stopped to swab barrels, hammer home balls against trees, or deal with other malfunctions. Veterans damp swabbed every five rounds or so to prevent stoppages. New recruits, reluctant to stop shooting to swab, experienced most problems. Barton stopped to assist several in clearing and loading fouled weapons.[605]

In the confusion, excited soldiers loaded atop unnoticed misfires, rendering those arms useless. Stuck bullets required pulling. There was no time for that. Grabbing a serviceable musket from the fallen was the best expedient.

Fighting raged along the 1.5-mile-long front. The 57th Virginia pressured the Union line on the west side of Winfree's. The Union line gave a little then held fast. The 14th Virginia and 53rd Virginia charged across an open field multiple times to assault the crossroads at Winfree's without success.

The Winfree house in 2012, looking west-southwest from inside Union line. (Photo by Author)

The 38th Virginia held their ground. To their left, a battalion of the 13th Indiana ascended from a ravine and hit their open flank.

Colonel Cabell again worked to refuse his left while exhibiting the same, consistent gallantry he displayed in every fight. The Napoleon sprayed more iron. A canister ball ripped through Cabell's abdomen.[606] Lt. Colonel Griggs took command and ordered Cabell carried to the rear. Griggs launched his refused companies in a desperate counterattack with fixed bayonets. In Company B, a clubbed musket broke Daniel Craddock's arm. Vicious hand to hand fighting forced the Hoosiers back, killing about fifteen and capturing fifty.

Federal artillery went into battery at Dr. Howlett's house on the James River. The enfilade fire harassed Barton's entire line. Shell fire kindled locomotive fuel stacked along the turnpike.[607]

The Pittsylvania Regiment was sorely pressed. Their flank was vulnerable. Weapons fouled. Ammunition was low. Casualties mounted. Energies waned. Colonel Cabell was down. The regiment neared its breaking point. Barton intervened. He refused half the 9th Virginia in support of the 38th Virginia. He then reverse wheeled the entire 38th Virginia parallel to the turnpike. This stabilized the line and allowed fighting withdrawal.

Barton had no staff officer present and still needed horses to remove the captured Napoleon. He left the situation in Griggs's capable hands and galloped off to Ransom.

Smoke from burning forest and gunfire obscured the battlefield. General Ransom had no clear view of the action. Bloody, sweat-soaked, black-powder-smeared wounded streamed from the burning woods, where cannons boomed, muskets rattled, and shells exploded.

Ransom occasionally glimpsed Darden riding Barton's high-strung horse back and forth across the smoky turnpike. Anger mounted as Ransom assumed it was Barton trotting around "without object."

A litter passed with a wounded officer. Ransom inquired. It was Colonel Cabell.

Barton galloped up the turnpike, reined his horse to a stop at Ransom, and announced his flank was turned again. Before Barton could address removing the captured gun, Ransom exploded and demanded Barton go back where he belonged. There was no reasoning with rage. Barton spurred his mount back into the fray.

The 7th Connecticut counterattacked from the crossroads. The 38th Virginia and 9th Virginia fell back. They reached the captured gun as Barton returned. They had no way to remove it and left it behind. Their attackers reclaimed the Napoleon and turned it upon the Rebels. The 38th Virginia and 9th Virginia broke and dashed down the slope and back across Purdue's spring branch.

Barton dismounted to pass an obstruction. As he placed his foot in the stirrup to remount, a cannon ball hit the horse squarely in the side. The impact killed the animal, splattered Barton with gore, and drove bone fragments into his boot.[608] Barton had not limped far when Darden rode up and returned Barton's original horse.

Ransom finally ordered Gracie to support, but it was too late. Ransom fumed and glared at Barton exiting the woods on his distinctive mount as he rallied his men back onto Osborne Road. Desultory fire followed. Their mission was finished. In Ransom's mind, so was Barton.

Both sides accepted a flag of truce to retrieve wounded. Litter bearers labored in the hot sun. Radiant heat from burning woods intensified the already sweltering upper-nineties. When the blaze threatened one wounded man, he crawled through the fire and burned his hands and face to a crisp.[609] Some wounded burned to death. Ransom ordered two railcars from Richmond to transfer the two hundred injured.[610]

Moans and cries of men grew louder as the shock of injuries wore off. Colonel Cabell languished beside the railway. He did not need the surgeon to tell him his perforated bowel was mortal. With last words, he dismissed doctors to tend those who might benefit. "I have done my duty; I am not afraid to die."[611] Cabell appeared engaged in prayer and resigned to his fate.[612] The young colonel lost consciousness and died. He was eighteen days shy of his twenty-fourth birthday. The blood of that noble warrior soaked the very land of his ancestor Powhatan.[613]

Trees and smoke had made it impossible for either side to accurately determine the strength of the other. Early in the fight, Barton's 1,600 men outnumbered defenders.[614] The Union assumed themselves attacked by a larger force. By end of the fight, Union reinforcements slammed the balance in their favor. By midafternoon, the bulk of the Union X Corps defended the position.

The 53rd Virginia captured a few new axes and entrenching tools.[615] Ultimately, Ransom's reconnaissance accomplished little at great cost. Ransom diverted attention from himself to Pickett's scapegoat. He blamed Barton for "general want of apparent vigor" and relieved him of command.[616]

While the Battle of Chester Station raged, General Beauregard arrived in Petersburg to relieve Pickett.[617] Beauregard stabilized the town's defense by evening. Pickett collapsed from stress. His breakdown confined him to bed for over a week.[618]

* * *

On May 11, Ransom replaced Barton temporarily with the recently exchanged Colonel Birkett D. Fry.[619] The date marked the second day of Sheridan's Raid. Cavalry clashed at Yellow Tavern, where the irreplaceable J. E. B. Stuart fell mortally wounded.

In the wee hours of May 12, Barton's brigade (Fry) deployed to counter Sheridan. They boarded steamers at Drewry's Bluff for Richmond. They marched to Mechanicsville and patrolled Meadow Bridge Road and Brook Turnpike.

Meanwhile, Fitzhugh Lee's cavalry clashed with Sheridan's force at the Meadow Bridge where the Virginia Central Railroad crossed the Chickahominy River. That same day Barton's brigade (Fry) marched back to Mechanicsville. The marching and countermarching continued two more days trending south to the York River Railroad. Lt. Colonel Griggs commanding the 38th Virginia attributed the apparently senseless movements to "a great want of generalship."[620] This was universally a footsore soldier's view of parrying cavalry with infantry.

Sheridan's Raid ended May 14 upon his reaching Haxall's Landing. The next day Barton's brigade (Fry) marched back to Rockett's Landing, steamed back to Drewry's Bluff, and bivouacked about midnight. The men slept a scant hour and a half before being roused and placed in line of battle east of the Petersburg Turnpike.

While Barton's brigade (Fry) marched after Sheridan, Union General Butler and his Army of the James had pushed toward Richmond. On May 13, Butler's assault took the outermost defense line at Drewry's Bluff and stalled. Union troops dug in while Butler established headquarters in the Half-Way House. Beauregard reinforced Drewry's Bluff with seven brigades under Major General Robert Hoke.

Beauregard arrived at Drewry's Bluff on May 14 to personally take command. He planned an attack for May 18. Pressure from President Davis moved the operation up to May 16. Beauregard with ten brigades in three divisions planned to strike Butler simultaneously head on and on both flanks. In addition, he ordered General Whiting from Petersburg with three brigades to Port Walthall Junction. Whiting was to march to the sound of the guns and attack the Union rear.

At four forty-five a.m. on a chilly May 16, first light illuminated dense fog. Preranged Confederate artillery commenced shelling. Ransom's division attacked with four brigades. Two brigades led abreast with no skirmishers posted. Two brigades followed. They moved forward quietly with orders to hold their fire until reaching the enemy's works.[621]

Barton's brigade (Fry) followed Hoke's brigade (Lewis) across Kingsland Creek and then through a heavy abatis. Once past the obstacle, Hoke's brigade (Lewis) began taking casualties. They increased their pace leaving a trail of dead and wounded. Their line outdistanced Barton's men by more than forty paces and disappeared in the fog. The brigade then split and uncovered Barton's (Fry) front.

Bullets whizzed wildly into Barton's (Fry) ranks from the dense, smoky fog. Officers encouraged men forward. Each thud, each cry signaled a comrade hit. The men assumed the friendly unit was still before them. Some may have sensed it odd that they had stopped stumbling over fallen Tar Heels.

Barton's brigade (Fry) blindly marched right up to the log and earth breastworks. They were only twenty yards away when muskets volleyed in their faces. Lt. Colonel Griggs of the 38th Virginia took a bullet in his left thigh. The line recoiled. Captain George Martin, Company I, assumed command and rallied the regiment. Other regiments re-formed likewise.

Barton's brigade (Fry) resumed the attack. They returned fire at muzzle flashes in the mist. The musketry exchange was horrific. Casualties mounted rapidly. One captain declared the firefight at close range worse than at Gettysburg.[622] The rest of Ransom's division rolled up the enemy's flank. Unable to see in the fog, Union regiments imagined themselves outnumbered. One after another, their units broke and fled.

The enemy before Barton's brigade (Fry) stood firm. The heavy musketry exchange continued. In Company B, 38th Virginia, 20 percent were hit. Franklin Collins fell dead. Samuel Dunn took a ball in the thigh. A bullet in his left leg doomed John L. Gregory to fatal amputation. Caleb Adkins and three more went down. Five others headed to the rear.

As ammunition ran low, the 9th Virginia misunderstood the command to retire. Instead, they charged with a yell.[623] The other regiments followed and overran the breastworks. The enemy threw down their rifles. They soon realized how few took them and vainly tried to retake their arms. The Rebels ushered them away.

The Union right had fallen. Ransom's division boasted three hundred prisoners and four stands of colors. An ammunition shortage thwarted further advance, but the division had achieved its objective. Ransom's attack took the enemy by such surprise that they fled leaving their frying pans and coffee pots on the fires. Many Rebels broke ranks for breakfast and their first real coffee in months, a welcome diversion from brewed parched wheat and other ersatz.[624]

The Union could not be corralled on three sides as Beauregard planned.[625] The battle continued with the divisions of Colquitt and Hoke respectively attacking the Union's center and the left. Corse's brigade pressed hard and turned the enemy's flank.[626] By ten o'clock the fog lifted. Improved visibility stiffened Federal resistance. Beauregard expected Whiting to hit the enemy from behind any moment, but that never happened.

General Whiting had secured Port Walthall Junction as ordered. He did not advance in support, for he missed the signal to attack. Due to acoustic shadow, Whiting and his men failed to hear the gunfire though only miles away. Whiting's failure to attack likely saved Butler's army.

The Union began withdrawing about noon. The Confederates occupied the vacated positions by four o'clock. By nine o'clock that night, Butler's men were safe in their Bermuda Hundred line. The next morning, Beauregard advanced his men and began digging parallel trenches from Dr. Howlett's house to the Appomattox River. Ransom's division dug in at Howlett's under fire from seven Union gunboats on the James River. The shelling destroyed the Howlett mansion. The Howlett Line confined Butler's army to the Bermuda Hundred peninsula. General Grant described Butler's situation as "in a bottle tightly corked."

On May 18, Bragg ordered Beauregard to reinforce Lee at Spotsylvania Court House with three brigades.[627] Barton's brigade (Fry) marched to Chester Station. They boarded trains for Richmond. There they transferred to the RF&P Railroad for transport north. After four hours on over forty miles of worn and hastily repaired track, the brigade detrained at Milford Station and marched for Spotsylvania Court House.[628] The 38th Virginia led the way without field officers. Captain George Martin commanded the regiment.

Apprehensions grew, for the men did not want to rejoin Lee's army.[629] They had already borne the brunt of Lee's greatest missteps at Malvern Hill and Gettysburg.[630] Many feared that rejoining Lee consigned them again to cannon fodder.

After marching fifteen miles, a courier delivered new orders. The battle that had raged at Spotsylvania Court House since May 8 had ended. The brigade reversed directions. On May 20, they arrived at Hanover Court House, hungry and exhausted. The brigade rested. They stood in reserve May 24 through 26 while Lee confronted Grant on the North Anna River. Over the next two weeks they subsisted on meager supplies and foraged rations.

Pickett recovered from his breakdown by May 27. On that date, he and his division reposted to Longstreet's Corps. However, Pickett's division became, as some historians note, a mobile reserve under Lee's direct command. Lee's new role for Pickett strangely paralleled Armistead's special appointment as provost marshal for the Maryland Campaign. The assignment accommodated Pickett's dubious fitness with decorum due his rank and class.[631]

Barton's brigade (Fry) continued to march and counter march between Hanover Court House, Mechanicsville, and Richmond in Lee's anticipations of Grant's next move. The brigade reunited with Pickett's division on May 29; thus ended its detachment since February.

Grant's cavalry seized the crossroads at Old Cold Harbor on May 31. Fighting ensued next day. Pickett's division held a line in support of artillery for the duration of the Battle of Cold Harbor.[632] On June 3, the day of the major Federal attack, Pickett's men found themselves, as at Fredericksburg, unopposed and fixed in place with tremendous fights on their left and especially their right. Grant's men suffered frightful losses. Both armies held their ground and consolidated lines. Mortars and howitzers lobbed shells into hot, dusty breastworks. Riflemen picked at each other under the brutal Virginia sun.

On June 9, Colonel Fry received promotion to brigadier general and took command of his old unit, which had been Archer's brigade.[633] Leadership of Barton's brigade again passed to Senior Colonel William Aylett, 53rd Virginia.

Grant's men disappeared on June 12. He had disengaged and maneuvered around Lee's right to Charles City Court House. Over the next several days, Grant and the Army of the Potomac crossed the James River on steam ferries at Wilcox's Landing and on a pontoon bridge at Weyanoke Point.[634]

Lee suddenly discovered his world upside down. It was as if one minute he had the Army of Northern Virginia interposed between Grant and Richmond, and the next, Richmond lay between it and Grant. Lee scrambled to move his men below Richmond. Barton's brigade (Aylett) marched to Chaffin's Bluff. On June 16, they crossed the James River on a pontoon bridge and took position at Drewry's Bluff.

At dawn June 17, the Union attacked Petersburg and breached the Dimmock Line. In desperation, Beauregard pulled Bushrod Johnson's division off the Howlett Line. This emptied the defenses across Bermuda Hundred and uncorked Butler's troops bottled up there. Lee rushed Pickett's and Field's divisions to fill the void. Before either could act, the Union occupied the abandoned Confederate works.[635] The main lines of communication with Richmond, Petersburg, and the rest of the South lay open and vulnerable.

Pickett's men sallied forth from Drewry's Bluff. Barton's brigade (Aylett) marched the Richmond-Petersburg Turnpike. The poignant route under hot summer sun took them over their scorched battlefields of May.

Barton's brigade (Aylett) joined Pickett's other brigades on the high ground at Winfree's house. Columns of regiments shifted into lines of battle. The 38th Virginia found themselves again at that fateful crossroads of thirty-eight days earlier. The terrain beyond Winfree's dropped and then rose to higher ground on Mrs. Clay's farm, across which, ran the works now occupied by the enemy.[636] Lee ordered Pickett and Field to assault the heights with their divisions. At three p.m. Pickett ordered, "Forward! March!"

Field received an order from Lee canceling his attack just as Pickett's division stepped off with the Rebel yell. "Pickett's men advanced as if the hill at Mrs. Clay's farm was another Cemetery Ridge."[637] They rushed the grassy green high ground crowned with orange clay breastworks. Those works, constructed to defend attack from the opposite direction, proved untenable. The wave of gray and butternut with red battle flags swept the position. The spectacle struck Field's men as irresistible. They, too, charged.

In a ten-minute flurry of musketry, Confederates shot down any who dared resist and captured those who remained. The rest fled to the safety of their original lines, leaving many overcoats, gum blankets, and other useful items.

As the smoke cleared, Pickett received Lee's order canceling the attack. It was too late. His men had already retaken the Howlett Line. One private presented a full canteen of rye whiskey to Colonel Aylett. He gave another to Colonel Henry A. Carrington, 18th Virginia.[638] The swift action incurred minimal casualties. The 38th Virginia suffered one killed and one wounded.

Lee arrived and set up headquarters in Mrs. Clay's house for the rest of the day. The Pittsylvania Regiment would remain on this trench line for nine miserable months.

* * *

June stretched into July with the discomfort, tedium, and monotony of trench warfare. Regiments rotated between camp and the front. Manning fire steps, improving earthworks, and building bombproofs summarized duty. There was always gunfire, shell bursts, bullets, heat, flies, mosquitos, dust or mud, filth, and vermin. Food and water were bad and never enough. Diarrhea was ubiquitous.

Nearby swamps bred malaria.[639] There was no soap and no safe place to bathe. There was no safe place for anything anytime.

There was little intelligence about the enemy in front of them. On July 24, Pickett offered a twenty-day furlough to any man producing an enemy prisoner by daybreak.[640] Patrols ventured out, but the results were undocumented.

At dawn July 30, the earth shook from a great distant explosion. Gunfire erupted in the direction of Petersburg. The Union had exploded a mine! Those on the Howlett Line stood their posts on heightened alert. No unusual activity occurred on their front as the Battle of the Crater played out.

On August 1, George Griggs returned, having recovered from his thigh wound. He resumed command with promotion to full colonel. Captain Martin, Company I, who had served as acting colonel in Grigg's absence, became acting lieutenant colonel.

George King Griggs, Colonel, 38th Virginia Infantry.
(Courtesy James W. Bruce)

Shortly before noon on August 9, shockwaves from another great explosion shook men on the Howlett Line. The blast occurred in the southeast, within enemy lines. Many assumed it another mine. Days later word circulated that Confederate saboteurs had blown up Grant's ammunition wharf at City Point with their newly invented horological torpedo (time bomb).[641]

On August 15, Lee asked Pickett for a brigade to reinforce Chaffin's Bluff, then threatened by Grant's forces at Deep Bottom. Rather than pull a proper brigade off the Howlett Line, Pickett slap-dashed together a brigade from reserve camps. He sent the 14th Virginia and 53rd Virginia along with the 18th Virginia under Colonel Henry A. Carrington.[642]

The 14th Virginia and 53rd Virginia returned to Pickett by August 25, when the division thrust itself forward to advance its picket line. The men attacked at dawn. In a lively musketry exchange, Pickett's men overran rifle pits and captured many prisoners. By nine o'clock the men returned to their original positions at considerable cost. The 38th Virginia suffered fourteen casualties, including two company commanders. Captain W. G. Cabaniss, Company K, was shot in the mouth. Captain Richard Joyce, Company A, was mortally wounded and left to languish in no-man's-land under full August sun. Both sides observed him rise, stagger, and fall throughout the day. A Union soldier heroically rescued Joyce after dark, but the captain died in enemy hands.[643]

* * *

On September 3, General George H. "Maryland" Steuart formally replaced Barton. Steuart had been recently exchanged following capture May 10 while defending the Mule Shoe salient at Spotsylvania Court House.

Senior Colonel William Aylett, 53rd Virginia, was furious. He had expected permanent command with promotion to brigadier general. Aylett had been a field officer in the brigade since Seven Pines. He led the brigade in the interim between Armistead and Barton. He had also commanded the brigade at New Bern and yet again since Fry departed. Aylett threatened to resign but remained in his post.

Steuart's brigade stood inspection for its new general on September 17. It was only brief respite from the front line.

Trench warfare was a hogpen-like existence with constant threat of slaughter. It taxed men physically and mentally to their limits. Desertions increased. Under cover of darkness on October 1, five men from Company I, 38th Virginia, crawled over to the enemy.

Captain Prichard, Company B, 38th Virginia, wounded at Chester Station, returned with a limp and one fewer finger. His thigh wound still gave him trouble. Prichard received temporary assignment as brigade recorder. 1st Lt. Benjamin Clement retained command of Company B.

On October 18, thirty-seven recruits, mostly conscripts, arrived for the 38th Virginia. Company B received six. They welcomed back Bill Hall, an 1861 volunteer who had served in Company B until discharged with a broken arm at Seven Pines. Authorities had reviewed his condition and recalled the twenty-one-year-old.[644] Also among the new arrivals was Raleigh Fuller, an 1861 volunteer discharged just prior to the Maryland Campaign because of age. The revised draft law raised the age limit and forced him to reenlist.[645] The same story applied to Tom Hines, who rejoined Company D.

Medical review recalled Stephen Holland to Company D. Be it remembered that Holland volunteered in 1861 but was immediately discharged from Camp Lee for being physically unfit for drill.[646] More and more, Virginia scraped the bottom of her manpower barrel. Four years of war had bled the Commonwealth dry.

Forty-two more replacements, all conscripts, arrived on October 20. Not everyone received a musket. Those without guns had to wait to acquire one from the captured or fallen.

The Pittsylvania Regiment observed General Lee at their position November 1. He walked their line and studied the enemy with his field glasses.

* * *

The future of the Confederacy was grim. Atlanta had fallen to Sherman on September 2. On October 19, Sheridan's Army of the Shenandoah soundly defeated Jubal Early's Army of the Valley at Cedar Creek. The last real hope for Southern independence hung on the U.S. presidential election. Democratic Party Candidate General George B. McClellan promised to negotiate peace if elected. However, Abraham Lincoln won reelection on November 8.

Union guns delivered the news of Lincoln's victory to Confederate lines with celebratory shot and shell. On November 15, Sherman began his ruthless march to the sea. The Confederate government had run out of options. Only denial of defeat remained.

On the night of November 17, the 38th Virginia and five other regiments swept forward and took the first Union line. The 38th Virginia netted twenty-two rifles and eighteen sets of accoutrements sorely needed by men in the unit. The raid cost the Pittsylvanians one wounded and one captured. It was their last sortie of the year.

Men of the 38th Virginia spent the remaining six weeks of 1864 alternating between the cold, muddy trenches of the Howlett Line and their cheerless camp near Chester Station. On Christmas Eve, Tom Hines, Company D, hoped against hope for a furlough. His understatement speaks volumes as he described his situation as being "on a tired old hill where no pleasure is to be seen."[647]

No Christmas cheer visited the 38th Virginia. Trench mud, filth, vermin, hunger, exposure, constant dangers, privations, sickness, and miseries of every description wore spirits down below thresholds refreshable by words and traditions. The soldiers craved deliverance and real peace, either in this world or the next. To growing numbers, it mattered little which.

CHAPTER FIFTEEN

Their Fight to the Finish

New Year's Day 1865 was cold. Temperatures hovered in the twenties. Sparse rations, frigid weather, constant sniping, shelling, and trench filth beat down the most stalwart. Realities trumped ideals. Optimism joined the long list of shortages. One positive aspect was that mud froze solid.

Soldiers relied heavily on provisions shipped from home. Pilferage grew to the point that one soldier in the 38th Virginia asked his wife to pack "small boxes" due to the uncertainty of receiving them.[648]

On January 19, Lee urged Longstreet to "correct the evils in Pickett's division."[649] Lee held Pickett responsible for a host of deficiencies from loose military discipline and training to inadequate provision for his sick. The division commander's melancholy tainted morale.

Flesh and blood had its limits. Lionheartedness extended those limits. It always had. Yet, as a torrent erodes solid rock, trench duty eroded that spirit.

Colonel Griggs assembled the Pittsylvania Regiment on January 25 in an effort to rally troubled hearts. Griggs then forwarded his wordy, group resolution to newspapers hoping also to counter growing despair at home.

> Whereas it has been represented to us that unworthy persons have circulated statements among those at home that the Army as a whole and ourselves as a regiment have wearied of the War and are willing to submit to such terms as the enemy may impose, that we have lost our confidence in our government and doubt our ability to maintain it:

Therefore, we as members of the 38th Va. Regt. in mass meeting assembled unwilling to submit tamely to these aspersions upon our manhood and fidelity and invoking the aid of Almighty God do resolve,

I. That those who are patriotic and have the good of the cause at heart should not receive with any degree of indulgence the statements of croakers who in prosperity sap the life blood of the country by speculation and extortion and when adversity comes would add to our gloom by their discordant notes asking of the hand of those at home the care of our wives and little ones, we trust we may ever be found defending the right and thus honoring Him who will ever uphold a just and righteous cause;

II. That though we would hail with unbounded joy the coming of peace, yet it can never be such as comes of subjugation and its conditions must be such as only men who have ever been and ever will be free can receive and to this end we pledge our lives, our fortunes and sacred honor;

III. That we still adhere in all confidence to our government and its authorities both civil and military and we hereby pledge them our unfaltering support fully believing that it is the only road to safety and is the only course to be pursued that can receive the smiles and aid of that God who has in keeping the welfare of nations;

IV. That this resolution be published in the Richmond daily and Danville papers.[650]

Even the most stouthearted sickened from poor nutrition and exposure. The list of men unfit for duty grew. On February 5, John Oakes's brother Charles, Company E, 57th Virginia, received medical discharge. Cpl. John Oakes, Company B, 38th Virginia, was the last of the four brothers in the field. Few cousins remained.

Soldiers walked away in growing numbers and took their muskets with them. Leniencies for deserters ended. A court-martial sentenced to death David Baise, Company E, 38th Virginia.[651] On February 10, Steuart's brigade formed three sides of a hollow square around an upright post. Baise marched to the center under guard, accompanied by Rev. Cridlin. After hearing sentence read, the prisoner kneeled and prayed with the chaplain. Baise rose to his feet and shook the preacher's hand. Guards then bound Baise to the pillar. On command, a squad drawn from various companies in the brigade raised their muskets and fired.

The tragic pageant made its point but did little to stem desertions. Personal duty focused increasingly more on survival for one's family. Martyrdom for the cause grew more pointless by the day.

Deserters fleeing south had difficulty avoiding arrest. Provost guards patrolled roads and monitored river crossings. The hills around Callands had sheltered a secret Confederate supply base since 1862.[652] Not surprisingly, the remote highlands provided excellent hideouts for fugitives.

From camp near Chester Station, Tom Hines, Company D, 38th Virginia, warned his wife to watch out for deserters stealing their goods. He also reported bad weather, poor health, and physical weakness. Most of all, he feared the Yankees would reach his home before he did. Hines mirrored the growing feeling that the South then had "no chance of whipping the North."[653]

* * *

On March 4, Mahone's division relieved Pickett's men from the Howlett Line. Steuart's brigade stood inspection on March 6. Pickett reviewed his division next day. They then marched to Drewry's Bluff to resume service as Lee's mobile reserve.

Fresh rumors spread among the Pittsylvanians of retreat to North Carolina through Danville.[654] On March 10, Pickett's division headed that direction. They broke camp, marched to Manchester, and boarded the Richmond & Danville Railroad. Lee's mobile reserve once again moved to counter threats from Sheridan's cavalry.

The war had severely stressed Virginia's railroads. By 1865, wear and disrepair of engines, track, and rolling stock had reduced normal cruising speeds on the Richmond-Danville line to ten miles per hour.

Pickett's division arrived at Burkeville at four p.m. There they manually switched cars to other tracks. The process required five hours. At nine p.m. the train proceeded on the Southside Railroad.[655] The nighttime jaunt carried them through Rice's Depot. They crossed the Appomattox River over High Bridge and detrained at Farmville. There they bivouacked trackside and awaited orders. No enemy cavalry materialized.

This was the closest the Pittsylvania Regiment and Pickett's other Piedmont units had been to home since muster in 1861. This proximity proved the deciding factor for some war-weary souls. Hopping off a slow-moving railcar or slipping away at Burkeville or Farmville were equally easy. All occurred. When Pickett's division boarded the train on March 12 to return to Manchester, there were fewer heads.

That day, George Harvey, Company E, 38th Virginia, entered Farmville Hospital with a "sprained ankle." James Alfred Oakes, Company B, 38th Virginia, missed roll call. Oakes appeared five days later at Farmville Hospital with an injured hip.[656] Both men had likely jumped from the train.

Cumulative gloom invited intoxication. Numbers of men and officers downed liquor purchased in Farmville.[657] Colonel Griggs placed Captain Grubbs, Company C, under arrest for drunken disobedience.[658]

On March 14, the men cooked three days of rations, crossed the bridge to Richmond, and boarded the RF&P Railroad for the ten-mile ride to Atlee Station. They detrained late that night and bivouacked. The next day they skirmished near Ashland. They marched and countermarched for days. Their patrol ended with bivouac a mile beyond New Huntley Ford.[659]

On March 18, they reached the Mechanicsville Turnpike, marched all day, and halted behind the defenses atop Chickahominy Bluffs.[660] There Pickett reportedly suffered loose bowels. This common enough affliction was curiously convenient for Pickett. He placed his division under Steuart and then rode into Richmond to convalesce at home with his wife and baby son.[661]

Esprit de corps had atrophied in the Howlett Line. Willingness to fight had waned. Roll calls revealed 512 men had deserted Pickett's division since leaving Drewry's Bluff (145 from Steuart's brigade). This represented fully three quarters of all desertions in Longstreet's Corps for that same period.[662] As bad as comparisons with desertions in other divisions reflected on Pickett, the train ride to Farmville had effectively given potential deserters a ride halfway home.

On March 19, the division rose at three a.m. and marched to fortifications on the Charles City Road. The next day they shuffled to another camp behind the defenses on Nine Mile Road.

On March 21, Pickett's division (Steuart) stood review for the new Secretary of War Major General John Cabell Breckinridge.[663] Governor "Extra Billy" Smith and many ladies attended. The Pittsylvania Regiment, once staffed by the secretary's cousins, was then devoid of near kin. The regiment and brigade spent the next three days drilling in camp.

Spirits improved in the two weeks removed from the trenches. Determination to fight rekindled upon realization that, no matter what, the lions of the Dan had to keep themselves between the enemy and their homes. The lion analogy held as true as ever, for the darker the night, the bolder the lion.[664]

* * *

In a desperate gamble, Lee approved General John B. Gordon's plan to attack Fort Stedman. The Petersburg defenses spread Lee's forces dangerously thin. A breakthrough at that Union stronghold would shorten the defense line and concentrate manpower.[665] On March 24, Lee ordered Pickett's division to Petersburg to reinforce Gordon. He also warned Gordon that Pickett's men may not arrive in time to support the predawn assault scheduled next day.

Pickett's division (Steuart) started for Petersburg. Steuart's brigade (Aylett) was first to move. They stepped off a half hour after sunset. They marched into Richmond, rode railcars to Drewry's Bluff, and marched the Petersburg Turnpike through the night. At four a.m. gunfire flashed and thundered before them. The attack had begun. At sunrise, sounds of battle tapered off as Steuart's brigade (Aylett) reached town. The fight was over. Fort Stedman had joined the growing list of Confederate debacles.

Steuart halted the brigades of Terry and Corse at Swift Creek. Steuart's brigade (Aylett) rested at arms in Petersburg throughout the day. The next morning, they proceeded through town into the works at Battery No. 45 on the Boydton Plank Road. General Pickett returned to duty.

The elusive Sheridan and his cavalry joined Grant on March 29 and moved past the Confederate right. This threatened the Southside Railroad, Richmond's key supply line.

Lee required his mobile reserve to supplement his shortage of cavalry more than ever. Three of Pickett's brigades boarded the Southside Railroad for a short hop to Sutherlin Station.[666] The troops detrained late night and rested while Lee met with Generals Pickett, R. H. Anderson,[667] and Harry Heth.

Pickett was to move his men to the far right along with Wallace's and Ransom's brigades borrowed from Anderson's Corps. Fitz Lee's and Rosser's cavalry would support. The goal was to push the Union back to Dinwiddie Court House, away from the Southside Railroad.

Lee ordered Hunton's brigade, Pickett's detached unit, to Manchester. There it could more easily deploy to Burkeville to defend the Richmond & Danville Railroad or shift to Petersburg as needed.[668] By the time Hunton moved, the situation demanded his brigade detrain at Sutherlin Station to reinforce Bushrod Johnson's division on White Oak Road.

March 30 was cold and rainy. Pickett's column advanced about noon down White Oak Road. They skirmished with the enemy the whole four miles in a cold drizzle and waded water on muddy roads. They reached Five Forks late afternoon, positioned their lines of battle at the crossroads, and remained at arms throughout the night.

On March 31, Pickett pushed toward Dinwiddie Court House. Corse's and Terry's brigades advanced against stubborn resistance while Steuart's brigade followed in reserve. The enemy yielded reluctantly. Just to the east, Anderson's Corps fended off attacks along White Oak Road as Union advances attempted to isolate Pickett. The fighting halted at dark.

Probes revealed Pickett faced massive Union cavalry supported by infantry. Rather than remain in an exposed position, Pickett ordered his men back to Five Forks. They readied themselves in predawn darkness and moved at first light. Brightening sky gave shape and color to surroundings as they trudged the mud back to the crossroads.

The men reached the intersection midmorning. Pickett telegraphed his situation to Lee. Lee responded:

> Hold Five Forks at all hazards. Protect road to Ford's Depot and prevent Union forces from striking the Southside Railroad. Regret exceedingly your forced withdrawal, and your inability to hold the advantage you gained.[669]

Cold, wet, hungry men spent hours digging rifle pits in red mud with bayonets, tin plates, cups, and bare hands. Steuart's brigade held the center. On their right, three guns under noted artillerist Willie Pegram went into battery at the forks. Three other guns covered the extreme Confederate right and four guns posted to General Ransom on the extreme left. Artillerists thought their deployment at the crossroads offered a dubious field of fire. One later commented, "Pickett knew far more about brands of whiskey than he did about the uses of artillery."[670]

About noon, Custer's cavalry probed the Confederate right and center. Artillery and musketry repelled the enemy at all points. Choruses of "Dixie" and "The Bonnie Blue Flag" burst forth from Steuart's men and others at the forks.[671] Their resolve was evident.

The smoke cleared. The sun came out from behind white clouds in blue sky and glowed warm. Red mud roads and earthworks crisscrossed the green landscape. Gray hardwoods bore their first yellow-green shoots. Apple and peach orchards bloomed within sight of the line. Hours passed. It was as if a truce had been declared to enjoy that spring day. Some napped while others kept vigil.

During that lull, a lone courier trotted up and delivered a message to Pickett. He read it, put Steuart in charge, and, without explanation, trotted away down Ford's Depot Road. Pickett was on his way to a shad bake on the far side of Hatcher's Run.

Steuart inspected defenses while Pickett enjoyed shad and whiskey.[672] Meanwhile, Union infantry, outnumbering Pickett's men three to one, moved undetected into the gap on the Rebel's left. They struck at four o'clock.

The leftmost brigade under Matt Ransom gave way upon the opening volley. Wallace, next in line, reverse wheeled his brigade away from their works into the open to face the onslaught pouring around Ransom. In desperation, Steuart directed Colonel Griggs and his 38th Virginia behind Ransom in an attempt to check the blue flood. Griggs pushed his men at the double quick, deployed the 38th Virginia in a single rank, and poured fire into the blue tide. The 38th Virginia made a stand with little ammunition. Courage alone was not enough.

Pickett? Where was Pickett? No one knew.

Griggs sent a runner to Steuart to report his flank turned. By then Union troops fired into the rear of the 38th Virginia. Heavily outnumbered, ammunition depleted, and their one and only escape route throttled, there was no remedy for panic. The 38th Virginia broke as Griggs ordered retreat. A few fought their way free with clubbed muskets. The rest were overwhelmed and threw down their arms.

Pickett arrived after evading capture on his two-mile return ride. When he reached the field, his left had already been forced back half a mile. Pickett was "thoroughly 'rattled.'"[673] Griggs presented his plight. The general replied, "I know it. Can't help it. I've done all I can."[674] A wagon rumbled past at speed bearing the mortally wounded Willie Pegram from his abandoned guns.

Virtually all of Wallace's and Ransom's brigades were captured. The remnants of Steuart's and Terry's ran for their lives. Only Corse's brigade retired in any semblance of order and acted as rearguard.

The Union V Corps captured over three thousand prisoners, the four guns of Pegram's battery, and eleven battle flags. Among the flags taken from Steuart's brigade were those of the 9th Virginia, 14th Virginia, and likely that of the 53rd Virginia. Sheridan's cavalry captured an additional three guns and 1,500 prisoners.

Pickett's shattered command splashed across Hatcher's Run. Union cavalry flushed men from the woods until nightfall. Those who escaped made their way to the Southside Railroad. The scant remnants of the 38th Virginia rallied around Colonel Griggs and the regiment's colors. Its companies resembled squads.

Most of Company B had been captured including 2nd Lt. Whitmell Adkins, Bill Hall, and Henry B. Fuller. Hall had been recalled to duty in October after having been discharged for injury at Seven Pines. Fuller was one of the five Gettysburg captives from Company B exchanged just weeks before. All five had not only survived the horrors of Fort Delaware and Point Lookout but refused furloughs to return to their company to fight.[675] Fuller and three other exchanged prisoners found themselves recaptured. The fifth repatriate, George Blair, lay dead on the field.

Only eight members of Company B escaped: 1st Lt. Benjamin Clement, 2nd Lt. James Warren, 3rd Cpl. John Oakes, Green Allen, Waddy and Raleigh Fuller, Chris Gregory, and Jake Hendrick.

Once re-formed, Pickett's units moved toward Exeter Mills. Pickett expected to cross the Appomattox River there and rejoin Lee's army. They marched Ford's Depot Road (now Courthouse Road, Rt. 627) to Exeter Mill Road (Rt. 611). Days of rain had swollen the Appomattox. Upon reaching Exeter Mills at daybreak, the water was too high to cross.[676] They had to seek another crossing upstream.

Artillery had boomed throughout the night. They knew not what it meant. Grant had broken Lee's defense line.[677] Lee ordered retreat.

* * *

News of Grant's breakthrough reached Secretary of War Breckinridge by midmorning. He relayed the message to President Davis as he sat in church.[678] Breckenridge arranged for government evacuation to Danville by rail. Davis fled Richmond about eleven p.m. on the last train.[679]

Major Isaac Carrington, Provost Marshal of Richmond, ordered the tobacco warehouses on Cary Street burned.[680] Confederates also blew up the arsenal and ammunition stores on Brown's Island. Flames spread quickly and engulfed the city's business district.

Thus, men with ties to the 38th Virginia figured prominently in the last hours of the Confederate capital. Isaac Carrington was the unit's first major. Both Breckenridge and Carrington were near kin to each other and the Cabells.

* * *

Pickett's remnants moved west. Steuart's brigade waded Horsepen Branch and made their way to Deep Creek (Rt. 623 to Rt. 708, then Rt. 622 and Rt. 612). There they discovered both the river and creek unfordable. The men halted for the night. A courier brought word of Richmond's evacuation and Lee's retreat toward Amelia Court House.

Their march west resumed late morning April 3. They backtracked (Rt. 612 to Rt. 708) and crossed Deep Creek upstream (Rt. 153). On April 4, they formed a line of battle to fend off cavalry at Tabernacle Church just before Beaverpond Creek. They marched early April 5 (Rt. 153 to Rt. 38) and reached Amelia Court House at dawn.

They had reconnected with the army. Weary soldiers rested, but empty stomachs received nothing.

The march proceeded that night parallel to the Richmond & Danville Railroad to Jetersville and then to Amelia Springs (U.S. Rt. 360, then Rt. 642). They continued without rest April 6 to Deatonsville (the intersection of Rts. 616 and

617). Cavalry harassed them at Holt's Corner (the intersection of Rts. 617 and 618). They fended off attackers and then proceeded (Rt. 617). They passed the Hillsman house and crossed Sailor's Creek.[681] The remnants of Pickett's division ascended the hill to Marshall's Crossroads (the intersection of Rts. 617 and 620). There they formed lines of battle.

Three distinct fights developed. Union infantry attacked Ewell's position overlooking the Hillsman house, cavalry attacked Pickett, and infantry attacked Gordon's column at the Lockett house.[682] Each fight was quick and desperate.

Custer's cavalry overran the crossroads. Pickett's command disintegrated. Pickett escaped.

When Steuart's brigade re-formed, each regiment numbered less than one hundred, scarcely company strength. Both the 38th Virginia and 57th Virginia had lost their colors. Cavalry had captured Raleigh Fuller and Jake Hendrick. This reduced Company B, 38th Virginia, to six men.

The survivors trudged through Rice's Depot (Rt. 600) and on to Farmville. Desperate for food, they arrived late in the night only to discover that they had missed the supply train. It had stopped, briefly dispensed rations to a few troops, then moved a safer distance to Pamplin. Again, as at Amelia Court House, empty stomachs received nothing.

On April 7, weak from starvation, they crossed the Appomattox River and slogged northward (Rt. 45). They pushed past Cumberland Church and turned west (Rt. 636). Gunfire sounded behind them as they bivouacked beyond New Store. Up at first light April 8, they turned south on the courthouse road (Rt. 24) and halted about a quarter mile west of New Hope Baptist Church, about three miles shy of Appomattox Court House. The 38th Virginia, alongside the other remnants of Pickett's division, dug in across the road. Those few with bayonets picked at the dirt while weary, bare hands scooped it out.

On April 9, they abandoned their puny works about nine a.m. They moved about a mile to a reserve position on high ground at the village ironically named Pleasant Retreat. They stood at arms into the afternoon.

At three forty-five p.m., Lee surrendered.

* * *

On April 10, dark skies cast gloom over Danville. It rained throughout the day. The Confederate government had moved there a week earlier to keep the capital in Virginia. President Davis lodged at the home of Major William T. Sutherlin. The striking new mansion built two years before the war overlooked the town from the top of Main Street.

In 1861, Sutherlin owned the second largest tobacco factory in the state. He was mayor of antebellum Danville and a delegate at Virginia's secession convention. His health kept him from active service, but he held the rank of major as quartermaster for Danville. His once bustling tobacco factory served as a prison for Union soldiers.[683] Sutherlin lost his brother George early in the war, a second lieutenant in the 38th Virginia.

A courier arrived about three o'clock in the afternoon to report Lee's surrender. President Davis conveyed the news to his cabinet. There was no planned contingency as there had been for their flight from Richmond.[684] The government scurried throughout the afternoon and evening to load an evacuation train south. Although recently completed, the Piedmont Railroad was a different gauge and inferior to the Richmond-Danville line. It terminated in Greensboro just fifty miles away, but it remained the best escape option.

The gray, overcast sky forced early darkness. Governor "Extra Billy" Smith arrived in Danville and sought the president. The two men greeted each other. Davis informed Smith of Lee's surrender.[685] Smith had fled Richmond via Lynchburg. It was the first news he had of Lee.

Davis needed to flee and focused on packing. Smith excused himself and repaired two blocks down to the home of Witcher Keen.

Sutherlin's servants loaded Davis's effects into the carriage. Once satisfied, Davis bid farewell to his hostess, Jane Sutherlin. She asked the president if he had money other than Confederate paper. The president affirmed he did not. She offered a pouch containing $1,000 in gold. Davis declined the offer. He fatalistically added he reckoned he should not need anything for very long.[686] Davis stepped from the porch of his last capitol. Confederate Virginia was history.

Major Sutherlin accompanied Davis to his train. Four years earlier, Sutherlin was one of four secession convention delegates who personally escorted Robert E. Lee to the capitol for his formal appointment as commander of Virginia's military.[687] Thus, W. T. Sutherlin was a unique presence at the beginning and the end.

The carriage followed its lantern beams down Sutherlin's driveway. Directly ahead in the impenetrable darkness was the vacant lot where the Danville Military Academy had stood until razed in 1864.[688] The military school existed for only one year and three months. It closed at the start of the war. Its principal, Edward C. Edmonds, raised the 38th Virginia Volunteer Infantry, the Pittsylvania Regiment. The gallant young colonel perished at Gettysburg with Armistead.

On the same azimuth just over the brow of the hill was Grove Street Cemetery. There lay Edmonds's premier cadet and successor, Colonel Joseph R. Cabell, and his brother Lieutenant Benjamin E. Cabell, both officers in the 38th Virginia, both sacrificed to the cause. Both men lay buried at the feet of their father, Major General Benjamin W. S. Cabell, the cornerstone of early Danville. He, too, was arguably a casualty of the war. Six sons fought for the Confederacy. The Cabells were descendants of the great Chief Powhatan through his daughter Pocahontas.

The carriage turned right onto Main Street. Mud muffled hoof clops. In two-tenths of a mile, the solemn passengers reached the corner of Jefferson Avenue. On their right was the Episcopal church. The two men had observed Palm Sunday there the day before. That dismal night, the locked, dark building with its bullet-shaped doorways appeared as Godforsaken as their cause.

Directly opposite the church was the residence of Witcher Keen, host to Governor Smith. Witcher's brother Elisha Keen was the major whose battalion became the core of the 57th Virginia, Lewis Armistead's first Confederate command, and later, a regiment in Armistead's brigade.

Thus, the carriage rolled past unperceived tokens of noble hearts, daring deeds, devotions to duty, and personal sacrifices—of heroisms second to none. Defeat brought their collective efforts to naught. That thought was unbearable.

In coming years, lost cause myths emerged to facilitate reconciliation. Selective remembrances of "Pickett's Charge" marginalized the soldiers of Pettigrew and Trimble. They elevated Armistead and Pickett to niches in the Southern pantheon of heroes and eclipsed the better men they commanded. The lives of Edmonds, Whittle, Griggs, the Cabells, the Carringtons, and other lions of the Dan emerge for consideration a century and a half later.

* * *

Lee's men bided their time until the completion of paroles and formal surrender ceremony. Lee's headquarters pitched tents with Longstreet's Corps. Circumstances prevailed upon Waddy Fuller, Company B, 38th Virginia, to cook for headquarters. Cpl. John Oakes carried three pones of cornbread to General Lee. Oakes had had nothing to eat since before Sailor's Creek. Temptation proved too great. Oakes wolfed down one of the pones, thinking it would never be missed.

Lee asked Oakes how many pieces were on the plate when he started out. Oakes, fearful of punishment, begged the general's pardon and confessed he had eaten one. Lee asked him when he had last eaten. Upon hearing the soldier's plight, Lee offered him another. Embarrassed, Oakes declined.[689]

All remnants of Company B, 38th Virginia, had served since June 1861. Their long, hard fight was over. Parole or no, some refused to abide the humiliation of formal surrender. Cpl. John Oakes and other like-minded veterans dissolved into the woods and started home.[690] They never deserted their colors. Their colors were no more.

Men from other commands also escaped Appomattox. Many of these avoided paroles to make their way south to continue the fight near their homes, where the war still raged.

On April 12, four years to the day after the firing on Fort Sumter, Lee's Army formally stacked arms for the last time. There were surprisingly few to stack. Some had dropped their muskets at Five Forks, some at Sailor's Creek. Some were too weak to carry them on retreat and dropped them along the road. Others broke them against trees and scattered the pieces rather than yield them to Yankees. Pickett's division surrendered about a thousand men. Among them were only fifty-three muskets and not a single battle flag.[691]

Colonel Griggs, being the only remaining field-grade officer in the unit, surrendered Steuart's brigade. The brigade had once been Armistead's.[692]

The 38th Virginia, the Pittsylvania Regiment, numbered only nine officers and eighty-one men, the equivalent of a company. Only four represented Company B: Capt. Prichard, who returned from staff to surrender with his company; 2nd Lt. James Warren; Waddy Fuller, the cook; and Christopher Gregory, often detailed as brigade blacksmith. Be it remembered that Gregory was severely wounded while carrying the colors at Malvern Hill. He was also the lone survivor of four brothers.

Most companies boasted similar numbers. Company K had the most, with fourteen.

The lions of the Dan headed home ragged. Many were barefoot. Pittsylvanians trudged through Campbell Court House (now Rustburg). They turned south along what was in colonial times the tobacco rolling road. They consumed what was in their haversacks and begged morsels along the way. There was much foot traffic, for it was the main route home for many of Lee's men returning to the Deep South.

Ward's Bridge (Rt. 640) over the Staunton River had been burned, forcing them downstream a mile to Dew's Ferry.[693] Once across the river, they were back in Pittsylvania County. At least another two-day walk remained to reach Callands or Danville. The Pittsylvanians were home again and at peace.

* * *

Although the war had destroyed much in Virginia, Pittsylvania soldiers returned to find their farms much as they had left them. Many households suffered acute food shortages, but no battles or raids ravaged their county. Infrastructure remained intact. Moreover, wartime Danville had benefited economically, largely the result of businesses relocated there from threatened areas.[694]

John Oakes would have beaten his friends home, but a Union patrol caught him without parole papers and sent him to Richmond until he took the oath of allegiance.[695] John had enlisted on first call in 1861 and fought all four years. Defeat for him was bitter indeed.

John's brother Charles was already home, having received medical discharge months prior. Brother James lay yet in a hospital in Thomasville, North Carolina, recovering from the canister wound received the previous year at Chester Station.[696] James Oakes was released upon surrender of Joseph Johnston's army on April 26, making him the last of the Pittsylvania Regiment.[697]

The Oakes brothers resumed their tobacco farming as before the war but without brave Thomas, last seen on Cemetery Ridge. The war forever affected their lives but did nothing to alter their way of life. Their soil was indifferent to whether its tillers won or lost.

Friends and neighbors whom the war had not crippled or maimed also returned to prewar routines. Those most blessed still possessed a draft animal and the physical wherewithal to work their fields. Former drudgeries acquired fresh perspectives. Plowing behind a farting mule now evoked thanksgiving to God.

Those who faired best, in life and death, relied on Him who doeth all things well. Survivors gloried in the Lord, their Deliverer, not in deliverance by their own hand or fickle fate. These put the war behind them and moved on.

Captain William Bond Prichard, the commander of Company B, 38th Virginia, went on to serve as an assistant professor at VMI for several years. He then moved to California and purchased a ranch. He married the youngest daughter of the late General Albert Sydney Johnston.[698] Prichard worked in San Francisco as a civil engineer and served as superintendent of Golden Gate Park and city assessor. He also grew fruit.[699]

Captain John "Jack" Taylor Averett, the prewar educator who served as quartermaster for the Pittsylvania Regiment, returned to Danville. In 1867, Averett became headmaster of the Danville Male Academy. He later served as principal of Danville's first public school system. He and his brother Samuel cofounded Averett College, which is today Averett University.[700]

Colonel George King Griggs, the last commander of the 38th Virginia, returned to his farm. Being "distinctly a man of great executive force and judgement," Griggs went to work for the Danville & Western Railroad. He advanced to general superintendent and treasurer. He was a pillar of his Baptist church, a prominent Mason, and a trustee of Averett College.[701]

Last, but not least, Colonel Powhatan Bolling Whittle returned to Georgia and resumed his law practice.[702] He served in that state's legislature and was judge of the Macon Corporation Court.

It is noteworthy to add that Powhatan's brother Lt. William Conway Whittle Jr. was executive officer aboard the commerce raider CSS *Shenandoah*. On November 6, 1865, the ship docked in Liverpool, England and lowered the last Confederate flag. William Whittle was the last descendant of Chief Powhatan to surrender.[703]

* * *

The 38th Virginia Volunteer Infantry Regiment, the Pittsylvania Regiment, was but one pride of lions of the Dan. They were unique and yet representative of the Armistead-Barton-Steuart brigade and Southside Virginia soldiers in general.

After being declawed and defanged at Appomattox, the lions returned to their habitats unmolested and so remained to the end of their days. The threats that had driven them to bay were no more.

Thirty years after the war a former private of Armistead's brigade wrote, "That we believed then we were right and that we believe now that we were right then."[704] The twice asserted "then" relegated past conviction to popular delusion.[705]

The lions of the Dan endured four bloody years in the vortex of national upheaval. Each had as much say in the matter as their tobacco seedlings in where to be planted. Often commanded by jackasses and governed by snouts in the trough, they fought as lions. Collectively, they were the best of men "snared in an evil time."

* * *

North and South had sowed the wind and reaped the whirlwind.[706] Federal authority triumphed. The war overthrew secession and ended bond slavery. Regional animosities persisted. FFV oligarchy still dominated Virginia's politics, learning, and culture.[707] Nowhere did black freedmen find acceptance as equals.[708] Another century would pass before the latter two situations changed.

Historians and hobbyists still debate the war. Generally, Northerners assert it was all about slavery. Southerners claim it was over states' rights—albeit, an inbred aristocracy's right to preserve wealth and class through slavery. Fundamentally, had there been no secession, there would have been no war.

President Lincoln exercised federal authority by force of arms to preserve the Union. Economics drove support for the war as much as any ideals victors advanced to the fore. One need only recognize cotton as the primary feed stock for the Industrial Revolution to know that is true.

Although slavery was an abomination, a stench in the nostrils of God, the federal government placed financial interests above abolition. Lincoln issued the Emancipation Proclamation primarily to avert foreign recognition of the Confederacy.[709]

Ever since the first English colonists landed at Jamestown, money has always been the warp and weft of national fabric. Much of the fabric is coarse and ugly. It reeks of tobacco and rum. Greed stained it with the blood, sweat, and tears of every race. Nevertheless, true hearts in each generation embroidered patches of magnificence upon it to the glory of God. The frequency and degree to which this occurred makes the United States of America truly unique. May true hearts always prevail.

If one requires a single reason for the American Civil War, the author believes one need look no further than wise King Solomon's observation three millennia before Fort Sumter: "…money answereth all things."[710] That has been true ever since the Phoenicians invented money.

For soldiers North and South, it was a rich man's war and a poor man's fight.

Their devotion and courage still resonate.

Soli Deo Gloria!

A PARTING THOUGHT:

Furled, but Not Forgotten

Every battle flag of the Armistead-Barton-Steuart brigade was either destroyed or captured in desperate fights. The federal government eventually returned the captured flags to the Commonwealth of Virginia. Many are preserved today at the American Civil War Museum in Richmond, Virginia.

The battle flag of the Army of Northern Virginia endures as the preeminent symbol of the Southern Confederacy. Most refer to its likeness simply as the *Confederate flag*. The pattern evokes strong emotions today: reverence or contempt, pride or hate. Beholders may justify them all.

The author personally views the Confederate flag with ambivalent awe. The device represents an evil time that trapped a nation. Ancestor James Lafayette Oakes, a private in Company B, 38th Virginia, and relatives on both sides lived that inescapable nightmare.

Although designers arguably incorporated Christian symbolism per heraldic tradition, the true symbolism of the Confederate flag is inescapable. The cruciform constellation represented slave states. Their bleached-white stars shined profanely from a night sky of slave-cultivated indigo.

The Confederate flag is a war prize, a national trophy. In defeat, its blood-red field boasts the dark Southern Cross upon which the Confederate star cluster is forever crucified.

Author with battle flag of the 38th Virginia Infantry captured at Gettysburg. (Photo for author by Cathy Wright, Curator, American Civil War Museum)

ENDNOTES

Introduction

1 "And if a house be divided against itself, that house cannot stand" (Mark 3:25 KJV).

2 The diary of Colonel George King Griggs was last sold at auction in 2013 for $11,000.00. The Eleanor S. Brockenbrough Library maintains a photocopy for study.

3 As it happens, the bibliography of G. Howard Gregory's *The Thirty-Eight Virginia Infantry* includes this writer's embarrassing embryonic effort, a monograph circa 1978 entitled "The Oakes Family in the Civil War."

4 *Murder at Green Springs: The True Story of the Hall Murder Case, Firestorm of Prejudices.*

Chapter One: Southside Virginia: An Antebellum Primer

5 Time-honored myths dissolve before modern scholarship. Pocahontas's story surfaces more as tragedy than romance. Her kidnapping by Jamestown colonists and her hostage status brought an end to the First Anglo-Powhatan War. Her questionable conversion to Christianity and subsequent marriage to John Rolf were both political and economic expediency. Dr. Custalow presents a credible case for Pocahontas as a victim of both rape and murder. Read Price as well as Custalow and Daniel. See Isenberg, p. 9.

6 Isenberg, pp. 17–42.

7 At the Louisa County Historical Society meeting on December 8, 2002, Louis M. Markwith, chief development officer for the Jamestown-Yorktown Foundation, described strong archaeological evidence for African Christians at Jamestown. Markwith attested to discovery of a crucifix unearthed at Jamestown with a Christ bearing breasts! Markwith reported such objects were characteristic of evangelized, matriarchal societies along the Ivory Coast.

8 "The standard justification of slavery in the seventeenth century was that

captives taken in war had forfeited their lives and might be enslaved." Morgan, p. 233. Jews, Moors, and Mohametans were all accounted heathens. Ballagh, p. 63.

9 Morgan, p. 297.

10 Ballagh, p. 44.

11 Ballagh, p. 48.

12 Ibid., p. 53.

13 Conflict with Virginia Puritans and Maryland Royalists culminated in the Battle of the Severn in 1655. Some historians argue this action on American soil as the last battle of the English Civil War.

14 Isenberg, p. 27. The Bible recognized slaves as a social class with rights. The New Testament admonishes Christians under Roman rule to "Give servants (slaves) what is just and fair" (Colossians 4:1). However, slave laws in Virginia bore no such intent, nor did they anywhere in the South. Furthermore, the Fugitive Slave Laws of 1793 and 1850 established by the U.S. Constitution, Article IV, Section 2, Clause 3, again mirrored traditional Roman bond servitude, not those of Scripture. The Book of Deuteronomy defies all defenses of fugitive slave laws. "You shall not give up to his master a slave who has escaped from his master to you" (Deut. 23:15). There is simply no biblical support for Southern style slavery. None!

15 Ballagh, p. 91.

16 Englishmen of means considered the poor, black or white, bound or free, as racial inferiors. Morgan, pp. 321–329.

17 Ironically, some historians consider the Battle of the Severn March 25, 1655, the victory of Puritan militia over Maryland's Governor Stone, as the last battle of the English Civil War.

18 Garber, p. 12.

19 Siegel, p. 72.

20 Farmer, "Patterns of Country Trade: Merchants, Locations, Structures," pp. 113–134.

21 At this writing, the original Pittsylvania County clerk's office and court house/gaol stand restored and preserved at Callands. These are generally open to the public during the Callands Festival each October.

22 The naming of present-day Chatham is confusing. Depending on the source, its original name, Competition, predates relocation of the county seat there. Even so, it was not until 1807, years after it became the county seat that Vir-

ginia's legislature officially named the town Competition. Although Civil War era maps list the town as Competition or Competition C.H., citizens of Competition appear to have referred to their town as Chatham before, during, and after the war. The Virginia General Assembly did not officially rename the town Chatham until 1874.

23 The marriage ceremony was conducted by Moses Hoge, then president of Hampden-Sydney.

24 Site is now the NE corner of Main and Craighead Street.

25 *History of Danville*, p. 12.

26 *Sketch Book*, p. 20.

27 The boat basin was immediately behind Cabell's house.

28 Clement, p. 240.

29 *The Telegraph* founded in 1822 lasted nine years. *The Reporter* cofounded by Cabell in 1833 evolved into *The Danville Register and Bee*. *History of Danville*, p. 104. *The Danville Register and Bee* is still published at this writing.

30 Colonel William J. Lewis served in the Virginia Legislature. He was also a U.S. congressional representative 1817–1819. Alexander Brown, pp. 240–241. Colonel Lewis married Elizabeth Cabell in 1828 and died shortly thereafter.

31 Bridgewater occupied the current site of Piedmont Mall.

32 Hampden-Sydney College was the last college founded before the Revolutionary War and was named after John Hampden and Algernon Sydney. Both were Puritan leaders and martyrs of religious freedom. Sydney was beheaded by Charles II for involvement in an alleged assassination plot.

33 Ironically, the Great Eclipse of 1831 occurred on February 12, Lincoln's birthday.

34 Subsequent to Nat Turner, Methodist minister Poindexter in Louisa County and a few others freed their slaves. Thomas Jefferson Randolph submitted legislation to abolish slavery. The Slavery Debate of 1832 in the Virginia General Assembly resulted in oppressive slave restrictions, criminalization of abolitionist activity, and prohibition of manumission.

35 Daniels, p. 281.

36 Farmer, pp. 61–62.

37 The Cabell family maintained close contact with their Kentucky kin. Joseph Cabell Breckinridge, father of John Cabell Breckinridge, and B. W. S. Cabell were first cousins. At this writing, John C. Breckinridge remains the youngest man

ever elected to vice president of the United States.

38 Carmichael, *The Last Generation*, p. 51.

39 At least one reference suggests that General Cabell obtained William's appointment to West Point through friendship with President James K. Polk. Nevertheless, Cabell had multiple connections through which to secure such.

40 In 1840, Pittsylvania produced 6,439,000 pounds of tobacco. The county boasted twenty tobacco factories manned by four hundred slaves. Aaron, p. 84.

41 Virginia's white population in 1860 was 1,047,299, of whom only 52,128 owned slaves. Half of that number owned between one and four slaves. Only 114 owned multiple hundreds. See Daniels, p. 282.

42 Siegel, p. 117.

43 B. W. S. Cabell's daughter Pocahontas Rebecca Cabell married Colonel John Tyler Hairston at Bridgewater on August 25, 1836. Alexander Brown, p. 471.

44 Glatthaar, pp. 54–55.

45 Farrow, Lang and Frank provide convincing evidence in *Complicity: How the North Promoted, Prolonged and Profited from Slavery.*

46 In addition to limited employment opportunities, New Jersey passed laws prohibiting free blacks from residing there. Illinois did the same. Indiana's and Oregon's state constitutions prohibited negros and mulattos from settling in those states. Free black transients who remained in Massachusetts longer than two weeks could be flogged. Many Northern states banned resident blacks from voting. Kennedy, pp. 54–57. Such laws forced the Undergound Railroad to compensate. By midcentury, routes that once terminated in free states had become through-express to Canada. By 1860, the term *free state* implied *free white state.*

47 States were then sovereign entities and the people citizens of their respective states. State secession was a recognized right. The Virginia Act of Ratification specifically stated that the powers delegated by the people to the United States may be resumed by them "whensoever perverted to their injury or oppression." Powers belonging to the citizens of the Commonwealth were thus delegated to the federal government, never surrendered. Kennedy, p. 162.

48 The preeminence of Virginians in federal government disenfranchised the New England states to great extent. Thus, New England blamed Madison and the preceding dominance of Virginian presidents, i.e., "The Virginia Dynasty," for causing the War of 1812.

49 Garber, p. 11.

50 Isenberg, p. 177.

51 Robert Williams (slave), Hurmence, p. 26. Also, Charles Crawley (slave) testified, "Old Marse was more hard on them poor white folks than he was on us niggers." Hurmence, p. 5.

52 One needs only read *The Narrative of the Life of Frederick Douglass, an American Slave* to glimpse the brutal life of field hands in the Chesapeake Bay region. However, cotton production in the Deep South depended on the slave trade from southeastern "breeder states" like Virginia. Slaves purchased for south-western labor camps toiled to meet ever increasing cotton quotas and experienced terrors and cruelties to rival any of the notorious slave labor camps of the twentieth century.

53 Melville, "An Antebellum Tragedy on the Old Richmond and Danville Railroad," *The Pittsylvania Packet*, Winter 1993, pp. 3–4.

54 The Danville Blues were established in 1841.

55 Sutherlin was first to employ water driven tobacco presses in his factories. Cooperation of Cabell and Sutherland in establishing the Danville Military Academy is conjecture.

56 Hagan, p. 80, lists the second military instructor as "Major Jesse S. Jones." One notes sufficient errors in Hagan's other information about the Danville Military Academy to cast doubt on Jones. The author finds no record elsewhere of "Major Jesse S. Jones" per se. There are men with similar names, but none correlate sufficiently. Verification of Major Jones remains elusive at this writing. The author submits the possibility that the second instructor may have been John Taylor Averett, headmaster of the Ringold Military Academy. That school may have been assimilated into the Danville Military Academy. Averett was already a trustee of the Union Female College in Danville.

57 Margaret was sister of Edmond's VMI classmate Eli Tutweiler. Per C. Edmonds Allen, the couple met at a cotillion.

58 The Sutherlin mansion was completed in 1859. At this writing, the Mid-Town Market at 1 Chambers Street occupies the site of the Danville Military Academy.

59 Records of the Danville Military Academy are unknown and references sparse. Sutherlin's and General Cabell's role in its creation are speculation based on sundry inferences.

60 This action is speculation consistent with the purpose of the academy.

61 Allen, *The Edmonds Family.*

62 On January 6, 1861, Mayor Wood of New York City proposed partition and formation of an independent city-state. The measure was approved by city council. Implementation was problematic. Commencement of hostilities in April put an end to the plan.

63 Furguson, pp. 32–34.

64 Although Governor Floyd eventually sided with Jackson and Union, Floyd considered advantages to Virginia as the key power in a Southern Confederacy. At the time of the 1832–1833 secession crisis, "Virginia's neighbors worried that they might be trading the tyranny of the North for the tyranny of Virginia." Meacham, p. 234.

65 Furguson, p. 36.

66 John B. Jones, vol. 1, p. 21. Note that although the device was first fashioned in 1831 for state troops mustered against the Nat Turner Rebellion, technically the Commonwealth of Virginia had no official state flag until it was adopted weeks later on April 30, 1861.

67 The Confederate Congress received the bill to move their capital on May 1, passed it on May 20, and adjourned on May 23 to reconvene in Richmond on July 20. North Carolina seceded May 20, 1861. Tennessee seceded June 8, 1861. A convention in Russellville, claiming to represent the people of Kentucky, adopted a secession resolution on November 20, 1861.

68 Furguson, p. 43. The treaty contained provision that it be voided should the public referendum reject secession. Freeman, *R. E. Lee*, vol. 1, p. 487. Even so, ratification of the treaty in the heat of the moment was bound to prejudice referendum votes.

Chapter Two: The Second Revolution

69 Those on the rolls listed as "students" and mustered in on April 23 and 24, 1861, are assumed from the Danville Military Academy. Three appear in each company. Joseph R. Cabell is so listed and known to have been among those from the academy. There may have been others. Not everyone listed occupations.

70 Withers, p. 130.

71 Withers, pp. 128–130. The U.S. Customs House survived the Richmond fire at the end of the war and still serves federal purposes at this writing.

72 Alexander Brown, p. 475.

73 The site of Millbank and Whittle's Mill are located seven miles north of South Hill, Virginia, on Rt. 636 at the Meherrin River. Powhatan Bolling Whittle is buried there.

74 McClurken, p. 14.

75 The actual name of the company organized at Kentuck by Captain Daniel C. Townes on August 20, 1860, is unknown at this writing largely due to its acceptance into Confederate service on May 30, 1861, predated association with the Pittsylvania Regiment. The name Kentuck Grays is the author's assumption. County units created prior to and after John Brown's raid but before the secession crisis were generally designated "Blues" or "Grays" units. The Kentuck company was likely one or the other.

76 Hayes, p. 32. Scant mention of the Ringgold Military Academy exists. It appears the Ringgold Military Academy also formed in reaction to John Brown's raid and just prior to organization of the Danville Military Academy. Since the Averett family was prominent in establishment of the Union Female College in Danville, and John was a trustee, it is reasonable that the Ringgold school may have been absorbed into the Danville Military Academy. At the very least, the Ringgold Military Academy appears to have closed when headmaster Averett joined the Kentuck company May 1861.

77 The Oakes family house near Callands still stands at this writing on the East side of Woodview Drive (Rt. 814), 0.2 miles South of Glenview Drive (Rt. 812).

78 The period term *roundabout* is synonymous with shell jacket, a skirtless version of the military frock coat. For photos of these uniforms, see *Pittsylvania County Virginia Heritage, 1767–2006*, vol. 2. p. 89.

79 Weeks before, the Cascade Rifles spent the night in the hotel in Danville the night before they boarded the train. The author assumes the Pittsylvania Vindicators did likewise. Some may well have been invited into private homes.

80 Camp Lee was named for General Henry "Light-Horse Harry" Lee of Revolutionary War fame, former governor of Virginia and father of Robert E. Lee.

81 Griggs was from Henry County. He attended VMI two years then moved to Cascade in Pittsylvania County and married Sallie B. Boyd. Gregory, *38th Virginia*, pp. 5–6. His leadership of the battalion recorded in Griggs, June 5, 1861.

82 For photos of Hutson and others, see *Pittsylvania County Virginia Heri-*

tage, 1767–2006, vol. 2. p. 89.

83 James Mathew Cabaniss, letter dated June 16, 1861 describing camp life and Holland's discharge.

84 William Bond Prichard. *The Confederate Veteran*, vol. 24. p. 9. VMI Historical Rosters Database.

85 Griggs, June 5, 1861. The pistol was likely a Colt Navy Model 1851 .36 caliber revolver.

86 Henry M. Talley, letter July 6, 1861.

87 Richmond *Dispatch*, June 13, 1861, p. 2.

88 Richmond *Enquirer*, June 15, 1861, p. 3.

89 James Mathew Cabaniss, letter dated June 16, 1861.

90 Powhatan Whittle, letter to James Whittle dated June 22, 1861.

91 McFall, p. 12. McFall suggests the name honored its captain, but it seems more likely it was in honor due General Cabell and/or his family.

92 Gregory, *38th Virginia*, p. 6.

93 Powhatan Whittle, letter to James Whittle dated June 22, 1861.

94 Gregory, *38th Virginia*, p. 6.

95 Governor Letcher transferred all Virginia State forces to Confederate service on June 8, 1861. It appears that new units joined Confederate service as they completed camps of instruction.

96 Henry M. Talley, letter July 6, 1861.

97 Robertson, *Stonewall Jackson*, p. 122.

98 [30] Richmond's Broad Street Station was later built on the site of Camp Lee. At this writing, it is the Science Museum of Virginia. This writer remembers visiting the Confederate locomotive *General* there on brief public display during the Civil War Centennial.

Chapter 3: Elusive Glory

99 Griggs, July 11, 1861.

100 The 4th Brigade of the Army of the Shenandoah under Brigadier General Edmund Kirby Smith consisted of the 1st Maryland, 3rd Tennessee, 10th Virginia, 13th Virginia, and 38th Virginia infantry regiments.

101 William G. Cabaniss, letter dated July 12, 1861.

102 James Booker, letter July 14, 1861.

103 Common practice with revolvers was to rest the hammer on an empty cylinder to prevent accidental discharge. Fully loaded, "battle ready" revolvers and single-shot pistols were always dangerous hazards.

104 James Booker, letter July 14, 1861.

105 Lewis Edmonds purchased Belle Grove farm in 1842. Daughter Amanda Virginia Edmonds mentioned visits by cousin "Ned" in her diary in 1858 and 1859 (see Edmonds, p. 250, n. 21). *Belle Grove* is currently Sky Meadows State Park, 11012 Edmonds Lane, Delaplane, Virginia 20144.

106 Gregory, *38th Virginia*, p. 8. Source of the cow is assumed.

107 Harrell, chapter 4.

108 The 1st Tennessee was among the regiments barred from the fight because of train mishaps. See Watkins, p. 24.

109 Henry M. Talley, letter July 23, 1861.

110 Pittsylvania was the grand mansion built by Landon Carter Jr. (1738–1801), grandson of Robert "King" Carter. Landon Jr.'s son Moore Fauntleroy Carter (1771–1820) married Judith Lee Edmonds. They had seven children. The oldest was Judith, who married Dr. Isaac Henry. The youngest was Helen, who married first cousin Dr. John R. Edmonds. They were parents of Colonel Edward Claxton Edmonds.

111 James "Gentleman Jim" Robinson was the biological son of Landon Carter Jr., Edmonds's great-grandfather. Thus, Robinson was Edmonds's half second great-uncle.

112 J. William Jones, p. 267.

113 Thomas J. Hines, letter dated July 25, 1861.

114 Henry M. Talley, letter July 29, 1861.

115 Cadmus Marcellus Wilcox graduated from West Point in 1946 with Stonewall Jackson, George McClellan, and George Pickett. His brigade consisted of the 8th Alabama, 9th Alabama, 10th Alabama, 11th Alabama, 19th Mississippi, and 38th Virginia.

116 John Henry Hutson, personal information and photo in uniform. *Pittsylvania County Virginia Heritage, 1767–2006*, vol. 2. p. 89. Hutson is mistakenly listed as Hudson in Gregory, p. 103.

117 Ibid.

118 McClurken, p. 16.

119 Ibid., p. 18.

120 2nd Lt. George Sutherlin died December 13, 1861. Gregory, p. 126.

121 McClurken, p. 20.

122 Thomas J. Hines, letter dated September 25, 1861.

123 Gregory, *38th Virginia*, p. 9.

124 Sole source for the court-martial of Col. Edmonds is George K. Griggs, diary entries October 7–14.

125 Edmonds, p. 61, supplies details place of memorial service. Judith Carter Henry is buried in the family plot on Henry Hill.

126 The neighborhood relationships are factual. The personal relationships are probable. Armistead's actual presence at Judith Henry's funeral is conjecture, but consistent with known events and considered highly likely.

127 Though the Armistead listed their address as Upperville, their estate was only four miles by road from both Upperville and Paris.

128 Forty-seven-year-old Dr. John R. Edmonds committed suicide in 1854 over financial difficulties. Allen, "The Edmonds Family," p. 7.

129 Elizabeth Stanly Armistead died September 30, 1861. She is buried in the Armistead cemetery located on Rt. 710 two miles east of U.S. Rt. 17 on a knoll on the far side of Gap Run.

130 Wilcox received promotion to brigadier general on October 21, 1861.

131 Gregory, *38th Virginia*, p. 7. For Griggs's faith, see J. William Jones, p. 480.

132 McClurken, p. 15.

133 The design was adapted from William Miles design for a national flag. Miles first envisioned a St. George's cross. Jewish citizens objected to the blatant incorporation of the "cross of Christ." St. Andrew's cross proved acceptable. See Coski, pp. 5–11. A thirteenth star was added after admission of Kentucky to the Confederacy in December 1861.

134 Kent Brown, *The Confederacy's First Battle Flag*, p. 70.

135 These were known as "second issue silk battle flags."

136 Coski, p. 10.

137 Griggs mentioned receipt of the state flag when reviewed by Governor Letcher. Strangely, Griggs failed to mention issue of the new battle flag even though he records the division review by Generals Johnston and Beauregard.

138 James Brooks, letter dated December 15, 1861.

139 Danville had all leading church denominations except Roman Catholic.

Withers, p. 124. Pittsylvania County hosted mainly Baptist, Methodist and Presbyterian.

140 Ann Cary Carter, wife of Robert Mottram Lewis of Portici, was half sister to Helen Carter Edmonds (Colonel Edmonds's mother). They had no issue. At the time of the Battle of Manassas, other kin resided at Portici.

141 James Booker, letter dated December 15, 1861.

Chapter Four: Advance to the Rear

142 Samuel A. Swanson, letter dated January 22, 1862. Tiedeken, Papers, section 4.

143 J. William Jones, p. 268.

144 Fort Donelson in Tennessee surrendered February 16, 1862, and opened the Cumberland River to invasion. The fort was named for Daniel Smith Donelson. His grandfather Colonel John Donelson once lived in Pittsylvania County, Virginia. John was father to Rachel Donelson, who was born in Pittsylvania County in 1767. Rachel was wife of President Andrew Jackson.

145 Lt. Benjamin Cabell died at Chimborazo Hospital March 17, 1862. General Cabell sickened upon receiving the news and died April 19, 1862.

146 Withers, p. 167.

147 Thomas J. Hines, letter dated March 18, 1862.

148 Withers, p. 167.

149 "In the year 1740 Elias and William Edmunds were among the first settlers in Fauquier County. They settled near what is now Warrenton and began producing tobacco of excellent quality, which soon came to be known as 'Edmonium Tobacco.'" Herndon, p. 8. Edmonium was on current site of Loretta. See National Register of Historic Places 030-0035, located northeast of Warrenton town limits on east side of U.S. Rt. 17. Edmonds's stop there is conjecture.

150 Gregory, *38th Virginia*, p. 11, writes that the officers found it necessary to "destroy a great deal of liquor." The context is uncertain, but assumed literal rather than figurative.

151 The famous resort served as refuge for the state legislature in 1849 to avoid a cholera outbreak in Richmond.

152 Samuel A. Swanson, letter dated March 26, 1862. Tiedeken, Papers, section 4.

153 *The War of the Rebellion: A Compilation of the Official Records of the Union and Confederate Armies* (hereafter *OR*), serial 108, chap. 63, p. 534.

154 James Allen Oakes was cousin to brothers Thomas Clement Oakes and John Kerr Oakes already with the regiment.

155 Eyewitness in the 11th GA on the same night. Krick, *Civil War Weather in Virginia*, p. 52.

156 The Battle of Hampton Roads fought March 8–9, 1862. First day, the ironclad CSS *Virginia* (formerly the USS *Merrimac*) sank the USS *Cumberland* at Newport News, fired the USS *Congress*, and ran the USS *Minnesota* aground. Second day the USS *Monitor* and CSS *Virginia* fought the first battle of ironclad ships.

157 The Battle of Shiloh (known as Pittsburg Landing in the South) was fought April 6–7, 1862. The Confederates overwhelmed Union forces on the first day. The Union won the field on the second day. At the time, the Union victory was the bloodiest battle fought in North America.

158 Edwin A. Penick, letter dated April 12, 1862.

159 Thomas J. Hines, letter dated April 11, 1862.

160 Camp Winder was located at current site of Richmond's Byrd Park.

161 Turkey Island, beneath the bluffs of Malvern Hill, was the family seat of George Edward Pickett. The plantations passed included Shirley, Berkeley, Flowerdew Hundred, and Westover, among others. Fort Pocahontas on Jamestown Island was then garrisoned by the 14th Virginia Infantry, later assigned to Armistead's brigade.

162 At this writing, the original Lebanon Church built in 1859 still stands as part of Lebanon Christian Church across the road from Endview, which also remains. Despite its lofty name, the Great Warwick-Hampton Highway was a typical dirt road from Williamsburg, which had served as main overland artery for the Peninsula since colonial times.

163 This was Magruder's second defense line. His initial line ran between Deep Creek and the Poquoson River. The first line was much longer, weaker, and virtually untenable.

164 The brigade of Robert A. Toombs consisted of the 1st Georgia, 2nd Georgia, 15th Georgia, and 17th Georgia regiments.

165 Details of regiment's action at Dam No. 1 extracted from Penick, letter begun April 15, 1862.

166 The Confederate earthworks are preserved at this writing in Newport News City Park. Much of the battle site is flooded by the Newport News City Reservoir.

167 Edwin A. Penick, letter begun April 15, 1862.

168 Sears, *To the Gates of Richmond*, p. 56.

169 Drummer boy Julian A. Scott and Captain Samuel E. Pingree of the 3rd Vermont braved shot and shell to assist the wounded, for which actions they each received the Congressional Medal of Honor.

170 The Battle of Dam No. 1 was McClellan's sole attempt to test the Yorktown line. It is also known in Union reports as the Battle of Lee's Mill and the Battle of Burnt Chimneys. This is different from the action on April 5, 1862, which Confederates called the Battle of Lee's Mill.

171 Thomas J. Hines, letter dated April 18, 1862.

172 Tucker sent from Yorktown April 20, 1862, to Richmond, died in the hospital and was buried on or about June 10, 1862. Gregory, *38th Virginia*, p. 128.

173 On April 17, the Confederates launched their hot air observation balloon with Captain John Bryan from Lee Hall mansion. The multicolored patchwork of donated silk dresses was in free flight high and a mile and a half behind the frontline. The tether had been cut to free man tangled in the line. The 2nd Florida fired on it as it drifted over its camp. It eventually landed near the York River. Bryan landed unharmed but considerably shaken by the friendly fire. The same balloon had been launched before at Yorktown. This was probably its last ascent. The Confederate Air Force ended with the capture of the illumination gas balloon captured July 4, 1862, aboard the tug *Teaser*, which had become stranded by a falling tide on the James River near Malvern Hill.

174 Edwin A. Penick, letter begun April 15, 1862.

175 Griggs, April 20, 1862.

176 Edwin A. Penick, letter dated April 24, 1862.

177 Gunn, p. 19.

178 Edwin A. Penick, letter dated April 21, 1862.

179 Report, General John Bankhead Magruder, Headquarters, Lee's Farm, April 23, 1862. http://1stky.org/correspondence/dam_number_1_correspondence.htm. Last viewed April 16, 2008.

180 Colonel Henry Coalter Cabell was son of Virginia Governor William

H. Cabell. He was promoted to colonel and chief of artillery under General Magruder in spring 1862. Colonel H. C. Cabell was uncle to Major Isaac Carrington and second cousin once removed from the Cabell brothers in the 38th Virginia Infantry.

181 Gunn, p. 16.

182 Edwin A. Penick, letter dated April 27, 1862.

183 *Coot* was soldier slang for accoutrement.

184 Edwin A. Penick, letter dated April 25, 1862.

185 Congress passed the Conscription Act April 16, 1862 while the Battle of Dam No. 1 was fought.

186 See Watkins, chap. 3, Corinth.

187 The Virginia Secession Convention's policy for Virginia troops was that company officers be elected, but field officers be appointed by the governor. Freeman, *R. E. Lee*, vol. 1, p. 486. However, the Confederate government initially prescribed election of both field and company officers. The reelection of officers in the spring of 1862 were among the last ever held. The Confederate government soon outlawed the election of officers.

188 Venable, Andrew Reid, 3rd Virginia Cavalry, letter dated May 1, 1862. Carrington Family, Papers, section 10.

189 Sears, *To the Gates of Richmond*, p. 61.

190 Ibid., p. 62.

191 Before departing Yorktown, Brigadier Gabriel J. Rains placed a number of contact fused "sub-terra explosive shells" in roadways, which killed a number of Union cavalry. This was the first use of victim-activated land mines. Rains was known to have booby-trapped aboveground items in the Seminole War. His handiwork was apparent. General McClellan cried foul. General Longstreet condemned the practice as "unsportsmanlike." The Confederacy refrained from further use until 1863 when President Jefferson Davis reconsidered the devices as force multipliers. Davis then authorized use. General Rains became head of the Confederate Torpedo Bureau on Brown's Island in Richmond, where formal manufacture of sub-terra torpedoes (land mines) proceeded. This author suspects that Union leadership intentionally placed United States Colored Troops in the forefront of attacks against Confederate forts known to be defended by mine fields. This seems apparent in actions at Fort Wagner, South Carolina; Fort Harrison, Virginia; Fort Gilmer, Virginia, and others.

192 Lee Hall served as General J. B. Magruder's headquarters during the siege.

The Lee Hall mansion and Endview remain and are open to the public. Lebanon Church remains an active congregation. The original brick sanctuary constructed in 1859 still stands. After the siege, Union cavalry used the church as a stable.

193 The Williamsburg Female Academy occupied the site of the colonial capitol building. The academy had closed and become a hospital well before the battle. The route taken to Fort Magruder, now cut by modern railroad, is approximated by current York Street to Penniman Road.

194 Maury, p. 9.

195 Ibid., p. 10.

196 Note that Early's men shouted, "Bull Run!" even though Confederates normally referred to the battle as "Manassas."

197 Maury, p. 14.

198 Details about Whittle's coat per Henry M. Talley, letter dated May 11, 1862.

199 Years after the war, D. H. Hill said, "I can not think of it, till this day without horror. The slaughter of the Fifth North Carolina regiment was one of the most awful things I ever saw, and it was caused by a blunder." Longstreet, p. 78.

200 Artist and Medal of Honor winner Julian Scott of the 3rd Vermont painted Hancock's repulse of Early's assault at Williamsburg titled *The Superb*. See "Master Index," *The Civil War*, Time-Life Books, pp. 14–15.

201 A Wisconsin soldier handed the flag of the 5th North Carolina to George Armstrong Custer. It was the first Confederate battle flag captured in the eastern theater. The twelve-star, pink silk flag was one of those issued November 1861 at Centerville and identical to that carried by the 38th Virginia. It returned to the state of North Carolina in July 2002 and is housed at the North Carolina Museum of History in Raleigh.

202 This movement was contrary to Hill's orders and believed inconsistent with Lt. Colonel Whittle; therefore, the author attributes the movement to another. Since Major Carrington appears to have made the retreat to Richmond, this writer assumes he had recovered from his illness and returned to duty before abandonment of the Yorktown line. Either Carrington took command or leadership defaulted to the senior captain.

203 Gregory, *38th Virginia*, p. 17.

204 Wall, p. 22.

205 *OR*, part 1, series 12, chap. 23, p. 605.

206 One assumes Delaney received some assistance along the way. All other wounds to soldiers in the 38th Virginia involved upper extremities.

207 The retreat from Barhamsville to the Forge Road was likely via the Roper's Church Road, which then cut through the current site of the Diascund Reservoir.

208 Union forces under Brigadier General Wm. B. Franklin landed at Brick House and moved inland toward Barhamsville. Confederates under Major General Gustavus W. Smith checked the threat in a heavy skirmish. Union forces retired and established camp at Eltham's Landing, hence the name the Battle of Eltham's Landing. The fight is also known as the battles of Barhamsville and West Point.

209 Thomas J. Hines, letter dated May 11, 1862.

210 In 1863, Major Isaac H. Carrington inspected and reported on conditions at Libby Prison and unsheltered prisoners of war held on Belle Isle. Furgurson, p. 234.

211 Gregory states that Carrington lost reelection and was dropped from the roll May 12, 1862. Gregory, *38th Virginia*, p. 85. Note the reorganization election was held April 29, 1862. Gregory, *38th Virginia*, p. 13. George K. Griggs in his diary states that Carrington resigned on May 10. This is consistent with the roll removal of May 12, 1862. One concludes that Carrington voluntarily resigned after leading the 38th Virginia on its retreat from Williamsburg.

212 The site description places camp on or near present day Montrose Heights along Gillie Creek.

213 Thomas J. Hines, letter dated May 18, 1862.

214 Henry M. Talley, letter dated May 19, 1862.

215 Lewis Delaney, Company E, 38th Virginia, was admitted to Chimborazo Hospital May 11, died of gangrene May 21, and was buried in Oakwood Cemetery, Richmond. Gregory, p. 90. Delaney was his regiment's only recorded fatality due to action at Williamsburg.

216 Thomas J. Hines, letter dated May 18, 1862.

217 Gregory, *38th Virginia*, p. 17, surmised that the regiment "had had quite enough of Jubal Early." This comment is suspect since the 38th Virginia was only under Early for five days, inclusive of his wounding.

218 Samuel A. Swanson, letter dated May 30, 1862. Tiedeken, Papers, section 4.

Chapter 5: Seven Pines: Day One

219 See Krick, *Civil War Weather in Virginia*, pp. 56–57.

220 The writer knows of no other instance requiring blanket issuance of a distinct "battle badge." Though unsubstantiated at this writing, this one speculates Hill issued the order because some units may still have worn prewar blue militia uniforms.

221 The original outer defense line later became the intermediate defense line. After the Battle of Seven Pines, Lee established a new outer defense line, which crossed Williamsburg Road near where Garland's brigade formed for attack.

222 At this writing, the position of the 38th Virginia is approximated by the intersection of Oakleys Lane and International Trade Drive.

223 Considering the early stage of the war, the percentage of uniforms actually dyed butternut vs. mud-discolored gray is open to speculation. Observers perceived either as butternut or brown.

224 Maine Infantry, p. 43.

225 Private William C. Cole of the 23rd North Carolina Infantry stopped to replace his barrel with a new one when the vent became hopelessly plugged. Walls, p. 27.

226 Gregory, *38th Virginia*, p. 18.

227 Maine Infantry, p. 46.

228 Ibid., p. 39.

229 The Southern Historical Society Papers and several recent works mistakenly infer Griggs captured the regimental colors of the 104th Pennsylvania. This is clearly not the case. Griggs indeed captured a flag, but it was the flank marker of the 104th PA, not the regiment's colors. *OR*, part 1, series I, vol. 11, p. 964. See also Griggs, May 31, 1862.

230 In 1894 Color Sergeant Hiram Purcell of the 104th PA received the Congressional Medal of Honor for saving his regiment's colors on May 31, 1862. The Bucks County Historical Society commissioned artist William Trego to commemorate the event in his 1899 painting *Rescue of the Colors*.

231 Granddaughter Edith Oakes Chapman, interview, 1982.

232 Captain Edgar Wirt Carrington, youngest of six brothers, a seminary graduate of Union Theological Seminary, Hamden-Sydney College enlisted as 1st lieutenant in the Charlotte Cavalry. He later transferred to Company H, 38th Vir-

ginia, to serve under his brother Major Isaac H. Carrington. He was elected captain of Company H in December 1861. He sought transfer after his brother left the regiment. At the time of his death he had lateral transfer orders in his pocket to General Floyd's division of Cavalry. See "Notes on E. W. C. by Samuel Joseph Price," n.d., Carrington Family, Papers, Section 4. Captain Carrington's sword is preserved at the American Civil War Museum, cat. no. 0985.13.00410.

233 The blood kinship and closeness of Company B members was typical for Civil War units recruited from small communities. At Seven Pines, Company B listed 117 men on its roll with only seventy different last names. The middle names of cousins Thomas Clement Oakes and James Allen Oakes evidence ties respectively to the Clement and Allen families. Many individuals with unique family names were, nevertheless, cousins and/or in-laws to those with common names. Those not kinfolk were lifelong friends and had interacted with each other in one way or another before the war.

234 Great-uncle Elmo Whitlock often told the story of one of his grandmother's sons at Seven Pines. When asked why she had not checked the casualty lists for his name, she answered that she knew that if there were seven pines out there, her son was hiding behind one of them.

235 "Burying Soldiers Prematurely," *Richmond Dispatch*, April 28, 1862.

236 Gregory, *38th Virginia*, p. 20.

237 *OR*, part 2, series 1, vol. 11, p. 826. The degree of ceremony suggests Hill presented Tarpley a replacement flag. The ferocity of Seven Pines fight, including a dash through abatis, justifies suspicion that the silk flag of the 38th Virginia was severely damaged. These and other circumstances convince the writer that Hill presented the 38th Virginia with a cotton bunting flag such as would have been issued at that time from the division quartermaster.

238 Gregory, *38th Virginia*, p. 126.

239 Although most of Christendom meets for worship on Sunday, referring to it as the Sabbath is common error that was prevalent in nineteenth-century America. The biblical Sabbath as revealed to ancient Israel has and always been Friday sunset to Saturday sunset.

240 Much has been written about the influence of Sir Walter Scott's *Ivanhoe* (1820) on the Civil War. To a lesser extent, but still a notable influence on Cavalier mindsets, was Thomas Babington Macaulay's poem "Horatius at the Bridge," published in *Lays of Ancient Rome* (1842).

241 Frederick Douglass most eloquently defines and separates slaveholding religion from Christianity proper. See Douglass, pp. 118–122.

242 Griggs, June 14, 1862. Although flags with "Big Bethel," "Eltham's Landing," and certainly "Manassas" exist, those and actions at Yorktown, Lee's Mill, and Dam No. 1 predate the general recognition of battle honors. Most surviving examples of battle flags with "Seven Pines" and "Williamsburg" honors display black block letters on white cloth sewn onto flags. It appears those cloth battle honors were not authorized and distributed until late July 1862. However, Griggs clearly states that the battle honors for "Seven Pines" and "Williamsburg" were painted on their flag in June 1862.

243 Interestingly, Edmonds's colonelcy predated Armistead's by at least three months. Had the two been serving in the same division at the time, Edmonds might have been promoted to brigadier general rather than Armistead. "The Confederacy was born in chaos and never fully outgrew it." Robertson, *Stonewall Jackson*, p. 327.

Chapter Six: The 57th Virginia, Armistead, and His Brigade

244 Elisha F. Keen died in 1868. His widow, Nancy Perkins Keen, later married Chiswell Dabney Langhorne, a tobacconist and auctioneer. Two of their five children attained international fame. Nancy Langhorne became Lady Astor, the first woman to sit in the British House of Commons. Irene Langhorne married artist Charles Dana Gibson and was an original "Gibson Girl."

245 Camp Belcher was located on the Belcher farm near the Fairfield Race Course. The site fronted Mechanicsville Turnpike and today approximated by the northeast quadrant of the Interstate 64 and Route 360 interchange.

246 George Watson Carr, a native of Roanoke, resigned his first lieutenant commission in the 9th U.S. Infantry to side with the Confederacy. He was married to Emma G. Watts, second cousin to John C. Breckinridge. Her father, G. Edward Watts, was a lawyer and speaker of the Virginia legislature.

247 Krick in Gallagher, p. 95.

248 Lewis Addison Armistead was born in the Stanly House, currently 307 George Street, New Bern, North Carolina. The house, originally on New Street, has been moved twice. Armistead's grandfather John Wright Stanly Jr. was a U.S. Congressman. The house once hosted George Washington and served as General

Ambrose Burnside's first headquarters in New Bern.
249 Garber, p. 29. Lewis Armistead was killed at Fort Erie. Addison Armistead died defending Savannah. Colonel Walker Keith Armistead deserves much credit for the American victory at Craney Island June 22, 1813. As army engineer, he oversaw the defenses there and successfully argued against their abandonment three days before the British assault. See "The Decision at Craney Island" by Christopher Pieczynski, *Hallowed Ground* (magazine of the Civil War Trust) 19, no. 1 (2018).
250 This is not to be confused with Ben Lomond of the Carter family in Prince William County.
251 Motts, p. 13. Some accounts reference a sugar bowl rather than a plate.
252 Ibid., pp. 28–29.
253 Ibid., p. 31.
254 Krick in Gallagher, p. 104.
255 Ibid., p. 105.
256 Ibid., pp. 109–111.
257 Motts, p. 37.
258 Howard's Grove was a popular prewar public picnic area in Richmond. In 1861, it became a troop staging area until spring 1862, when the Howard's Grove hospital complex was built. The site is bounded today by Mechanicsville Turnpike, Q Street (extended), Redd Street, and Coalter Street.
259 When retreat became imminent, Brigadier General Henry A. Wise ordered Elizabeth City burned. Confederates fired part of the town before being driven off. Union capture saved the town.
260 Richmond *Dispatch*, February 17, 1862.
261 See atlas to the *OR* plate 138 for Manney's Ferry. The same location was site of the patriot settlement of Wyanoke Ferry burned by loyalist militia on July 17, 1781. Only a simple ferry existed there in 1862.
262 John Bowie Magruder, letter dated March 9, 1862.
263 Sublett, p. 6.
264 Withers, p. 162.
265 Wallace, p. 143.
266 Withers, pp. 161–162. Withers mistakenly associates Carr with the 19th Virginia, which had not yet formed. However, Major Carr commanded a battalion at Harpers Ferry that included units that became Companies A and B of the 19th

Virginia.

267 Sandy Cross is the intersection of Sandy Cross Road (Rt. 1413) and Acorn Hill Road (Rt. 1002) in Gates County, North Carolina, near present-day Hobbsville. At this writing, a little green sign at the crossroads declares "Sandy Cross." Nearby is the Sandy Cross Baptist Church.

268 William H. White, 14th Virginia was commissioned major at Sandy Cross on May 17, 1862. Crews and Parrish erroneously list date as 1861, p. 150. Other than this mention, there is little record of involvement of the 14th Virginia at Sandy Cross.

269 Krick in Gallagher, p. 117 alludes to Armistead at Sandy Cross April 27, 29, 1862. Therefore, this writer infers that Armistead likely conducted the inspection recorded by Carr's men at Gatesville.

270 Sublett, p. 7.

271 Lewis, p. 23.

272 Ibid., p. 24.

273 Withers, pp. 176–177.

274 Apparently, D. H. Hill did not issue white strips of cloth to be worn as battle badges for the second day of battle as he had required on the first day.

275 Lewis, pp. 25–26.

276 *OR*, part 1, series 12, chap. 23, p. 982.

277 Gregory, *53rd Virginia*, p. 25.

278 One wonders if the friendly troops would have fired on each other if they had been wearing battle badges as required by Hill on the first day. There is no mention known mention of battle badges on the second day.

279 Withers, p. 178.

280 Motts, p. 38.

281 Lewis, p. 30.

282 Garland's brigade shed the 38th Virginia, 2nd Florida, and 2nd Mississippi battalions. It retained the 5th North Carolina and 23rd North Carolina and received the 12th North Carolina, 13th North Carolina, and 20th North Carolina regiments. Garland's brigade remained in D. H. Hill's division and joined Lee's strike force to push north of the Chickahominy River. Hill's division then fought at Mechanicsville and anchored the Confederate left at Gaines's Mill.

283 Gregory, *38th Virginia*, p. 20.

284 John Oakes, the progenitor of the Oakes family of Pittsylvania County,

was born in England about 1640 and entered the Virginia Colony at Yorktown. He raised tobacco on his farm in York County. John Oakes was among those arrested for destroying tobacco plants in the Tobacco Riots of 1682. Oakes was pardoned and sent home. A number were convicted of treason and hanged. See "A Traitor in the Family Tree?" *The Pittsylvania Packet*, Spring 2018, p. 23. *The Executive Journal, Council of Colonial Virginia* 1, no. 27 (September 30, 1682) records the arrest warrant issued for John Oakes.

Chapter Seven: Malvern Hill

285 Joseph T. Payne, letter dated June 21, 1862.

286 Although the light division of Theophilus Holmes was also south of the Chickahominy, it was nearest the James River and removed from the major thrust.

287 The Battle of Oak Grove is also referred to as the Battle of King's Schoolhouse and the Battle of French's Field. Virtually the entire site is now occupied by Richmond's Byrd International Airport.

288 The Battle of Beaver Dam Creek is also known as the Battle of Mechanicsville and the Battle of Ellerson's Mill.

289 Burton, p. 82.

290 Gregory, *53rd Virginia*, p. 30.

291 Benjamin W. Scott, letter dated July 26, 1862. Union corpses Scott referenced as "Seven Pines" dead were in fact killed in the Oak Grove fight just days before.

292 At this writing, the site of the Battle of Savages Station is the interchange of I-64 and I-295. Modern tracks of the York River Railroad mark the original railroad right of way.

293 The Battle of Frayser's Farm was known by at least six names. Before the war, the Frayser family owned a farm called Glendale at the edge of White Oak Swamp. Glendale was at the intersection of Charles City Road, Long Bridge Road, and Willis Church Road, where there was also a blacksmith shop run by a man named Riddle. The Frayser family had moved away years before the war. Glendale was still referred to locally as Frayser's farm, although owned by the Nelson family. Southern troops generally referred to the battle as Frayser's Farm, with several alternate spellings. The North referred to the battle as Glendale. Some accounts refer to the fight as the Battle of White Oak Swamp, Charles City Crossroads, Nelson's

Farm, or Riddle's Shop.

294 Malvern Hill had a history of use as a defensive position. Military encampments and musters occurred there in the Revolutionary War and the War of 1812.

295 Freeman, *R. E. Lee*, vol. 2, p. 200.

296 Dowdey, p. 327.

297 *OR*, part 2, series 1, vol. 11, Peninsula Campaign, p. 802.

298 Sears, *To the Gates of Richmond*, p. 317.

299 William P. Judkins, 22nd Georgia, claimed Armistead was behind a poplar tree shirking his duty and drinking. Motts, p. 39.

300 *OR*, serial 013, chap. 23, Peninsula Campaign, p. 824.

301 Dowdey, p. 337.

302 Carmichael, *Lee's Young Artillerist*, p. 47.

303 Hudson, p. 70.

304 Benjamin W. Scott, letter dated July 26, 1862.

305 Captain R. T. Daniel is a noble commodity indeed. He was adjutant of the 5th KY regiment on furlough but volunteered to fight with Company F, 38th Virginia. Remarkably, Daniel survived his wounds. *OR,* series 1, vol. 11, part 2, p. 826.

306 Dowdey, p. 343.

307 Crocker, p. 99.

308 Krick, in Gallagher, p. 118.

309 See Withers, pp. 208–209.

310 In 2012, author examined subject battle flag captured at Gettysburg and was first to propose explanation for its uniqueness. All evidence points to preservation and incorporation of elements of the Malvern Hill flag into its replacement. The battle flag is preserved at the American Civil War Museum. A number of authorities concur with the author's reasoning. Until documentation surfaces proving the fact, conjecture must suffice.

311 1st Company G, 14th Virginia, was transferred to artillery service and replace by 1st Company I, 38th Virginia. Although the order was issued June 27, 1862, the transfer was not completed until after Malvern Hill. See Gregory, *38th Virginia*, p. 5; also Crew and Parrish, p. 27.

312 Edwin A. Penick, letter dated July 28, 1862.

313 Edwin A. Penick, letter dated August 5, 1862.

314 Confederates attacked McClellan's forces at Harrison's Landing on August 1, 1862 and were driven back. This accounts for the gunfire heard that day at Drewry's Bluff. On August 5, McClellan retook Malvern Hill, held it for one day, and withdrew.

315 Albert Moore, p. 50.

316 James Booker, letter dated August 3, 1862. Pvt. John P. Millner, Company D, paid substitute Michael Kelly to take his place in ranks. The 38th Virginia discharged Milner on July 29, 1862. Kelly deserted August 1, 1862. Gregory, p. 106, p. 111.

317 Motts, p. 39. "Poplar" is, of course, word play on *popular*, which in turn mocks Armistead, who was anything but popular.

318 William H. Cocke, Company K, 9th Virginia. Letter dated July 14, 1862.

Chapter Eight: The Second Manassas and Maryland Campaigns

319 Henry Gwynn, Lt., 9th Virginia, letter dated July 20, 1862.

320 General Order No. 5 established vouchers which amounted to outright confiscation of civilian property. General Order No. 7 held local citizens responsible for injuries. Houses used for hostile acts were to be burned. Citizens within a five-mile radius of partisan damage were to be assembled and forced to make repairs. General Order No. 11 required an oath of allegiance or exile south. Hennessy, pp. 14–19.

321 Hennessy, p. 44.

322 Gregory, *38th Virginia*, p. 24.

323 Rappahannock Bridge was near Rappahannock Station, now Remington, Virginia.

324 Hennessy, p. 117.

325 Hazel Plain was home to the Chinn family, relatives of the Carters.

326 Prichard retained Webster's personal affects and returned them to his widow after the war. VMI Historical Rosters Database.

327 Hennessy, p. 424.

328 Freeman, *R. E. Lee*, vol. 2, p. 337.

329 Edwin A. Penick, letter dated September 29, 1862.

330 Thomas J. Hines, letter dated September 2, 1862.

331 Harsh, p. 13.

332 Gregory, *38th Virginia*, p. 25.

333 Thomas J. Hines, letter dated September 2, 1862. The numbers suggest the 38th Virginia was the leftmost regiment in the brigade.

334 Hennessy, p. 456.

335 See Harsh for in-depth treatment of Lee's strategy.

336 Floris is at the intersection of Routes 657 and 608 in Fairfax County. From 1726 to 1892 the community was known as Frying Pan.

337 Gregory, *38th Virginia*, p. 25.

338 The George W. Ball farm. Harsh, p. 92.

339 Harsh, p. 74.

340 Online resource *Encyclopedia Virginia* states, "During the Maryland Campaign, Robert E. Lee, *recognizing Armistead's qualities*, appointed him provost marshal for the army" (author's emphasis). Indeed contemporary descriptions of Armistead include "strict disciplinarian" and his belief in "obedience to duty" being the "first qualification of a soldier." Although true, military rigidity is not as likely the reason for Armistead's appointment to provost as much as the post sidelined a mediocre general officer. Freeman states than Lee had no serious questions regarding the courage of any general officer except for one brigadier. *R. E. Lee*, vol. 4, pp. 182–183. Freeman failed to identify the individual. It may well have been Lewis Armistead.

341 James Booker, letter dated September 30, 1862.

342 Freeman, *R. E. Lee*, vol. 2, p. 412.

343 Murfin, p. 96.

344 John W. Mahan, letter dated October 6, 1862.

345 Harsh, p. 106.

346 Murfin, p. 104.

347 Henry Talley of the former Company I, 38th Virginia. Crews and Parrish, p. 30.

348 Ecclesiastes 9:4 (KJV).

349 Gregory, *38th Virginia*, p. 82. John M. Bohanon enlisted May 1861. He was promoted to color sergeant in October and ensign in January 1862. On the march through Maryland, he simply walked off the stage of history. His fate is unknown. Listed as deserted September 15, 1862, Leesburg, the date and location

are questionable.

350 Blackford's Ford is also known as Boteler's Ford and Pack Horse Ford.

351 Motts, p. 40. The specific foot is not recorded.

352 Crews and Parrish, p. 31.

353 Edwin A. Penick, letter dated September 29, 1862.

354 Lewis, p. 45.

355 Murfin, appendix D.

356 Edwin A. Penick, letter dated September 29, 1862.

357 *OR*, series I, vol. 19, part 2, Antietam, p. 613.

358 Freeman, *R. E. Lee*, Vol. 2, p. 407.

359 See McGrath for a thorough account.

360 Murfin, p. 308.

361 McClellan anticipated the possibility and had already dispatched troops to Williamsport. Thus, he had made recrossing the Potomac impossible for Lee.

362 Gregory, *38th Virginia*, p. 28.

363 William R. Aylett, letter to wife dated October 20, 1862.

364 The Quaker church built in 1759 still stands and is in active use at this writing.

365 In his postwar memoirs, secessionist and colonel of the 18th Virginia Dr. Robert Withers of Danville wrote that he knew secession meant war, but whether or not the secession vote passed or failed, "slavery in Virginia was doomed." Withers, p. 126. Oliver Wendell Holmes Jr. wrote his father after First Manassas, "this defeat tends more and more to throw the war into the hands of the radicals, and if it lasts a year, it will be a war of abolition." Robertson in *Soldiers Blue and Gray*, p. 30.

366 James Booker, letter dated October 17, 1862.

367 James Booker, letter dated September 30, 1862.

368 Murfin, p. 324.

Chapter Nine: Pickett's Division and Fredericksburg

369 John W. Mahan, letter dated October 4, 1862.

370 John W. Mahan, letter dated October 6, 1862.

371 John W. Mahan, letter dated October 9, 1862.

372 Gregory, *38th Virginia*, p. 28.

373 The site was likely at or near present day Morgans Ford Bridge (Rt. 624) over the Shenandoah River.

374 Lewis, p. 54.

375 Ibid.

376 Gordon, p. 14.

377 James Tilton Pickett was born December 31, 1857. His mother died weeks later from delivery complications. Maternal grandparents cared for the boy for a while. By the time George Pickett left for Virginia, he had placed the boy in care of friends. Pickett knew the mixed-race child would never have been accepted in Virginia society. Although he continued to support the boy financially, he never saw him again.

378 Gordon, p. 73.

379 Haskell, p. 32.

380 Withers, p. 188.

381 Gordon, p. 91.

382 Sublett, p. 19.

383 William R. Aylett, letter to wife dated December 3, 1862.

384 William R. Aylett, letter to wife dated December 7, 1862.

385 John Roy Cabell returned home and eventually married Mrs. Kate Clement of Clement Hill. He was murdered August 26, 1897 on his Callands farm by Edward Hankins, a disgruntled renter. Hankins hanged for the crime. *Richmond Dispatch*, November 12, 1897.

386 Gregory, *38th Virginia*, p. 30.

387 Sublett, p. 20.

388 Glatthaar, p. 334.

389 "Observation has taught me that a commander may acquire sufficient caution by receiving hard blows, but he cannot acquire boldness. It is a gift from Heaven. A soldier whose quality of caution far exceeds that of boldness, can never be eminent in war." John Bell Hood, p. 157.

390 Tagg, p. 244.

391 James resigned July 28, 1862, and Keen resigned July 31, 1862, per Sublett, pp. 66, 68.

392 Gallagher, p. 118.

393 William R. Aylett, letter to wife dated January 25, 1863.

394 Burnside and his IX Corps landed at Newport News.

395 Chimborazo Hospital was the largest in the Confederacy. It was comprised of 150 unpainted 30 × 150 foot wood frame wards and as many as 150 Sibley tents on forty acres of land. Samuel Moore, pp. 63–64. The site at this writing is Chimborazo Park. On April 20, James Lafayette Oakes was transferred to the general hospital in Danville.

396 Gregory, *53rd Virginia*, p. 47.

397 Letter Book, March 3, 1863.

398 Krick in Gallagher, p. 119. Also Tagg, p. 244.

399 Grammer went on to serve as surgeon for the 26th Battallion and the 62nd Virginia Mounted Infantry.

400 George Washington met Martha Dandridge Custis at Montville while on a visit to the Aylett family.

401 Letter Book, March 11, 1863.

402 Letter Book, March 16, 1863.

403 Gilliam eventually resigned June 19, 1863, due to "dropsy and debility." Robert Krick, *Lee's Colonels*, p. 143.

404 Letter Book, March 35, 1863.

405 Lt. W. Keith Armistead is cited as his father's aide-de-camp on February 19, 1863. List of Staff Officers of the Confederate Army, p. 6.

406 Poindexter, p. 5.

Chapter Ten: The Siege of Suffolk

407 Davis's brigade was commanded by Brigadier General Joseph R. Davis, President Jefferson Davis's nephew. Cormier, p. 54.

408 2 Samuel 11:1 (KJV).

409 Joseph T. Payne, letter dated April 3, 1863.

410 Joseph T. Payne, letter dated March 15, 1863.

411 Joseph T. Payne, letter dated January 23, 1863.

412 John W. Mahan, letter dated March 29, 1863.

413 The bridge on South Quay Road (Rt. 189) approximates the point of Pickett's crossing. At the outbreak of the Revolutionary War, South Quay was Virginia's largest inland port. A customs house supported international trade. It boasted a fledgling shipyard. The British burned South Quay in 1781. South Quay and New South Quay appear on Civil War–era maps on opposite banks of the

Blackwater River. The community ceased to exist by 1900. Other than the name South Quay Road, virtually nothing remains to suggest its existence.

414 The pontoon bridge was alleged Union origin, captured at Seven Pines. Cormier, p. 84.

415 Comier, p. 86.

416 The village of Leesville no longer exists. The location is suggested at this writing by the modest mile-long country lane called Leesville Road (Rt. 663).

417 Over thirty Suffolk homes burned during the siege. Most were looted and torched. A few were ignited by shellfire. All house burnings displaced families. In addition, two mills and a church as well as homes along the Blackwater River were also burned. For a comprehensive, list see *The Quiet Regiment*, p. 13.

418 The three forts were Fort Nansemond, Fort McClellan, and Fort Union.

419 Comier, p. 220.

420 Captain George K. Griggs wrote that the woman was "wantonly" shot by the enemy; however, each side blamed the other. Evidence supports Judith Smith was shot by accident while fleeing the firefight. Mrs. Smith died April 13. Gregory reports the event as April 14.

421 Gregory, *38th Virginia*, p. 33.

422 Comier, pp. 219–220.

423 Joseph T. Payne, letter dated April 16, 1863.

424 Letter Book, April 15, 1863.

425 William G. Cabaniss, letter dated April 26, 1863.

426 Joseph T. Payne, letter dated April 26, 1863.

427 William G. Cabaniss, letter dated April 26, 1863.

428 Letter Book, April 29, 1863.

429 Griggs, April 29, 1863.

430 Pickett met LaSalle nightly at her aunt's home at Barber's Cross Roads in Isle of Wight County. Gordon, p. 98. Author estimates fifteen miles one way from Pickett's headquarters. See *The Official Military Atlas of the Civil War*, Plate 26. Thirty miles at a trot equates to about four hours' traveling time, about the daily range for a horse.

431 Gordon, p. 92.

432 Joseph T. Payne, letter dated May 10, 1863.

433 Freeman, *R. E. Lee*, vol. 2, p. 562.

434 Freeman, *R. E. Lee*, vol. 3, chap. 2.

435 *Savannah Republican*, August 2, 1863.

436 John W. Mahan, letter to wife dated May 28, 1863.

437 William R. Aylett, letter to wife dated June 9, 1863. Montville is located one mile southwest of Aylett on U.S. Route 360.

438 Mathew 19:30 and 20:16.

Chapter Eleven: Gettysburg

439 Joseph T. Payne, letter dated June 11, 1863.

440 Rev. Ransel W. Cridlin replaced Rev. John F. Poulton who was stricken from the roll June 8, 1863 due to prolonged absence. The 38th Virginia added Cridlin to its roster on June 9, 1863. Gregory, *38th Virginia* p. 89, p. 118.

441 McClurken, p. 16.

442 Norman Oakes, son of James Lafayette Oakes, said, "My daddy told me the heat was so bad on the way to Gettysburg that a lot of them died from it." Interview by author, June 1978.

443 Gregory, *38th Virginia*, p. 35.

444 Edmonds, p. 154. Amanda Edmonds specifically mentioned Longstreet and Pickett by name and "several relations" in Pickett's division. The reference would have certainly included her Cousin Ned Edmonds. Circumstances presuppose Armistead's presence.

445 Joseph T. Payne, letter dated June 26, 1863.

446 William R. Aylett, letter to wife, June 23, 1863. For comprehensive history and description of period matches, refer to monograph by this writer titled "'Lucifers'–A Match Not Made in Heaven," *Camp Chase Gazette*, vol. 17, no. 7 (1990).

447 *Savannah Republican*, July 20, 1863, p. 2, c. 2.

448 James Booker, letter dated June 30, 1863.

449 Krick in Gallagher, p. 119.

450 Sublett, p. 25.

451 Motts, p. 41.

452 John A. Herndon, letter dated July 11, 1863.

453 Although lead units arrived then, the mountain trek in hot weather, likely against opposing traffic, no doubt created delays. Evidence suggests elements of Pickett's division arrived piecemeal throughout the night. Guelzo, p. 380.

454 Modern approximation of Pickett's route is from Cashtown, turn right off Chambersburg Turnpike onto Knoxlyn Road, then left onto Black Horse Tavern Road. The road jogs right at Black Horse Tavern (Hood's division hospital) and continues past site of Bream's Mill (Pickett's division hospital) to Sachs Bridge. \

455 Kent Brown, *Retreat from Gettysburg*, p. 55.

456 Guelzo, pp. 321–333.

457 Wert, p. 94.

458 Longstreet's opposition to Lee's plan is legendary. See Freeman, *R. E. Lee*, vol. 3, chap. 8, "It's All My Fault."

459 Sears, *Gettysburg*, p. 383.

460 Hess, p. 50.

461 Guelzo, p. 395.

462 The total number of Confederate artillery pieces participating in the bombardment is debatable. For a comprehensive map of 163 Confederate artillery positions, see Trudeau, *Gettysburg*, pp. 445–446. Priest in his appendix A provides astute arguments for a total of 155 Confederate artillery pieces in action on the afternoon of July 3.

463 Poindexter, p. 6.

464 Stewart, p. 33.

465 John A. Herndon, letter dated July 11, 1863.

466 William R. Aylett, letter to his brother Patrick Henry Aylett, dated July 16, 1863.

467 Per C. Edmonds Allen, the listed items are still in the family's possession.

468 Captain Farinhold in Gregory, *53rd Virginia*, p. 52. Armistead seeming to be "in the best mood under fire" implies a lesser mood otherwise.

469 Wert, p. 196.

470 Hess, p. 166.

471 Ibid.

472 Ibid.

473 Lewis, p. 97.

474 Song of Solomon, 6:4, 6:10 (KJV).

475 Hess, pp. 170–171.

476 Wert, p. 119.

477 Sears, *Gettysburg*, p. 444.

478 Major Joseph R. Cabell, report, *OR* Supplement, series 1, vol. 5, p. 332.

One historian suggests that some of these fence lines also presented added nuisances of trees, brush, and poison ivy entanglements. See Stewart, p. 97.

479 Trudeau, *Gettysburg*, p. 489. One wonders what might have happened had Longstreet moved Armistead's brigade in line with Garnett, as Armistead had requested and thus closed the distance with Pettigrew's men before the assault.

480 Hess, p. 171.

481 Page, p. 150.

482 The Compte de Paris, ibid.

483 Punctuation revised by author.

484 Stopping to fire was the fatal mistake of British troops at Bunker Hill. Proper bayonet tactics are discussed in Lockhart, pp. 266–267. Garnett, Kemper, and Armistead all had sufficient military training to have known not to halt a bayonet charge to fire or return fire. One wonders what difference it might have made had they not.

485 Sears, *Gettysburg*, p. 448.

486 Wert, p. 112. Lieutenant Colonel Henry A. Carrington served as commander of the 18th Virginia after Colonel Withers's wounding at Gaines's Mill. Carrington received formal promotion to full colonel in August 1864.

487 Poindexter, pp. 7–9.

488 Letter Book, July 11, 1863.

489 Page, p. 152.

490 John A. Herndon, letter dated July 14, 1863.

491 Letter Book, July 11, 1863.

492 No description exists on how Whittle returned from the field in his condition. He must have been carried back in similar manner as General Kemper.

493 John Corbett Timberlake, *OR* Supplement, series I, vol. 5, p. 336.

494 The flags of the 3rd Virginia and 7th Virginia of Kemper's brigade and those of the 28th Virginia and 56th Virginia of Garnett's brigade were captured inside the Angle. Trudeau, *Gettysburg*, p. 512.

495 Coski, p. 31.

496 First Lieutenant Alonzo Hersford Cushing was posthumously promoted to brevet lieutenant colonel for bravery on July 3, 1863. On November 10, 2014, he deservedly received the Congressional Medal of Honor, though 151 years after the fact.

497 Hess, p. 262.

498 Wounds documented by Dr. Daniel G. Brinton. Wert, p. 247.

499 Sergeant Thomas Booker Tredway, Company I, 53rd Virginia, was a VMI alumnus and veteran of the Battle of Big Bethel. He was left on the field wounded. He died in a Gettysburg hospital July 13, 1863. Gregory, *53rd Virginia*, p. 196.

500 John Corbett Timberlake, *OR* Supplement, series I, vol. 5, p. 336.

501 The July 11, 1863, report of Major Cabell alone is sketchy and confusing at best. This may explain why it was never officially submitted and appears in the *OR* Supplement. Use of "lane," in context, cannot be assumed to mean "road." "Fence" may either be wood or stone. Proximity to "enemy works" removes assault action away from Emmitsburg Road rather than on it, as some have assumed. The action of the 38th Virginia as described by writer is believed the best bit fit of all details composited from the brigade Letter Book, the letters of Captain Herndon, and other eyewitness accounts as well as multiple on-site surveys conducted personally.

502 John A. Herndon, letter dated July 14, 1863.

503 John A. Herndon, letter dated July 11, 1863.

504 Stewart, p. 230.

505 Letter Book, July 11, 1863.

506 Sgt. Daniel Miller received the Congressional Medal of Honor for capturing the colors of the 38th Virginia and 24th North Carolina. Many received the Medal of Honor that day for turning in colors taken by the rank and file or simply picked up off the ground. Thus, the actual party who grabbed the 38th Virginia flag remains in doubt.

507 Freeman, *R. E. Lee*, vol. 3, p. 136.

Chapter Twelve: The Aftermath of Gettysburg

508 Sears, *Gettysburg*, p. 456.

509 Hess, p. 326.

510 Sears, *Gettysburg*, p. 465.

511 Edward H. Estes, Letter dated July 11, 1863.

512 Freeman, *R. E. Lee*, Vol. 3, p. 131.

513 Captain James Edward Poindexter, Company H, 38th Virginia was wounded and captured. He endured captivity at Fort Delaware and Point Lookout until exchanged in March 1865. Gregory, *38th Virginia*, p. 117.

514 Wert, p. 291.

515 Brown, *Retreat from Gettysburg*, pp. 73–74. Captain John Herndon confirms this was route taken by 38th Virginia in letter dated July 14, 1863.

516 Trudeau, *Gettysburg*, p. 541.

517 Brown, *Retreat from Gettysburg*, p. 355.

518 Ibid., p. 296.

519 Capt. John Herndon, Company D, 38th Virginia, letter dated July 14, 1863, Bunker Hill, Virginia.

520 Brown, *Retreat from Gettysburg*, p. 315.

521 Other works infer Lt. Col. White, 14th Virginia had command of the brigade until Aylett's return. For instance, the roster in Crews and Parrish on p. 150 erroneously lists White in command of the brigade from July 3 to July 18. This is most unlikely because White was seriously wounded July 3. Their text on p. 46 states White did not return to the unit until the "last quarter of 1863." The Letter Book of the Armistead-Barton-Steuart brigade includes a report from Aylett dated July 11, 1863, stating specifically that Major Joseph R. Cabell had command of the brigade until Aylett assumed command.

522 Regarding Union raids in and around Ayletts, "Their track was marked by pillage, plunder, and the destruction of several houses by firebrand of the incendiary upon the homes of peaceful citizens." Excerpt from report of Captain J. Washington Williams, Holcome's Legion, South Carolina, Volunteer Cavalry on their expedition from Yorktown to Ayletts to counter Union incursion. Supplement to *OR*, part 1, vol. 5, p. 476.

523 Carmichael, *The Last Generation*, p. 198. The number twelve may have corresponded to the number of dwellings torched and ransacked.

524 Capt. John Herndon, Company D, 38th Virginia, dated a letter July 11 at Williamsport, Maryland, and another letter from Bunker Hill, Virginia (West Virginia) on July 14. Considering the twenty-six-mile trek, the 38th Virginia must have crossed no later than July 12.

525 Georg and Busey, p. 424. The General Receiving Hospital, General Hospital No. 9, was also known as Seabrook's Hospital. It was the Seabrook Warehouse, a tobacco warehouse owned by the City of Richmond at the start of the war. Located on Grace Street between 17th and 18th Streets, it was near the Virginia Central Railroad and sufficient in size to serve as a receiving hospital. Samuel Moore, p. 57. At this writing, the site of General Hospital No. 9 is a parking lot.

526 3rd Sgt. Thomas Clement Oakes died at the II Corps hospital and was buried in Yard B, Row 2, between the Schwartz and Bushman farms. His remains were disinterred in 1872 and placed in Box #213 destined for the mass reburial of Gettysburg Dead in Hollywood Cemetery, Richmond, Virginia. Georg and Busey, p. 423.

527 Five Shelhorse brothers served in Company I, 53rd, Virginia. In July 1863 Jacob, James, and John were on active roll. Jacob developed bronchitis and missed the Gettysburg campaign. James made the charge and returned. John was shot in the right leg near the ankle, captured and exchanged. All were descended from Johannes Bernhardt Schellhase, 2nd Company, Erbprinz Regiment. Schellhase escaped prisoner of war captivity, married a Pennsylvania Dutch woman and migrated to Pittsylvania County, where his name was anglicized Bennett Shelhorse.

528 Brothers Richard Leake Dunkum and William B. Dunkum served in Company A, 57th Virginia. Richard was wounded in the charge, captured and exchanged. William was captured and sent to Fort Delaware, where he died October 26, 1863, presumably of either smallpox or typhoid. In 1905, Richard's sons, David Asa Dunkum and Richard "Buck" Dunkum, bought a store at Green Springs Depot, Louisa County, Virginia. In 1914, their families and businesses were focus of the Hall murder case. See *Murder at Green Springs: The True Story of the Hall Case, Firestorm of Prejudices* by this author.

529 Stewart, p. 255.

530 Motts, p. 48.

531 Wert, p. 247.

532 Walker, p. 187.

533 At this writing Fort Delaware is maintained as Fort Delaware State Park, accessible by ferry from Delaware City. Initially, Confederate dead were buried on the island. The Union established a two-acre burial ground at Finn's Point, New Jersey, to accommodate the large numbers of Confederate dead. After the war, the early deaths at Fort Delaware were removed and reinterred at Finn's Point, which became a national cemetery in 1875. In 1910 the federal government erected a monument to the 2,436 Confederate who died at Fort Delaware.

534 Confederates soldiers who took the oath of allegiance and entered U.S. service were generally sent west to fight Indians rather than risk recapture.

535 Statistics vary depending on sources. This author uses a compilation of Gettysburg captives gleaned from Letter Book, July 11, 1863, and Gregory,

38th Virginia, pp. 77–133. The American Civil War Museum estimates the 38th Virginia suffered fifty-five killed, 135 wounded, and forty missing, for a casualty rate of 55 percent, which assumes four hundred men engaged. Considering a lower number engaged evaluated by subsequent roll call results in higher casualty rate.

Chapter Thirteen: Pickett Descends on New Bern

536 J. William Jones, pp. 247, 336.

537 See Tucker for insight into logistics of moving Longstreet's Corps, pp. 92–93.

538 At this writing, remains of the CSS *Neuse* as well as a full-scale replica are on display in Kinston, North Carolina.

539 William R. Aylett, letter to wife dated October 9, 1863.

540 Carmichael, *The Last Generation*, pp. 162, 198.

541 Thomas Bowerbank Barton, father of Seth Maxwell Barton, served as lieutenant in the War of 1812. He was Commonwealth attorney for Fredericksburg and Spotsylvania County. All four sons served in the Confederate army. When Confederates abandoned Fredericksburg in spring 1862, T. B. Barton and other members of the Fredericksburg town council negotiated peaceful occupation of the town. Union forces under General Erwin McDowell occupied Fredericksburg on April 19, 1862.

542 Robertson, *Stonewall Jackson*, p. 310.

543 William R. Aylett, letter to wife dated October 9, 1863.

544 On October 14, 1863, Lee's aggressive campaign against Meade and the Army of the Potomac culminated in his costly repulse at Bristoe Station.

545 Colonel Powhatan Bolling Whittle remained on General A. P. Hill's staff until admitted to Richmond General Hospital #4 on April 20, 1864. He then moved to CSA hospital in Petersburg on April 29, 1864. He received furlough and exited the war on June 22, 1864.

546 Henderson Lee never recovered sufficiently to return to duty.

547 Date for return to duty for James Lafayette Oakes is undocumented. Writer assumes his return by mid-November. This is reasonable and consistent with records. A study of more than sixty similar wounds suggests sixty to ninety days' average recovery time. Oakes returned to the ranks fit as a rifleman prior to May 1864. Oakes's 1884 pension application lists his shoulder wound as contribu-

tory to his latter-day disabilities but due mainly to his future leg wound. See Court Record, Pittsylvania County, vol. 58, p. 215.

548 Gregory, *53rd Virginia*, p. 68.

549 James Booker, letter dated January 1, 1864.

550 Ibid.

551 Ibid.

552 Wilson, p. 157.

553 Also known as Batchelor's Creek.

554 Barrett, p. 202.

555 At this writing, Chinquapin Chapel remains an active Baptist congregation just south of Phillips Crossroads on North Carolina Route 58.

556 Approximately forty pine trees yielded one barrel of tar.

557 The span and navigability of Brice's Creek is similar to that of the Blackwater River at South Quay over which Pickett had to employ a pontoon bridge to cross a similar force in his Suffolk operation. Failure to identify the water hazard and provide bridging for the operation ultimately rested with Pickett.

558 The same open expanse is the current site of Coastal Carolina Regional Airport.

559 Writer's speculation: period maps suggest Trenton as the most expedient crossing site for Barton's column. *OR* Serial 009, Operations in North Carolina, chap. 20, p. 337 confirms a bridge at Trenton. The distance is also consistent with Pickett's disappointment that the column had only reached Pollocksville next day.

560 Barrett, p. 207.

561 Most of those who made their way to Union lines at New Bern were sent to Fort Monroe. There they took the oath of allegiance and were set free.

562 Barrett, p. 206.

563 Responsibility for the conceived attack across Brice's Creek rested solely with Barton's superiors. Most commentaries to date unjustifiably presume Barton lost his nerve. One needs only visit the site to appreciate the situation.

564 Freeman specifically cites Barton as example when he wrote, "…only in the rarest instances did he [Lee] call for courts in inquiry." *R. E. Lee*, vol. 3, p. 225. Lee called for a court of inquiry in Barton's behalf after Lee's letter to President Davis failed to clear Barton.

565 Gordon, p. 129.

566 Patriotic locals rallied to defend North Carolina in 1861. These were

ready to fight for their state, but not necessarily the Confederacy. When the Union took New Bern in 1862, many of these men enlisted in local Union defense regiments.

567 Barrett, p. 208.

568 Toalson, p. 32.

569 General John J. Peck was the Union commander during the Siege of Suffolk. By 1864 he was in charge of Union occupied areas of North Carolina.

570 Gordon, p. 132.

571 Because of these twenty-two executions, Pickett was later investigated for war crimes. He fled to Canada and returned only upon certain assurances by President Grant.

572 "General Orders, No. 12. Petersburg, March 7th, 1864. Before a General Court Martial, Convened at Kinston, North Carolina," Academic Affairs Library, University of North Carolina at Chapel Hill. http://docsouth.unc.edu/imls/csaarmy/csaarmy.xml. Last viewed June 2009.

573 Gregory, *38th Virginia*, p. 103.

574 William R. Aylett, letter to wife dated February 17, 1864.

575 John Booker, letter dated March 1, 1864.

576 James Booker, letter dated March 16, 1864.

577 Krick, *Civil War Weather in Virginia*, p. 120.

578 Gordon, p. 135.

Chapter Fourteen: Chester Station, Drewry's Bluff and the Howlett Line

579 William Glenn Robertson, p. 46.

580 Gordon, pp. 136–137.

581 Pvt. John Q. Adams was wounded by Pvt. Joel Harris, both in Company K. Gregory, *38th Virginia*, p. 50. One assumes malice, but it may have been some improvised game of skill or other relief of boredom gone awry.

582 John B. Jones, Vol. 2, p. 182.

583 Gregory, *38th Virginia*, p. 50.

584 Gordon, p. 137.

585 The landing of the Army of the James at Bermuda Hundred was the largest amphibious landing of U.S. troops until D-day, June 6, 1944.

586 Many held Major General Robert Ransom Jr. in low esteem. See Toalson, p. 126. Ransom's treatment of Barton provides yet more justification for dislike.

587 Robert Ransom Jr. replaced Arnold Elzey Jones Jr. as head of the Department of Richmond when Elzey was relieved April 25, 1864.

588 J. William Jones, p. 480.

589 Schiller, p. 151.

590 The Winfree house still stands at this writing immediately adjacent to Sunset Memorial Park.

591 Archibald Gracie was a former New Yorker relocated to Alabama. Gracie's brigade made the final, victorious charge at Chickamauga.

592 *OR*, part 2, series I, vol. 36, pp. 230–231.

593 Although use of an entire regiment as skirmishers was unfamiliar to Barton and Gracie, the 38th Virginia served as skirmishers for McLaws's advance on Maryland Heights in September 1862.

594 Chester Station casualties included members from all ten companies of the 38th Virginia. Figures suggest that substantial numbers of Companies H and I missed the fight. Sundry members may have been incidentally attached to other companies. Likely regiments collected their pickets during the advance rather than recall them.

595 Less than a week later General Benjamin Butler used the Half-Way House as his headquarters during the Battle of Drewry's Bluff. The inn, circa 1760, hosted Washington, Lafayette, and many other notables. At this writing, the structure and detached kitchen are privately preserved and operated as the Half-Way House Restaurant.

596 *OR*, series 1, vol. 36, part 2, p. 215.

597 The Perdue house still stood in 1979 when author first surveyed battlefield. It was subsequently razed for new housing. The Perdue family cemetery prominently remains at the end of what is now Warfield Ridge Drive. The Perdue house stood about twenty yards northeast of the cemetery.

598 William Glenn Robertson, p. 124.

599 The two guns belonged to the 4th New Jersey Artillery.

600 *OR*, series 1, vol. 36, part 2, p. 215.

601 J. D. Darden was assistant adjutant-general on Barton's staff.

602 Captain Thom, assistant adjutant and inspector general on Barton's staff.

603 "My daddy said that the ball hit a tree first, then hit him. If it hadn't,

it would have killed him." Norman Oakes, Sr., interviewed June 1978. The 1.5-inch-diameter iron canister ball removed from James Oakes's leg is the possession of Terry L. Oakes, Blairs, Virginia. At this writing, it is on display at the Pittsylvania County Historical Society, Chatham, Virginia.

604 Pvt. Tolbert Barker died September 24, 1864, at Chimborazo Hospital. Gregory, p. 80. The writer assumes hammer fall on a cap as reason for the ramrod blown through the hand. Premature ignition in a hot barrel may have occurred as perhaps also loading on a cartridge ember (if paper was rammed, as common with a Springfield rifle). Both types of accidents were rare.

605 *OR*, series 1, vol. 36, part 2, p. 218.

606 Gregory, *38th Virginia*, p. 52.

607 Schiller, p. 158.

608 *OR*, series 1, vol. 36, part 2, p. 233.

609 Gregory, *53rd Virginia*, p. 72.

610 Schiller, p. 159.

611 Alexander Brown, p. 477. Attending surgeon was likely the original source.

612 Per Rev. J. W. Walkup, chaplain, 9th Virginia in J. William Jones, p. 499.

613 Eight miles to the north on the other side of the James River was Tree Hiil Farm, the site of Powhatan's capital village. That is also the site where Richmond's mayor surrendered the city in 1865.

614 Returns put Barton's strength on paper at 1,945 men. William Glenn Robertson, p. 127. Per Barton, he left one-fifth behind. This put his effectives at Chester Station at about 1,600.

615 William R. Aylett, letter to wife dated May 11, 1864.

616 Ransom's charge against Barton strangely paralleled Pickett's accusation: "want of cooperation." Records make it apparent that Ransom exceeded his authority in relieving Barton. Universal support from Barton's subordinates eventually secured him another brigade command in Ewell's division. Barton was captured at Sailor's Creek and survived the war to become a noted chemist. He died in 1900 and is buried in Fredericksburg.

617 Schiller, p. 150; William Glenn Robertson, p. 122; and other sources agree on May 10. Gordon claims Beauregard arrived May 11. Gordon, p. 139.

618 Gordon, p. 139.

619 Colonel Birkett D. Fry was wounded and captured at Gettysburg while

leading Archer's brigade, the brigade of direction immediately to the left of Armistead's.

620 Gregory, *38th Virginia*, p. 54.

621 Crews and Parrish, p. 55.

622 Captain Stephen P. Read, Company F, 14th Virginia, ibid.

623 Ibid., p. 56.

624 Toalson, p. 121.

625 Schiller, pp. 240–241.

626 Major George Cabell was shot in the face while leading the 18th Virginia which included the Danville Blues, Danville Grays and Spring Garden Blues.

627 Robert Ransom was recalled to the War Department in Richmond. Schiller, p. 296.

628 Repairs to sections of the RF&P track destroyed by Sheridan's Raid had just been completed.

629 Toalson, p. 126.

630 "Next to that of Malvern Hill, the Battle of Gettysburg was the worst fought of all the engagements of General Lee." Freeman, *Lee's Lieutenants*, vol. 3, p. 187.

631 Freeman wrote, "Not once during the whole war did he [Lee] initiate court-martial proceedings against an officer, and only in the rarest instances did he call for courts of inquiry." *R. E. Lee*, vol. 3, pp. 224–225. Lee's method of handling mediocrity or incompetence was exclusively by reassignment within his command or transfer out of it. This work presents Armistead and Pickett as recipients of remedial duty reassignments dispensed by Lee.

632 Fry's men held a line on Rt. 633 (Colts Neck Road) between Rt. 615 and Rt. 635 in support of Frank Huger's Artillery Battalion. Gregory, *38th Virginia*, p. 55.

633 Fry's promotion to brigadier general was dated May 24, 1864.

634 For photographs of Wilcox's Landing and the pontoon bridge at Weyanoke Point, see Frassanito, *Grant and Lee*, pp. 205–209.

635 Trudeau, *The Last Citadel*, p. 43.

636 At this writing, the campus of John Tyler Community College occupies much of the hill that was Mrs. Clay's farm. Interstate 95 is built over the site of the abandoned Confederate works then occupied by the Union. Mrs. Clay's house was in the southeast quadrant of the intersection of I-95 and Old Bermuda Hundred

Road (Rt. 618).

637 Freeman, *Lee's Lieutenants*, vol. 3, p. 532. See also *R. E. Lee*, vol. 3, p. 418.

638 Pvt. William G. Morton, Company A, 53rd Virginia captured three canteens of rye whiskey. After the action, he presented one canteen to Col. Aylett and one to Col. H. A. Carrington, 18th Virginia. See Gregory, 53rd Virginia, p. 76. No doubt Morton kept the third canteen for himself.

639 Glatthaar, p. 385. Malaria plagued Pickett's men from August through October.

640 Sgt. Samuel Vest, Company C, 57th Virginia. Toalson, p. 178.

641 See "It Was Terrible—Awful—Terrific," Trudeau, *The Last Citadel*, pp. 131–141.

642 Trudeau, *The Last Citadel*, p. 154 and Gregory, *53rd Virginia*, p. 76.

643 Gregory, *38th Virginia*, p. 55.

644 Gregory, *38th Virginia*, p. 99.

645 On June 17, 1861, Raleigh W. Fuller enlisted at Callands in the Pittsylvania Vindicators, which became Company B, 38th Virginia. He was discharged September 4, 1862. In July 1863, the conscription age advanced to forty-five. Under imminent threat of conscription, Fuller reenlisted in his old company on October 6, 1864.

646 For initial discharge of Stephen J. Holland, Company D, 38th Virginia, see James Mathew Cabaniss, letter dated June 16, 1861. For Holland's reenlistment, see Gregory, *38th Virginia*, p. 102.

647 Thomas J. Hines, letter dated December 24, 1864.

Chapter Fifteen: Their Fight to the Finish

648 Thomas J. Hines, letter dated January 20, 1865.

649 Gordon, p. 146.

650 Gregory, *38th Virginia*, p. 60.

651 The last name also appears as Bays. Gregory, *38th Virginia*, p. 80. Variations on the family name in Pittsylvania County include, Baise, Baize and Bays.

652 Herman E. Melton, "The Willow Del Commissary: Pittsylvania's Secret Confederate Supply Base," *Pittsylvania Packet*, winter 1996, pp. 5–6.

653 Thomas J. Hines, letter dated February 23, 1865.

654 Thomas J. Hines, letter dated March 8, 1865.

655 The Richmond & Danville Railroad and Southside Railroads had the same gauge tracks. However, changing rail lines was an involved, manual affair employing slave labor. Use of "switching engines" was not even suggested until February 1865. See Glatthaar, p. 444.

656 James Alfred Oakes, Company B, 38th Virginia exited the war under curious circumstances. Oakes was admitted to Farmville Hospital on March 17, 1865, five days after the regiment had left there. Oakes's complaint was coxalgia, a painful hip condition (see "A. Oak," Gregory, p. 115). He returned to duty on March 22, 1865, only to be admitted to Chimborazo hospital with anchylosis (immobility) of the right knee. See *Pittsylvania County Virginia*, vol. 1, p. 258. The times, locations, and ailments make one suspect Oakes injured himself jumping from the train.

657 The liquor was probably manufactured illegally. The Confederate government had passed prohibition laws to conserve grain for food and animal feed.

658 Gregory, *38th Virginia*, p. 62.

659 New Hundley [*sic*] Ford (Gregory, p. 62) is likely reference to river crossing near what was then the Huntley farm and at or near present day Nelson's Bridge. Bivouac site below the ford is most likely near the present-day intersection of River Road (Rt. 605) and Summer Hill Road (Rt. 644).

660 Chickahominy Bluffs is consistent with "on the Mechanicsville Turnpike about two miles north of Richmond" per Gregory, p. 62.

661 George Edward Pickett Jr., born July 17, 1864, had just turned eight months old. The Pickett residence was on the southwest corner of 6th and Leigh Streets. Samuel Moore, p. 36. At this writing, neither the house nor the intersection exist. The site is currently on the grounds of the Richmond Coliseum bordering East Leigh Street.

662 *OR*, part 3, series 1, vol. 46, p. 1332.

663 General John C. Breckinridge became secretary of war on February 6, 1865, replacing John Seddon.

664 "The darker the night the bolder the lion;...there is almost no limit to its daring in black, stormy weather." Theodore Roosevelt and Edward Heller, *Life Histories of African Game Animals* (New York: Charles Scribner's Sons, 1914), p. 173.

665 Desperation is clearly evidenced by the fact that Lee could not possibly

concentrate his forces along a shared front without also concentrating Grant's.

666 Freeman, *Lee's Lieutenants*, vol. 3, p. 659.

667 Upon Longstreet's wounding at the Battle of the Wilderness, Richard H. Anderson assumed command of I Corps and given temporary rank of lieutenant general. When Longstreet returned in October, Anderson reverted to major general and was given command of the IV Corps organized during the siege of Petersburg.

668 Bearss and Calkins, p. 21.

669 Freeman, *Lee's Lieutenants*, vol. 3, p. 661.

670 Carmichael, *Lee's Young Artillerist*, p. 161.

671 Ibid.

672 Sources differ as to whether or not whiskey was actually involved. If whiskey was available, George Pickett would have partaken with near absolute certainty.

673 Ibid., p. 163.

674 Author modified quote to reflect a proper first-person response. Pickett as quoted by Griggs appears: "He knew it, but could not help it—had done all he could." Gregory, p. 64.

675 All five returning Gettysburg captives in Company B, 38th Virginia, appear to have responded to Lee's request that exchanged prisoners waive their customary furlough. See Freeman, *R. E. Lee*, vol. 3, p. 544.

676 Exeter Mills was located at the end of present day Lakeland Road (a private road) on the Appomattox River.

677 At this writing, the site of Grant's breakthrough is preserved in Pamplin Military Park.

678 At this writing, one may visit the pews of Jefferson Davis and Robert E. Lee in St. Paul's Episcopal Church at 815 East Grace Street, Richmond.

679 Furguson, p. 325.

680 Ibid., p. 334.

681 Oldest maps show the stream as Sailor's Creek. Sayler's is a later spelling.

682 At this writing, bullet holes are still visible in the original siding of the Lockett house.

683 Union prisoners of war were held in six Danville prisons. Four were at Union and Spring Street. One at High and Floyd Street. Prison No. 6 was Sutherlin's tobacco factory at Lynn and Loyal Street. Hayes, p. 23. At this writing, the Sutherlin factory/prison building still exists at that location.

684 *Virginia at War 1865*, p. 80.

685 Hagan, p. 16.

686 Mrs. Sutherlin, Richmond *Dispatch*, December 11, 1889.

687 Freeman, *R. E. Lee*, vol. 1, p. 464.

688 Hagan, p. 68. Sutherlin probably had the old brick building dismantled to improve the view from his home. At this writing, the Midtown Market at 7 Chambers Street occupies the site.

689 Edith Oakes Chapman, granddaughter of John K. Oakes, interviewed by author, 1982.

690 1st Lt. Benjamin Clement and Pvt. Green Allen were two others from Company B, 38th Virginia, who escaped Five Forks and Sailor's Creek. They are not listed among those paroled at Appomattox. Author assumes they were also among those who walked away before formally surrendered.

691 Marvel, p. 197. Lesley Gordon states that sixty men surrendered "weapons," p. 154. Freeman also states Pickett had sixty armed men at Appomattox, *R. E. Lee*. Vol. 4, p. 118. Lee officially relieved Pickett of command following Sailor's Creek. Controversies will forever endure over whether or not Pickett received the order and whether or not he was present at Appomattox. After Lee surrendered, Pickett fled to Canada with his family and lived there under the assumed name of Edwards. Samuel Moore, p. 36. Pickett returned to the United States only upon assurances from President Grant that he would not be prosecuted for his war crimes at Kinston. He became an insurance agent in Norfolk. Pickett died July 30, 1875, from an abscessed liver (alcohol-induced cirrhosis?). He was buried in Hollywood Cemetery in Richmond. As the Pickett myth upstaged so many better men in his command, this writer finds it fitting to conclude him here as an endnote.

692 Brigadier General Steuart surrendered at Appomattox. Since Griggs surrendered Steuart's brigade, one assumes Steuart surrendered Pickett's division. See preceding note.

693 Gregory, *38th Virginia*, p. 67.

694 Siegel, p. 153.

695 Edith Oakes Chapman, granddaughter of John Kerr Oakes, interviewed by author 1982.

696 The substantial flesh wound and length of recovery suggests osteomyelitis, a bone infection that often accompanies gunshot wounds.

697 Despite his short, irregular tenure with the 38th Virginia, one may argue

Lt. Colonel George A. Martin was the last of the Pittsylvania Regiment. Captain George A. Martin of Norfolk joined the 38th Virginia when with his "St. Brides Artillery" became 2nd Company I, 38th Virginia, in May 1864. He served as acting colonel for three months after Drewry's Bluff during Colonel Griggs's recuperation and served thereafter as Griggs's second in command. Martin was sick sometime winter 1864–1865. He officially received promotion to lieutenant colonel March 28, 1865. Hartley, p. 147, records that while Martin recuperated from fever, he assisted in defense of Lynchburg. On April 9, 1865, he left Lynchburg hospital. He joined Jefferson Davis in Charlotte, North Carolina, and accompanied Davis as far as Washington, Georiga. Martin surrendered in Augusta, Georgia. See Gregory, *38th Virginia*, p. 109. In any event, James Lafayette Oakes appears the last Pittsylvanian of the Pittsylvania Regiment.

698 Freeman notes that after the war, Colonel William Preston Johnston, eldest son of General Albert Sydney Johnston, was a professor of history and literature at Washington College (now Washington and Lee University). *R. E. Lee*, vol. 4, p. 299. It is highly likely that Prichard gained introduction to Margaret Strother Johnston through acquaintance with the colonel since both instructors taught concurrently at neighboring schools in Lexington. Miss Johnston may have been Prichard's primary reason to move to California.

699 Blake, p. 62.

700 Samuel Wooton Averett served in the Confederate Navy. He was a junior officer aboard the CSS *Florida* in October 1863. He was later detailed to carry dispatches to and from Bermuda and thus avoided capture with that ship in October 1864. Hayes, p. 32.

701 Hill, p. 180, and Hayes, p. 32.

702 At this writing, the stirrups worn by Powhatan Bolling Whittle are preserved by the American Civil War Museum. Catalogue no. 0985.13.01109a.

703 A photograph of William C. Whittle appears in *The American Civil War Museum Magazine*, Summer 2017, p. 14.

704 Lewis, p. 92.

705 "Men, it has been well said, think in herds; it will be seen that they go mad in herds, while they recover sense slowly, and one by one." Charles Mackay in his 1852 preface to *Extraordinary Popular Delusions and the Madness of Crowds*.

706 Hosea 8:7.

707 Louisa County, Virginia, serves as best example of the social order of *Old*

Virginia surviving well into the twentieth century. See *Patronage and Poverty in the Tobacco South: Louisa County, Virginia, 1860–1900* by Crandall A. Shifflett. Also *Murder at Green Springs: The True Story of the Hall Case, Firestorm of Prejudices* by J. K. Brandau.

708 All Western civilization in the nineteenth century considered the black man inferior. It took the emergence of men like Frederick Douglass to prove that belief wrong.

709 In context of the war, emancipation was a political expedient for Lincoln, not a solution. The president wrestled with solutions. On August 14, 1862, weeks prior to the Emancipation Proclamation, Abraham Lincoln met with a "committee of colored men" at the White House to discuss the colonization of negroes in Central America. Lincoln stated, "It is better for us both [whites and blacks], therefore, to be separated." Ayers, pp. 205–209.

710 Ecclesiastes 10:19 (KJV).

BIBLIOGRAPHY

Published Sources

Aaron, Larry G. *Pittsylvania County Virginia: A Brief History*. Charleston, SC: History Press, 2009.

Ayers, Edward L., ed. *America's War: Talking about the Civil War and Emancipation on their 150th Anniversaries*. Chicago: American Library Association; National Endowment for the Humanities, 2012.

Ballagh, James Curtis. *White Servitude in the Colony of Virginia: A Study of the System of Indentured Labor in the American Colonies*. Baltimore: Johns Hopkins University Press, 1895.

Bearss, Ed, and Chris Calkins. *The Battle of Five Forks*. Lynchburg, VA: H. E. Howard, 1985.

Blake, Evarts I. *San Francisco: A Brief Biographical Sketch of the Most Prominent Men Who Will Preside over Her Destiny for at Least Two Years*. San Francisco: Press Pacific Publishing Company, 1902.

Brock, Robert Alonzo. *Virginia and Eminent Virginians*. Signal Mountain, TN: Mountain Press, 1988.

Brown, Alexander. *The Cabells and Their Kin: A Memorial Volume of History, Biography and Genealogy*. Cambridge, MA: Riverside Press, 1895.

Brown, Kent Masterson. *The Confederacy's First Battle Flag: The Story of the Southern Cross*. Gretna, LA: Pelican Publishing Company, 2014.

Brown, Kent Masterson. *Retreat from Gettysburg: Lee, Logistics, and the Pennsylavnia Campaign*. Chapel Hill: University of North Carolina Press, 2005.

Burton, Brian K. *Extraordinary Circumstances: The Seven Days Battles*. Bloomington: Indiana University Press, 2001.

Carmichael, Peter S. The Last Generation: Young Virginians in Peace, War, and Reunion. Chapel Hill: University of North Carolina Press, 2005.

Carmichael, Peter S. *Lee's Young Artillerist: William R. J. Pegram*. Charlottesville: University of Virginia Press, 1995.

Confederate Veteran. Nashville, TN: 1893–1932.

Clement, Maud Carter. *The History of Pittsylvania County*. Lynchburg, VA: J. P. Bell Company, 1929.

Cormier, Steven A. *The Siege of Suffolk: The Forgotten Campaign April 11–May 4, 1863*. Lynchburg, VA: H. E. Howard, 1989.

Coski, John M. *The Confederate Battle Flag. America's Most Embattled Emblem*. Cambridge, MA: Harvard University Press, 2005.

Crews, Edward R., and Timothy A. Parrish. *14th Virginia Infantry*. Lynchburg, VA: H. E. Howard, 1995.

Crocker, James F. *Gettysburg, Pickett's Charge, and Other War Addresses*. Portsmouth, VA: W. A. Fiske, 1915.

Custalow, Linwood, and Angela Daniel. *The True Story of Pocahontas: The Other Side of the Story*. Golden, CO: Fulcrum Publishing, 2007.

Daniels, Jonathan. *The Randolphs of Virginia: America's Foremost Family*. Garden City, NY: Doubleday and Company, 1972.

Davis, William C., and James I. Robertson Jr., eds. *Virginia at War 1865*. Lexington: University Press of Kentucky, 2012.

Davis, William Watts Hart. *History of the 104th Pennsylvania Regiment, from August 22nd, 1861 to September 30th, 1864*. Philadelphia: Jas. B. Rodgers, Printer, 1866.

Douglass, Frederick. *Narrative of the Life of Frederick Douglass, an American Slave*. Dublin: Webb and Chapman, G.T. Brunswick-Street, 1846.

Dowdey, Clifford. *The Seven Days: The Emergence of Robert E. Lee*. New York: Fairfax Press, 1978.

Edmonds, Amanda Virginia. *The Journals of Amanda Virginia Edmonds: Lass of the Mosby Confederacy, 1857–1867* (1st ed.), ed. Nancy Chappelear Baird. Delaplane, VA: N. C. Baird, 1984.

Farmer, Charles J. *In the Absence of Towns: Settlement and Country Trade in Southside Virginia, 1730–1800*. Lanham, MD: Rowman and Littlefield, 1993.

Farrow, Anne, Joel Lang, and Jenifer Frank. *Complicity: How the North Promoted, Prolonged, and Profited from Slavery*. New York: Ballantine Books, 2006.

Frassanito, William A. *Grant and Lee: The Virginia Campaigns, 1864–1865*. New York: Charles Scribner's Sons, 1983.

Freeman, Douglas Southall. *Lee's Lieutenants: A Study in Command.* New York: Simon and Schuster, 1972.

Freeman, Douglas Southall. *R. E. Lee: A Biography.* New York: Charles Scribner's Sons, 1934–1935.

Furgurson, Ernest B. *Ashes of Glory: Richmond at War.* New York: Vintage Books, 1997.

Gallagher, Gary W., ed. *The Third Day at Gettysburg and Beyond.* Chapel Hill: University of North Carolina Press, 1994.

Garber, Virginia Armistead. *The Armistead Family, 1635–1910.* Richmond, VA: Whittet and Shepperson, Printers, 1910.

Georg, Kathleen R., and John W. Busey. *Nothing but Glory: Pickett's Division at Gettysburg.* Hightstown, NJ: Longstreet House, 1987.

Glatthaar, Joseph T. *General Lee's Army: From Victory to Collapse.* New York: Free Press, 2008.

Gordon, Lesley J. *General George E. Pickett in Life and Legend.* Chapel Hill: University of North Carolina Press, 1998.

Govan, Gilbert, and James Livingwood. *Joseph E. Johnston, C.S.A.: A Different Valor.* New York: Bobbs-Merrill Company, 1956.

Gregory, G. Howard. *38th Virginia Infantry.* Lynchburg, VA: H. E. Howard, 1988.

Gregory, G. Howard. *53rd Virginia Infantry.* Lynchburg, VA: H. E. Howard, 1999.

Guelzo, Allen C. *Gettysburg: The Last Invasion.* New York: Alfred A. Knopf, 2013.

Gunn, Ralph White. *24th Virginia Infantry.* Lynchburg, VA: H. E. Howard, Inc., 1987.

Hagan, Jane Gray. *The Story of Danville.* New York: Stratford House, 1950.

Harsh, Joseph L. *Taken at the Flood: Robert E. Lee and Confederate Strategy in the Maryland Campaign of 1862.* Kent, OH: Kent State University Press, 1999.

Hayes, Jack Irby, Jr. *The Lamp and the Cross: A History of Averett College.* Macon, GA: Mercer University Press, 2004.

Herndon, George Melvin. *Tobacco in Colonial Virginia: "The Sovereign Remedy."* Williamsburg, VA: Virginia 350th Anniversary Celebration Corporation, 1957.

Hess, Earl J. *Pickett's Charge: The Last Attack at Gettysburg.* Chapel Hill: University of North Carolina Press, 2001.

Hennessy, John J. *Return to Bull Run: The Campaign and Battle of Second Manassas.* New York: Simon and Schuster, 1993.

Hill, Judith Parks America. *A History of Henry County, Virginia with Biographical Sketches of its Most Prominent Citizens and Genealogical Histories of Half a Hundred of its Oldest Families.* Bowie, MD: Heritage Books, 2003.

Hudson, Carson O. *Civil War Williamsburg.* Williamsburg, VA: Colonial Williamsburg Foundation, 1997.

Hurmence, Belinda, ed. *We Lived in a Little Cabin in the Yard.* Winston-Salem, NC: John F. Blair Publisher, 1994.

Irons, Charles F. *The Origins of Proslavery Christianity: White and Black Evangelicals in Colonial and Antebellum Virginia.* Chapel Hill: University of North Carolina Press, 2008.

Isenberg, Nancy. *White Trash: The 400-Year Untold History of Class in America.* New York: Viking, 2016.

Jones, John B. *A Rebel War Clerk's Diary.* Philadelphia: J. B. Lippincott and Co., 1866.

Jones, J. William. *Christ in the Camp or Religion in the Confederate Army.* Harrisonburg, VA: Martin and Hoyt Co., 1904.

Jordan, Ervin L., Jr., and Herbert A. Thomas Jr. *19th Virginia Infantry.* Lynchburg, VA: H. E. Howard, 1999.

Kennedy, James Ronald, and Walter Donald Kennedy. *The South Was Right!* Gretna, LA: Pelican Publishing Company, 2006.

Krick, Robert K. *Civil War Weather in Virginia.* Tuscaloosa: University of Alabama Press, 2007.

Krick, Robert K. *Lee's Colonels: A Register of the Field Officers of the Army of Northern Virginia.* Dayton, OH: Morningside Bookshop, 1979.

Lewis, John H. *Recollections from 1860 to 1865.* Dayton, OH: Morningside House, 1983.

List of Staff Officers of the Confederate States Army. Washington, DC: U.S. Government Printing Office, 1891.

Lockhart, Paul. *The Whites of Their Eyes: Bunker Hill, the First American Army, and the Emergence of George Washington.* New York: HarperCollins Publishers, 2011.

Loehr, Charles T. *War History of the Old First Virginia Infantry Regiment, Army of Northern Virginia.* Richmond, VA: Wm. Ellis Jones, Book and Job Printer, 1884.

Longstreet, James. *From Manassas to Appomattox: Memoirs of the Civil War in America*. Bloomington: Indiana University Press, 1960.

Maine Infantry, 11th Regiment. *The Story of One Regiment: The Eleventh Maine Infantry Volunteers in the War of the Rebellion*. New York: J. J. Little & Co., 1896.

Marvel, William. *Lee's Last Retreat: The Flight to Appomattox*. Chapel Hill: University of North Carolina Press, 2002.

Masur, Louis P. *1831: Year of Eclipse*. New York: Hill and Wang, 2001.

Maury, Colonel Richard L. *The Battle of Williamsburg and the Charge of the 24th Virginia, Early's Brigade*. Richmond, VA: Johns and Goolsby, Steam Printers, 1880.

McClurken, Jeffrey W. *Take Care of the Living: Reconstructing Confederate Veteran Families in Virginia*. Charlottesville: University of Virginia Press, 2009.

McFall, F. Lawrence, Jr. *Danville in the Civil War*. Lynchburg, VA: H. E. Howard, 2001.

McGrath, Thomas A. *Shepherdstown: Last Clash of the Antietam Campaign, September 19–20, 1862*. Lynchburg, VA: Schroeder Publications, 2008.

Meachum, Jon. *American Lion: Andrew Jackson in the White House*. New York: Random House, 2008.

Moore, Albert Burton. *Conscription and Conflict in the Confederacy*. Columbia: University of South Carolina Press, 1996.

Moore, Samuel J. T., Jr. *Moore's Complete Civil War Guide to Richmond*. Richmond, VA: Samuel J. T. Moore Jr., 1978.

Morgan, Edmund S. *American Slavery, American Freedom: The Ordeal of Colonial Virginia*. New York: W. W. Norton & Company, 1975.

Motts, Wayne E. *"Trust in God and Fear Nothing," Gen. Lewis A. Armistead, CSA*. Gettysburg, PA: Farnsworth House Military Impressions, 1994.

Murfin, James V. *The Gleam of Bayonets: The Battle of Antietam and Robert E. Lee's Maryland Campaign, September 1862*. Baton Rouge: Louisiana State University Press, 1965.

Newton, Steven H. *The Battle of Seven Pines: May 31–June 1, 1862*. Lynchburg, VA: H. E. Howard, 1993.

Page, Charles D. *History of the Fourteenth Regiment, Connecticut Vol. Infantry*. Meriden, CT: Horton Printing Co., 1906.

Pittsylvania County Heritage Book Committee, *Pittsylvania County Virginia—Heritage 1767–2004 Vol. 1*. Waynesville, NC: County Heritage, 2004.

Pittsylvania County Heritage Book Committee, *Pittsylvania County Virginia—Heritage 1767–2006 Vol. 2*. Waynesville, NC: County Heritage, 2006.

Pittsylvania County Historical Society. *The Pittsylvania Packet*. Chatham, VA: Pittsylvania County Historical Society, published quarterly, 1991–2018.

Poindexter, James E. *Lewis A. Armistead, Brigadier General, CSA: A Graphic Account of Pickett's Charge at Gettysburg*. N.p.: n.p., 1909.

Pollock, Edward. *1885 Sketch Book of Danville, Virginia; Its Manufactures and Commerce* (facsimile of 1885 edition). Danville, VA: Womack Press, 1976.

Price, David A. *Love and Hate in Jamestown: John Smith, Pocahontas, and the Heart of a New Nation*. New York: Knopf, 2003.

Priest, John M. *Into the Fight: Pickett's Charge at Gettysburg*. Shippensburg, PA: White Mane Books, 1998.

Robertson, James I., Jr. *Soldiers Blue and Gray*. Columbia: University of South Carolina Press, 1988.

Robertson, James I., Jr. *Stonewall Jackson*. New York: Macmillan Publishing USA, 1997.

Robertson, William Glenn. *Back Door to Richmond: The Bermuda Hundred Campaign, April—May, 1864*. Newark: University of Delaware Press, 1987.

Richmond Dispatch. Microfilm, Library of Virginia.

Savannah Republican. Microfilm, Library of Congress.

Schiller, Herbert M. *The Bermuda Hundred Campaign*. Dayton, OH: Morningside House, 1988.

Sears, Stephen W. *Gettysburg*. Boston: Houghton Mifflin Company, 2003.

Sears, Stephen W. *To the Gates of Richmond: The Peninsula Campaign*. New York: Ticknor and Fields, 1992.

Sheehan-Dean, Aaron. *Why Confederates Fought: Family and Nation in Civil War Virginia*. Chapel Hill: University of North Carolina Press, 2007.

Siegel, Frederick F. *The Roots of Southern Distinctiveness: Tobacco and Society in Danville, Virginia 1780–1865*. Chapel Hill: University of North Carolina Press, 1987.

Stewart, George R. *Pickett's Charge: A Microhistory of the Final Attack at Gettysburg, July 3, 1863*. Boston: Houghton Mifflin Company, 1987.

Sublett, Charles W. *57th Virginia Infantry*. Lynchburg, VA: H. E. Howard, 1985.

Tagg, Larry. *The Generals of Gettysburg: Leaders of America's Greatest Battle*. Cambridge, MA: D Capo, 2003.

The Quiet Regiment. Suffolk, VA: Suffolk-Nansemond Historical Society, 1990.

The Civil War. Alexandria, VA: Time-Life Books, 1988.

Toalson, Jeff, ed. *No Soap, No Pay, Diarrhea, Dysentery, and Desertion: A Composite Diary of the Last 16 Months of the Confederacy from 1864 to 1865*. New York: iUniverse, 2006.

Trask, Benjamin H. *9th Virginia Infantry*. Lynchburg, VA: H. E. Howard, 1984.

Trudeau, Noah Andre. *Gettysburg: A Testing of Courage*. New York: HarperCollins, 2002.

Trudeau, Noah Andre. *The Last Citadel: Petersburg, Virginia June 1864–April 1865*. Baton Rouge: Louisiana State University Press, 1991.

Tucker, Glenn. *Chickamauga: Bloody Battle in the West*. Dayton, OH: Morningside House 1992.

United States, War Department, Department of the Army, Department of the Interior, Navy Department War Office. *The War of the Rebellion: A Compillation of the Official Records of the Union and Confederate Armies*. Washington: [s.n.], 1894.

United States, War Department. *The Official Military Atlas of the Civil War*. New York: Arno Press and Crown Publishers, 1978.

Walker, Charles D. *Memorial, Virginia Military Institute: Biographical Sketches of the Graduates and Eleves of the Virginia Military Institute Who Fell during the War between the States*. Philadelphia: J. B. Lippincott and Co., 1875.

Wall, H. C. *Historical Sketch of the Pee Dee Guards (Co. D 23rd N.C. Regiment) From 1861 to 1865*. Raleigh, NC: Edwards, Broughton & Co., Printers and Binders, 1876.

Wallace, Lee A. *A Guide to Virginia Military Organizations 1861–1865*. Lynchburg, VA: H. E. Howard, 1986.

Watkins, Sam R. *Co. Aytch: A Confederate Soldier's Memoirs*. New York: Collier Books, 1962.

Wert, Jeffry D. *Gettysburg, Day Three*. New York: Simon & Schuster, 2002.

Wilson, Greene A. *Civil War Petersburg: Confederate City in the Crucible of War*. Charlottesville: University of Virginia Press, 2007.

Withers, Robert Enoch. *Autobiography of an Octogenarian*. Roanoke, VA: Stone Printing and Mfg. Co. Press, 1907.

Unpublished Manuscripts

Allen, C. Edmonds, Jr. *The Edmonds Family*. N.p., n.d.

Aylett, William Roane. Aylett Family Papers, Virginia Historical Society.

Booker, James. Letters, Alderman Library, University of Virginia.

Booker, John. Letters, Alderman Library, University of Virginia.

Cabaniss, James Mathew. Letter. Library of Virginia.

Cabaniss, William George. Letters. Library of Virginia.

Carrington Family Papers, 1781–1939. Virginia Historical Society.

Cocke, William H. Cocke Family Papers. Virginia Historical Society.

Daniel Family. Papers, 1805–1877. Virginia Historical Society.

Estes, Edward H. Letters. Eleanor S. Brockenbrough Library, American Civil War Museum.

General Orders, No. 12. Petersburg, March 7th, 1864. Before a General Court Martial, Convened at Kinston, North Carolina. Academic Affairs Library. University of North Carolina at Chapel Hill. http://docsouth.unc.edu/imls/csaarmy/csaarmy.xml. Last viewed January 2018.

Griggs, George K. Personal diary. Eleanor S. Brockenbrough Library, American Civil War Museum.

Gwynn, Henry. Letter dated July 20, 1862. Catalogue item #0268 for auction closed January 22, 2004. Historical Collectible Auctions, Graham, NC.

Harrell, Charles T. *Too Few Trains: The Reinforcement of P. G. T. Beauregard at First Manassas*. N.p. 1999. http://nps-vip.net/history/too_few_trains4.htm. Last viewed January 2018.

Herndon, John A. Letter to brother dated July 11, 1863, Williamsport, MD. Carl L. Sell Jr., Franconia, VA.

Herndon, John A. Letter to brother dated July 14, 1863, Bunker Hill, VA. Gregory A. Coco Collection, Gettysburg National Military Park.

Hines, Thomas Jefferson. Letters. Library of Virginia.

Letter Book, Armistead/Barton/Steuart/ Brigade, Pickett's Division, February 14, 1863, to November 19, 1864. Eleanor S. Brockenbrough Library, American Civil War Museum.

Mahan, John W. Letters to his wife, Matilda A. Mahan, dated September 20, 1862, through May 28, 1863. D. M. Hensley as published on internet http://www.geocities.ws/CapitolHill/9145/Mahan_letters.html. Last viewed January 2018.

Moore Family. Papers, 1861–1865. Virginia Historical Society.

Payne, Joseph T. Letters 1861–1863. Anna M. Craik, Chatham, VA.

Penick, Edwin Anderson. Letters 1862. Virginia Historical Society.

Scott, Benjamin Wiley. Letters in Ella Merryman Papers, Virginia Historical Society.

Talley, Henry M. Personal Papers 1858–1865. Virginia Historical Society.

Tiedeken, Donald (collector). Papers, 1861–1865. Virginia Historical Society.

VMI Historical Rosters Database. http:///archivesweb.vmi.edu/rosters/record.php?ID-1099. Last viewed January 2018.

Whittle, Powhatan Bolling. Letter to James Whittle dated June 22, 1861. Richard J. Reid Papers 1770–1910 (MSS 550). Albert and Shirley Small Special Collections Library, University of Virginia.

INDEX

ABOUT THE AUTHOR

J. K. Brandau was born in Richmond, Virginia and grew up in Richmond's Southside. The life-long Civil War buff and eleventh generation Virginian graduated from Old Dominion University with a B.S. in Chemistry. Brandau retired in 2017 as lead chemist for Newport News Shipbuilding. His forty-five-year laboratory career supported nuclear ship construction and included chemical analyses of USS *Monitor* artifacts for conservation by the Mariners' Museum.

On the Surrender Field at Yorktown. (Photo by Sharon Brandau)

Fascination with history propelled personal research on three continents. Brandau has authored scores of privately shared monographs, some of which appeared in newsletters, magazines, and historical society journals. His first book *Murder At Green Springs, The True Story of the Hall Case, Firestorm of Prejudices*, published 2007, chronicles injustice and cover-up in one of Virginia's most sensational criminal trials.

J. K. "Ken" Brandau and wife Sharon retired to Williamsburg, a vertex of Virginia's Historic Triangle. Their son Zack, his wife Katie, and granddaughter Winnie live nearby.

CPSIA information can be obtained
at www.ICGtesting.com
Printed in the USA
LVHW041723060623
749021LV00003B/265